# Two Years in the Forbidden City

## Princess Der Ling

### Complete & Unabridged

Tutis Digital Publishing Private Limited

First published in 1911 as *Two Years in the Forbidden City*.

This edition published by
Tutis Digital Publishing Pvt Ltd, 2008.

# Foreword

THE author of the following narrative has peculiar qualifications for her task. She is a daughter of Lord Yu Keng, a member of the Manchu White Banner Corps, and one of the most advanced and progressive Chinese officials of his generation. Lord Yu Keng entered the army when very young, and served in the Taiping rebellion and the Formosan war with France, and as Vice Minister of War during the China-Japan war in 1895. Later he was Minister to Japan, which post he quitted in 1898 to become President of the Tsung-li-yamen (Chinese Foreign Office). In 1899 he was appointed Minister to France, where he remained four years. At a period when the Chinese Government was extremely conservative and reactionary, Lord Yu Keng labored indefatigably for reform. He was instrumental in reorganizing China's postal service on modern lines, but failed in efforts to revise the revenue system and modernize the army and navy, from being ahead of his times. He died in 1905. The progressive spirit of Lord Yu Keng was shown in the education of his children. When it became known that his daughters were receiving a foreign education – then an almost unheard – of proceeding among high Manchu officials-attempts were made to impeach him as pro-foreign and revolutionary, but he was not deterred. His children got their early education in missionary schools, and the daughters later attended a convent in France, where the author of this work finished her schooling and entered society. On returning to China, she became First Lady-in-Waiting to the Empress Dowager, and while serving at the Court in that capacity she received the impressions which provide the subject-matter of this book. Her opportunity to observe and estimate the characteristics of the remarkable woman who ruled China for so long was unique, and her narrative throws a new light on one of the most extraordinary personalities of modern times. While on leave from her duties to attend upon her father, who was fatally ill in Shanghai, Princess Der Ling took a step which terminated connexion with the Chinese Court. This was her engagement to Mr. Thaddeus C. White, an American, to whom she was married on May 21, 1907. Yielding to the urgent solicitation of friends, she consented to put some of her experiences into literary form, and the following chronicle, in which the most famous of Chinese women, the customs and atmosphere of her Court are portrayed by an intimate of the same race, is a result. THOMAS F. MILLARD. SHANGHAI, July 24, 1911.

# CHAPTER ONE

## Introductory

MY father and mother, Lord and Lady Yu Keng, and family, together with our suite consisting of the First Secretary, Second Secretary, Naval and Military Attaches, Chancellors, their families, servants, etc., – altogether fifty-five people, – arrived in Shanghai on January 2, 1903, on the S.S. "Annam" from Paris, where for four years my father had been Chinese Minister. Our arrival was anything but pleasant, as the rain came down in torrents, and we had the greatest difficulty getting our numerous retinue landed and safely housed, not to mention the tons of baggage that had to be looked after. We had found from previous experience that none of our Legation people or servants could be depended upon to do anything when travelling, in consequence of which the entire charge devolved upon my mother, who was without doubt the genius of the party in arranging matters and straightening out difficulties.

When the launch from the steamer arrived at the jetty off the French Bund, we were met by the Shanghai Taotai (the highest official in the city), the Shanghai Magistrate and numerous other officials, all dressed in their official robes. The Taotai told my father that he had prepared the Tien Ho Gung (Temple of the Queen of Heaven) for us to reside in during our stay in Shanghai, but my father refused the offer, saying that he had telegraphed from Hong Kong and made all arrangements to go to the Hotel des Colonies in the French Concession. We had had previous experience staying in this temple while on our way to Japan, where my father went as Minister in 1895, and did not care to try it a second time. The building is very old and very much out of repair. It was a beautiful place in its prime, but had been allowed to go to rack and ruin. The custom is that the magistrate has to find a place and supply the food, etc., for high officials when passing through, and it is not exactly the thing to refuse their kind offer, but my father was always very independent and politely declined all proffers of assistance.

At last we did safely arrive in the Hotel des Colonies, where my father found awaiting him two telegrams from the Imperial Palace. These telegrams ordered my father to go to Peking at once, but, as the river to Tientsin was frozen, it was out of the question for us to go by that route, and as my father was very old and quite ill at that time, in fact constantly under the doctor's care, the only accessible way, via

Chinwangtao, was equally out of the question, as it was a long and most tedious journey and quite beyond his strength. In view of all these difficulties, he telegraphed that, after the ice had broken up in the Peiho River, we would come by the first steamer leaving Shanghai for Tientsin.

We left Shanghai on the 22d of February and arrived at Tientsin on the 26th, and, as before, were met by the Customs Taotai of the port and numerous other officials (the same as when we arrived at Shanghai).

There is a very curious custom of reverence, which must be performed by all high officials on their return from abroad. Immediately upon landing on the shores of China, arrangements are made with the nearest Viceroy or Governor to receive their obeisance to Ching Sheng An (to worship the Emperor of Peace), a Taotai being considered of too low a rank for such an honor. As soon as we arrived, Yuan Shih Kai, who was then Viceroy of Chihli Province at Tientsin, sent an official to my father to prepare the time and place for this function, which is an extremely pretty one. When arrangements had been made, both my father and Yuan Shih Kai dressed in their full ceremonial robes, which is the dragon long robe, with a reddish black three-quarter length coat over it, chao chu (amber beads), hat with peacock feather and red coral button, and repaired at once to the Wan Shou Kung (10,000 years palace), which is especially built for functions of this kind, where they were met by a large number of officials of the lower grades. At the back centre of this Temple, or Palace, stands a very long narrow table on which are placed the tablets of the Emperor and Empress Dowager, on which is written, "Wan sway, wan sway, wan wan sway" (10,000 years times 10,000 years times 10,000 10,000 years). The Viceroy, or in this case Yuan Shih Kai, and the other officials arrived first. Yuan stood at the left side of this table and the others arranged themselves in two diminishing lines starting from the front corners of the table. Soon afterward my father came and knelt directly in front of the centre of the table and said, "Ah ha Ching Sheng An" (Your servant gives you greeting). After this ceremony was over my father immediately arose and inquired after Their Majesties' health, and Yuan replied that they were quite well. This closed the function.

We stayed in Tientsin for three days, arriving in Peking on the twenty-ninth. My father's condition was much worse and he begged for four months' leave of absence, in which to recuperate, which was granted by Her Majesty, the Empress Dowager. As our beautiful mansion, which we had built and furnished just before leaving for Paris, was burned during the Boxer Rising of 1900, entailing a loss of over taels 100,000, we rented and moved into a Chinese house. Our old house was not entirely new. When we bought the place there was a very fine but old Chinese house, the palace of a Duke, standing on the ground, and by some clever re-arrangement and building on, it was transformed into a beautiful foreign style house with all the fine hardwood carving of the old house worked into it. By using the words "foreign style," it is meant that, in so far as the Chinese house could be made to look like a foreign house, without tearing it down entirely, it was changed, that is the doors and windows, passageways, furnishings, etc., were foreign, but the arrangement of the house itself and courtyard was Chinese. This, like all Chinese houses in Peking, was built in a very rambling fashion, and with the gardens, covered about ten acres of ground. We had just finished furnishing it and moved in only four days when we left for Paris; and it has always been a great sorrow to my family that we should lose this magnificent place, after having spent so much time and money in building and beautifying it. However, this is only one of the many trials that a high official in China is called upon to bear.

The houses in Peking are built in a very rambling fashion, covering a large amount of ground, and our former house was no exception to the rule. It had sixteen small houses. one story high, containing about 175 rooms, arranged in quadrangles facing the courtyard, which went to make up the whole; and so placed, that without having to actually go out of doors, you could go from one to the other by verandas built along the front and enclosed in glass. My reader will wonder what possible use we could make of all of these rooms; but what with our large family, numerous secretaries, Chinese writers, messengers, servants, mafoos (coachmen), and chair coolies, it was not a difficult task to use them.

The gardens surrounding the houses were arranged in the Chinese way, with small lakes, stocked with gold fish, and in which the beautiful lotus flower grew; crossed by bridges; large weeping willows along the banks; and many different varieties of flowers in prettily arranged flower beds, running along winding paths, which wound in and out between the lakes. At the time we left for Paris, in the month of June, 1899, the gardens were a solid mass of flowers and foliage, and much admired by all who saw them.

As we now had no place of our own in Peking we did not know where to go, so, while we were at Tientsin, my father telegraphed to one of his friends to find him a house. After some little trouble one was secured, and it turned out to be a very famous place indeed. It was the house where Li Hung Chang signed the treaties with the Foreign Powers after the Boxer Rising and also where he died. We were the first people to live there since the death of Li Hung Chang, as the Chinese people were very superstitious and were afraid that, if they went there to live, something dreadful would happen to them. We soon made ourselves very comfortable, and while we lived there, none of the dreadful things happened to us that all of our good friends told us would be visited upon us if we dared to take this place. However, in view of our having lost our place by fire, I am inclined to think that their fears were well founded.

The loss sustained by having this house burned we never recovered, as my father, being an official of the Government, it would have been very bad form to have tried to recover this money, besides a possible loss of standing, as Government officials are supposed never to consider themselves or families in the service of their country, and any private losses in the service must be borne without complaint.

On the first of March, 1903, Prince Ching and his son, Prince Tsai Chen, came to see us and told us that Her Majesty wished to see my mother, my sister, and myself at once; that we should be at the Summer Palace (Wan Shou Shan) at six o'clock the following morning. My mother told Prince Ching that we had been wearing foreign clothes all these years, while abroad, and had no suitable Manchu clothes to wear. He replied that he had told Her Majesty all about us and also mentioned that he had seen us in European attire and she had said that it would not be necessary for us to wear Manchu costume to go to the Palace, that she would be glad to have us wear foreign clothes, as it would give her an opportunity to study the foreign way of dressing. Both my sister and myself had a very difficult time deciding what we should wear for this occasion; she wished to wear her pale blue velvet gown, as she thought that color suited her the best. My mother had always made us dress exactly alike, ever since we were little girls. I said that I preferred to wear my red velvet gown, as I had the idea it might please Her Majesty. After a long discussion I had my way. We had lovely red hats trimmed with plumes and the same color shoes, and stockings to match. My mother wore a lovely gown of sea green chiffon cloth embroidered with pale mauve iris and trimmed with mauve velvet; she wore her large black velvet hat with long white plumes.

As we lived in the central part of the city and the only means of travel was by sedan chair and the distance from our house to the Palace was about thirty-six Chinese li (a three-hour ride), we had to start at three o'clock in the morning, in order to be there at six. As this was our first visit to the Palace, Prince Ching's message threw us into a great state of excitement, and we were naturally anxious to look our best and to be there on time. It had been the dream of my life to go to the Palace and see what it was like, and up to this time I had never had an opportunity, as most of my life had been spent out of Peking, – in fact, out of China. Another reason why this chance had never come before was, that my father had never registered our names (my sister and myself) in the Government book for the registration of births of Manchu children, in consequence of which the Empress Dowager did not know until we came back from Paris that Lord Yu Keng had any daughters. My father told me the reason why he did not put our names in this book was, that he wished to give us the best education obtainable, and the only way he could do it was not to let the Empress Dowager know. Besides this, according to the Manchu custom, the daughters of all Manchu officials of the second rank and above, after reaching the age of fourteen years, should go to the Palace, in order that the Emperor may select them for secondary wives if he so desires, and my father had other plans and ambitions for us. It was in this way that the late Empress Dowager was selected by the Emperor Hsien Feng.

(comment: li is 1/3 mile or 1/2 km)

We started at three o'clock that morning in total darkness riding in four coolie sedan chairs, one on each side of the chair. In going such a long distance it was necessary to have two relays of chair coolies. This meant twenty-four coolies for the three chairs, not counting an extra coolie for each chair who acted as a sort of head chair bearer. Besides this there were three military officers on horses, one for each chair and two servants riding at the back of each chair. In addition there were three big Chinese carts following behind for the chair coolies to ride in and rest. This made a cavalcade consisting of fortyfive men, nine horses and three carts.

I had a rather nervous feeling riding along in the chair surrounded by inky blackness, with nothing to relieve the stillness of the night but the rough voices of the chair bearers calling back and forth to each other to be careful of stones and holes in the road, which was very uneven, and the clump, clump of the horses. To my readers who have never had the experience of riding a long distance in a sedan chair I would say that it is a most uncomfortable conveyance, as you have to sit perfectly still and absolutely straight, otherwise the chair is liable to upset. This ride was a very long one and I felt quite stiff and tired by the time I reached the Palace gates.

# CHAPTER TWO

## At the Palace

WHEN we reached the City gates, which were about half way between our house and the Summer Palace, they were wide open for us to pass. This quite surprised us, as all gates are closed at seven o'clock in the evening and are not opened except on special occasions until daylight. We inquired of the guard why this was, and were told that orders had been given for the gates to be opened for us to pass. The officials who had charge were standing in a double line dressed in full official dress and saluted us as we passed.

It was still quite dark when we had passed through the gate and I thought of the many experiences of my short life; but this was by far the strangest of them all. I wondered what Her Majesty would be like and whether she would like me or not. We were told that probably we would be asked to stay at the Court, and I thought that if that came to pass, I would possibly be able to influence Her Majesty in favor of reform and so be of valuable assistance to China. These thoughts made me feel happy and I made up my mind then and there that I would do all I could and use any influence I might have in the future towards the advancement of China and for her welfare. While I was still dreaming of these pleasant prospects, a faint red line appeared on the horizon heralding the coming of a most perfect day, and so it proved. As the light grew brighter and I could distinguish objects, a very pretty view gradually opened to me, and as we came nearer to the Palace I could see a high red wall which zigzagged from hill to hill and enclosed the Palace grounds. The tops of the wall and buildings were covered with yellow and green tiles and made a most dazzling picture in the bright sunlight. Pagodas of different sizes and styles were passed, and when we arrived at the village of Hai Tien, about four li from the Palace gates, we were told by the officers we only had a short distance further to go. This was good news, as I began to think we would never get there. This village was quite a pretty country place of one-story houses built of brick, which were very neat and clean as are most of the houses in the northern part of China. The children trouped out to see the procession pass, and I heard one remark to another: "Those ladies are going to the Palace to become Empresses," which amused me very much.

Soon after leaving Hai Tien we came to a pai lou (archway), a very beautiful piece of old Chinese architecture and carved work, and from here got our first view of the Palace gates, which were about 100 yards ahead. These gates are cut into the solid wall surrounding the Palace and consist of one very large gate in the center and two smaller ones on each side. The center gate is only opened when their Majesties pass in and out of the Palace. Our chairs were set down in front of the left gate, which was open. Outside of these gates, at a distance of about 500 yards, were two buildings where the guard stayed at night.

Just as we arrived I saw a number of officials talking excitedly, and some of them went into the gate shouting "Li la, doula" (have come, have arrived). When we got out of our chairs, we were met by two eunuchs of the fourth rank (chrystal button and feather). This feather which is worn by eunuchs of the fourth rank, comes from a bird called the magh (horse-fowl) which is found in Szechuen Province. They are grey and are dyed black, and are much wider than the peacock feather. These two eunuchs were accompanied by ten small eunuchs carrying yellow silk screens, which they placed around our chairs when we alighted. It appeared that Her Majesty had given orders that these screens (huang wai mor) should be brought to us. This is considered a great honor. They were ten feet long and twenty feet high and were held by two eunuchs.

These two eunuchs of high rank were extremely polite and stood at each side of the gate and invited us to enter. Passing through this gate we came into a very large paved courtyard about three hundred feet square, in which there were a great many small flower beds and old pine trees from which hung all kinds of birds in cages. On the side opposite to the gates we had entered was a red brick wall with three gates exactly like the others; on the right and left side were long rows of low buildings each containing twelve rooms, used as waiting rooms. The courtyard was full of people dressed in official robes of the different ranks, and, after the Chinese fashion, all seemed to be very busy doing nothing. When they saw us they stood still and stared. The two eunuchs who were showing us the way conducted us to one of these rooms. This room was about twenty feet square, just ordinarily furnished in black wood furniture with red cloth cushions and silk curtains hanging from the three windows. We were not in this room more than five minutes when a gorgeously dressed eunuch came and said: "Imperial Edict says to invite Yu tai tai (Lady Yu) and young ladies to wait in the East side Palace." On his saying this, the two eunuchs who were with us knelt down and replied "Jur" (Yes). Whenever Her Majesty gives an order it is considered an Imperial Edict or command and all servants are required to kneel when any command is transmitted to them the same as they would if in Her Majesty's presence, Then they told us to follow them and we went through another left gate to another courtyard laid out exactly the same as the former, except that the Ren Shou Dien (audience hall) is situated on the north side and the other buildings were a little larger. The eunuchs showed us into the east side building, which was beautifully furnished with reddish blackwood exquisitely carved, the chairs and tables covered with blue satin and the walls hung with the same material. In different parts of the room were fourteen clocks of all sizes and shapes. I know this, for I counted them.

In a little while two servant girls came and waited on us and told us that Her Majesty was dressing and that we were to wait a little time. This little time proved to be a matter of more than two hours and a half, but as this is considered nothing in China, we did not get impatient. From time to time eunuchs came and brought milk to drink and about twenty or more dishes of various kinds of food which Her Majesty sent. She also sent us each a gold ring with a large pearl in the center. Later the chief eunuch, Li Lien Ying, came dressed in his official clothes. He was of the second rank and wore a red button and peacock feather and was the only eunuch that was ever allowed to wear the peacock feather. He was a very ugly man, very old and his face was full of wrinkles; but he had beautiful manners and said that Her Majesty would receive us in a little while, and brought us each a jade ring which she had sent us. We were very much surprised that she should give us such beautiful presents before she had even seen us, and felt most kindly disposed toward her for her generosity.

Soon after Li Lien Ying had gone, two court ladies, daughters of Prince Ching, came in and asked the eunuchs who were attending us if we could speak Chinese, which we thought a great joke. I was the first one to speak, and told them of course we could speak our own language, although we knew several others. They were very much surprised and said: "Oh! how funny, they can talk the language as well as we do." We in turn were very much surprised to find such ignorant people in the Imperial Palace and concluded that their opportunities for acquiring knowledge were very limited. Then they told us Her Majesty was waiting to receive us, and we went immediately.

After walking through three courtyards very similar to those we had previously passed through, we came to a magnificent building just one mass of exquisite carving. Large lanterns made of buffalo horns hung all over the veranda covered with red silk from which red silk tassels were hanging and from each of these tassels was suspended a beautiful piece of jade. There were two smaller buildings flanking this large one, also one mass of carvings and hung with lanterns.

At the door of the large building we met a lady, dressed the same as Prince Ching's daughters, with the exception that she had a phoenix in the center of her headdress which distinguished her from the others. This lady came out to meet us, smiling, and shook hands with us in the most approved foreign fashion. We were told later that this was the Young Empress, wife of the Emperor Kwang Hsu. She said: "Her Majesty has sent me to meet you," and was very sweet and polite, and had beautiful manners; but was not very pretty. Then we heard a loud voice from the hall saying, "Tell them to come in at once." We went into this hall immediately and saw an old lady dressed in a beautiful yellow satin gown embroidered all over with pink peonies, and wearing the same kind of headdress with flowers on each side made of pearls and jade, a pearl tassel on the left side and a beautiful phoenix in the center made of purest jade. Over her gown she wore a cape, the most magnificent and costly thing I ever saw. This cape was made of about three thousand five hundred pearls the size of a canary bird's egg, all exactly alike in color and perfectly round. It was made on the fish net pattern and had a fringe of jade pendants and was joined with two pure jade clasps. In addition to this Her Majesty wore two pairs of pearl bracelets, one pair of jade bracelets, several jade rings and on her third and little fingers of her right hand she wore gold finger nail protectors about three inches long and on the left hand two finger nail protectors made of jade and about the same length. Her shoes were trimmed with small tassels made of pearls and embroidered with tiny pieces of different colored jade.

Her Majesty stood up when she saw us and shook hands with us. She had a most fascinating smile and was very much surprised that we knew the Court etiquette so well. After she had greeted us, she said to my mother: "Yu tai tai (Lady Yu), you are a wonder the way you have brought your daughters up. They speak Chinese just as well as I do, although I know they have been abroad for so many years, and how is it that they have such beautiful manners?" "Their father was always very strict with them," my mother replied; "he made them study their own language first and they had to study very hard." "I am pleased to hear their father has been so careful with them," Her Majesty said, "and given them such a fine education." She took my hands and looked into my face and smiled and kissed me on both cheeks and said to my mother: "I wish to have your daughters and hope they will stay with me." We were very much pleased at this and thanked her for her

9

kindness. Her Majesty asked all sorts of questions about our Paris gowns and said we must wear them all the time, as she had very little chance to see them at the Court. She was particularly in love with our Louis XV high heel shoes. While we were talking to her we saw a gentleman standing at a little distance and after a while she said, "Let me introduce you to the Emperor Kwang Hsu, but you must call him Wan Sway Yeh (Master of 10,000 years) and call me Lao Tsu Tsung (the Great Ancestor)." His Majesty shyly shook hands with us. He was a man about five feet, seven inches in height, very thin, but with very strong features; high nose and forehead, large, brilliant black eyes, strong mouth, very white, even teeth; altogether good looking. I noticed he had a very sad look, although he was smiling all the time we were there. At this juncture the head eunuch came, knelt down on the marble floor and announced that Her Majesty's chair was ready and she asked us to go with her to the Audience Hall, distant about two minutes' walk, where she was going to receive the heads of the different Boards. It was a beautiful day and her open chair was waiting. This chair is carried by eight eunuchs all dressed in official robes, a most unusual sight. The head eunuch walked on her left side and the second eunuch on her right side, each with a steadying hand on the chair pole. Four eunuchs of the fifth rank in front and twelve eunuchs of the sixth rank walked behind. Each eunuch carried something in his hand, such as Her Majesty's clothes, shoes, handkerchiefs, combs, brushes, powder boxes, looking glasses of different sizes, perfumes, pins, black and red ink, yellow paper, cigarettes, water pipes, and the last one carried her yellow satin-covered stool. Besides this there were two amahs (old women servants) and four servant girls all carrying something. This procession was most interesting to see and made one think it a lady's dressing room on legs. The Emperor walked on Her Majesty's right and the Young Empress on the left, as did also the Court ladies.

The Audience Hall was about two hundred feet long by about one hundred and fifty feet wide, and at the left side was a long table covered with yellow satin. When Her Majesty came down from the chair she went into the Hall and mounted her throne just behind this table, and His Majesty mounted a smaller one at her left side, the Ministers all kneeling on the floor in front of her and on the opposite side of the table.

At the back of the Hall was a large dais about twenty feet long by about eighteen feet wide, enclosed by a magnificently carved railing about two feet high running all the way round, open only in the front in two places just large enough for a person to pass through. These two openings were reached by a flight of six steps. At the back of this dais was a small screen and immediately in front of this, in the center, was Her Majesty's throne. Immediately behind was an immense carved wood screen, the most beautiful thing I ever saw, twenty feet long by ten feet high. In front of Her Majesty's throne was a long narrow table. At the left side was a smaller throne for the Emperor.

The theme of the carving and furnishings of this dais was the phoenix and peony most exquisitely carved in ebony wood, in fact the theme of the entire room was the same. On each side of Her Majesty's throne were two upright ebony poles on the top of which were peacock feathers made into the shape of a fan The upholstery was entirely of yellow Chinese velvet.

Just before Her Majesty took her seat on her throne she ordered us to go behind this screen with the Young Empress and the Court ladies. This we did, and could hear the conversation between Her Majesty and the Ministers very plainly, and as my readers will see later, I made good use of this.

# CHAPTER THREE

## A Play at the Court

THIS day to me was a medley of brilliant impressions. I was a great novelty among these exclusive Court ladies, brought up rigidly apart from foreign life and customs, and I was subjected to a rapid fire of questions. I soon found that these women were the same as others the world over in point of curiosity and love of gossip. The fourth daughter of Prince Ching (Sze Gurgur), a young widow and a strikingly handsome woman, spoke to me. "Were you brought up in Europe and educated?" she asked. "I am told that when people go to that country and drink the water there, they quickly forget their own country. Did you really study to acquire all those languages or was it drinking the water that gave them to you?" I mentioned that I met her brother, Prince Tsai Chen, in Paris on his way to London for the coronation of King Edward, and that we should have liked to have gone also, as my father had a special invitation, but were prevented from doing so by his urgent duties in Paris in settling the Yunnan question, to which the Princess replied: "Is there a king in England? I had thought that our Empress Dowager was Queen of the world." Her sister, wife of the brother of the Young Empress, a most intelligent, quiet and dignified lady, stood by smiling and listening to the eager questions. After numerous questions had been asked the Young Empress finally said: "How ignorant you are. I know that each country has its ruler and that some countries are republics. The United States is a republic and very friendly toward us, but I am sorry that such a common class of people go there, as they will think we are all the same. What I should like to see is some of our good Manchu people go, as then they would see what we really are." She afterwards told me she had been reading a history of the different countries, which had been translated into Chinese, and she seemed to be very well informed.

After the Audience was over, Her Majesty called us out from behind the screen and told us to go with her to see the theatre. She said, as it was such a beautiful day, she preferred to walk, so we started, walking a little behind her, as is the custom. Along the way she pointed out from time to time different places and things that were her particular favorites, and as she had to keep turning around all the time, she finally told us to come and walk alongside of her. This, as I afterwards found out, was a great condescension on her part and a thing that she very seldom ever did. She, like everybody else, had her pets and hobbies, such as flowers, trees, plants, dogs, horses, etc., and there was one dog in particular that was her favorite pet. This dog was with Her Majesty always and followed her wherever she went, and a more homely dog I never saw. It had absolutely nothing to recommend it in any way. Her Majesty thought it beautiful, and called it Shui Ta (Sea Otter).

A short distance from the Audience Hall we came to a large courtyard. On each side of this courtyard were two immense baskets fifteen feet in height, built of natural logs and literally covered with purple wisteria. They were simply gorgeous and great favorites of Her Majesty. She was always very proud of them when in bloom and took great delight in showing them to the people.

From this courtyard we entered a sort of passageway which ran along the sides of a big hill and led directly to the theatre, where we soon arrived. This theatre is quite unlike anything that you can imagine. It is built around the four sides of an open courtyard, each side being separate and distinct. The building has five stories. It is entirely open on the front and has two stages, one above the other. The three top stories are used for holding the drops and for store rooms. The stage on the first floor is of the ordinary kind; but that on the second floor is built to represent a temple and used when playing religious plays, of which Her Majesty was very fond.

On the two sides were long, low buildings with large verandas running their entire length, where the Princes and Ministers sat when invited by Her Majesty to witness the play. Directly opposite this stage was a spacious building, containing three large rooms, which was used exclusively by Her Majesty. The floor was raised about ten feet above the ground, which brought it on a level with the stage. Large glass windows ran along in front, so made that they could be removed in the summer and replaced with pale blue gauze screens. Two of these rooms were used as sitting rooms and the third, the one on the right, she used as a bedroom, and it had a long couch running across the front, on which she used to sit or lie according to her mood. This day she invited us to go to this room with her. Later I was told that she would very often come to this room, look at the play for a while and then take her siesta. She could certainly sleep soundly, for the din and noise did not disturb her in the least. If any of my readers have ever been to a Chinese theatre, they can well imagine how difficult it would be to woo the God of Sleep in such a pandemonium.

As soon as we were in this bedroom the play commenced. It was a religious play called "The Empress of Heaven's Party or Feast to all the Buddhist Priests to eat her famous peaches and drink her best wine." This party or feast is given on the third day of the third moon of each year.

The first act opens with a Buddhist Priest, dressed in a yellow coat robe with a red scarf draped over his left shoulder, descending in a cloud from Heaven to invite all the priests to this party. I was very much surprised to see this actor apparently suspended in the air and actually floating on this cloud, which was made of cotton. The clever way in which they moved the scenery, etc., was most interesting, and before the play was finished I concluded that any theatre manager could well take lessons from these people; and it was all done without the slightest bit of machinery.

As this Buddhist Priest was descending, a large pagoda began to slowly rise from the center of the stage in which was a buddha singing and holding an incense burner in front of him. Then four other smaller pagodas slowly rose from the four corners of the stage, each containing a buddha the same as the first. When the first Buddhist Priest had descended, the five buddhas came out of the pagodas, which immediately disappeared, and walked about the stage, still singing. Gradually from the wing came numbers of buddhas singing until the stage was full, and they all formed into a ring. Then I saw a large lotus flower, made of pink silk, and two large green leaves appearing from the bottom of the stage, and as it rose the petals and leaves gradually opened and I saw a beautiful lady buddha (Goddess of Mercy) dressed all in white silk, with a white hood on her head, standing in the center of this flower. As the leaves opened I saw a girl and a boy in the center of them. When the petals of the lotus flower were wide open this lady buddha began to gradually ascend herself, and as she ascended, the petals closed until she seemed to be standing on a lotus bud. The girl standing in the leaf on the Goddess' right side held a bottle made of jade and a willow branch. The legend of this is that if the Goddess dips the willow branch into the jade bottle and spreads it over a dead person it will bring the person to life. The boy and the girl are the two attendants of the buddha.

Finally the three came down from the flower and leaves and joined the rest of the buddhas. Then the Empress of Heaven came, a good old lady with snow-white hair, dressed from head to foot in Imperial yellow, followed by many attendants, and ascended the throne, which was in the center of the stage, and said: "We will go to the banquet hall." This ended the first scene.

The second scene opened with tables set for the feast to be given by the Empress of Heaven. These tables were loaded down with peaches and wine and four attendants guarding them. Suddenly a bee came buzzing near and scattered a powder under the nostrils of the attendants, which made them sleepy. When they had fallen asleep, this bee transformed itself into a big monkey and this monkey ate all the peaches and drank all the wine. As soon as he had finished he disappeared.

A blast of trumpets announced the coming of the Empress of Heaven and she soon arrived accompanied by all the Buddhist Priests and their attendants. When the Empress of Heaven saw all the peaches and wine had disappeared, she woke the attendants and asked them why they were asleep and where the peaches and wine had gone. They said that they did not know, that they were waiting for her to come and fell asleep. Then one of the guests suggested that she should find out what had become of the feast, and attendants were sent out to the guard to find out from the soldiers if anyone had gone out of the gate recently. Before the messenger had time to return, the Guard of Heaven came and informed the Empress that a big monkey, who was very drunk and carrying a big stick, had just gone out of the gate. When she was told this, she ordered the soldiers of heaven and several buddhas to go and find him at his place. It seems that this monkey had originally been made from a piece of stone and lived in a large hole in a mountain on the earth. He was endowed with supernatural powers and could walk on the clouds. He was allowed to come to heaven and the Empress of Heaven gave him a position looking after the Imperial orchards.

When they got to his place on the earth, they found that he had taken some of the peaches with him and he, with other monkeys, was having a feast. The soldiers challenged him to come out and fight. He immediately accepted this challenge, but the soldiers could do nothing with him. He pulled the hair out of his coat and transformed each hair into a little monkey and each monkey had an iron rod in its hand. He himself had a special iron rod, which had been given to him by the King of Sea Dragons. This rod he could make any size he wanted from a needle to a crowbar.

Among the buddhas who had gone with the soldiers was one named Erh Lang Yeh, who was the most powerful of them all and had three eyes. This buddha had a dog which was very powerful and he told the dog to bite this monkey, which he did, and the monkey fell down and they caught him and brought him up to heaven. When they got there the Empress of Heaven ordered that he should be handed to Lao Chun, an old taoist god, and that he should burn him in his incense burner. The incense burner was very large, and when they took the monkey to him he placed him inside this burner and watched him very carefully to see that he did not get out. After he had watched for a long time he thought the monkey must be dead and went out for a few minutes. The monkey, however, was not dead and as soon as Lao Chun went out, he escaped and stole some golden pills which Lao Chun kept in a gourd and went back to his hole in the mountains. These pills were very powerful and if one of them were eaten it would give eternal life, and the monkey knew this. The monkey ate one and it tasted good and he gave the little monkeys some. When Lao Chun came back and found both the monkey and the pills gone he went and informed the Empress of Heaven. This ended the second scene.

The third scene opened with the buddhas and soldiers at the monkey's place in the mountains and they again asked him to come out and fight. The monkey said: "What! Coming again?" and laughed at them. They started to fight again, but he was so strong they could not get the best of him. Even the dog who had bit him before was powerless this time, and they finally gave it up and returned to heaven and told the Empress of Heaven that they could not capture him the second time, as he was too strong. Then the Empress of Heaven called a little god about fifteen years old by the name of Neur Cha, who had supernatural powers, and told him to go down to earth to the monkey's place and see if he could finish him. This god was made of lotus flowers and leaves, that is, his bones were made of flowers and his flesh made of leaves and he could transform himself into anything that he wished. When Neur Cha got to the monkey's place and the monkey saw him, he said: "What! A little boy like you come to fight me? Well, if you think you can beat me, come on," and the boy transformed himself into an immense man with three heads and six arms. When the monkey saw this, he transformed himself also into the same thing. When the little god saw that this would not do, he transformed himself into a very big man and started to take the monkey, but the monkey transformed himself into a very large sword and cut this man into two pieces. The little god again transformed himself into fire to burn the monkey, but the monkey transformed himself into water and put the fire out. Again the little god transformed himself, this time into a very fierce lion, but the monkey transformed himself into a big net to catch the lion. So this little god, seeing that he could not get the best of the monkey, gave it up and went back to heaven, and told the Empress of Heaven that the monkey was too strong for him. The Empress of Heaven was in despair, so she sent for Ju Li, an old ancestor of the buddhas, who was the all-powerful one of them all; and Kuan Yin, Goddess of Mercy, and sent them down to the monkey's place to see if they could capture him. When they arrived at the hole in the mountain the monkey came out and looked at Ju Li, but did not say a word, as he knew who this god was. This god pointed a finger at him and he knelt down and submitted. Ju Li said: "Come with me," and took the monkey and put him under another mountain and told him he would have to stay there until he promised he would be good. Ju Li said: "You stay here until one day I lift this mountain up for you to come out to go with a Buddhist Priest to the West side of heaven and demand the prayer books that are kept there. You will have to suffer a great deal on the way and face many dangers, but if you come back with this Buddhist Priest and the prayer books, by that time your savage temper will be gone and you will be put in a nice place in heaven and enjoy life forever afterwards."

This finished the play, which was very interesting, and I enjoyed it from beginning to end. It was acted very cleverly and quite realistic, and I was very much surprised to know that the eunuchs could act so well. Her Majesty told us that the scenery was all painted by the eunuchs and that she had taught them about all they knew. Unlike most theatres in China, it had a curtain which was closed between the acts, also wing slides and drop scenes. Her Majesty had never seen a foreign theatre and I could not understand where she got all her ideas from. She was very fond of reading religious books and fairy tales, and wrote them into plays and staged them herself, and was extremely proud of her achievement.

Her Majesty sat talking, we standing, for some little time and she asked me if I understood the play, and I told her that I did and she seemed quite pleased. Then she said in such a charming way: "Oh! I am so interested in talking with you that I have forgotten to order my lunch. Are you hungry? Could you get Chinese food when you were abroad, and were you homesick? I know I would be if I left my own country for so long a time; but the reason why you were abroad so long was not your fault. It was my order that sent Yu Keng to Paris and I am not a bit sorry, for you see how much you can help me now, and I am proud of you and will show you to the foreigners that they may see our Manchu ladies can speak other languages than their own." While she was talking I noticed that the eunuchs were laying three large tables with nice white table cloths, and I could see a number of other eunuchs standing in the courtyard with boxes of food. These boxes or trays are made of wood painted yellow and are large enough to hold four small and two large bowls of food. After the tables were laid ready, the eunuchs outside formed themselves into a double line from the courtyard to a little gate running into another courtyard and passed these trays from one to the other up to the entrance of the room, where they were taken by four nicely dressed eunuchs and placed on the tables.

It seems that it was a habit of Her Majesty to take her meals wherever she happened to be, so that there was no particular place that she used as a dining room. I should also mention that these bowls were of Imperial yellow with silver covers. Some were ornamented with green dragons and some with the Chinese character Shou (Long Life).

There were about one hundred and fifty different kinds of food, for I counted them. They were placed in long rows, one row of large bowls and one row of small plates, and then another row of small bowls, and so on. As the setting of the tables was going on, two Court ladies came into the bedroom, each carrying a large yellow box. I was very much surprised to see Court ladies doing this kind of work and I said to myself, if I come here will I have to do this sort of thing? Although these boxes appeared to be quite heavy, they brought them in very gracefully. Two small tables were placed in front of Her Majesty, then they opened the boxes and placed a number of very cute plates containing all sorts of sweets, lotus flower seeds, dried and cooked with sugar, watermelon seeds, walnuts cooked in different ways, and fruits of the season cut and sliced. As these plates were being placed on the tables Her Majesty said that she liked these dainties better than meat and gave us some and told us to make ourselves at home. We thanked her for her kindness and enjoyed them very much. I noticed that she ate quite a quantity from the different plates and wondered how she would be able to eat her lunch. When she had finished, two of the Court ladies came and took the plates away and Her Majesty told us that she always gave what was left to the Court ladies after she had finished eating.

After this a eunuch came in carrying a cup of tea. This tea cup was made of pure white jade and the saucer and cover was of solid gold. Then another eunuch came in carrying a silver tray on which were two jade cups similar to the others, one containing honeysuckle flowers and the other rose petals. He also brought a pair of gold chopsticks. They both knelt on the floor in front of Her Majesty and held the trays up so that she could reach them. She took the golden cover off of the cup containing tea and took some of the honeysuckle flowers and placed them in the tea. While she was doing this and sipping the tea, she was telling how fond she was of flowers and what a delicate flavor they gave to the tea. Then she said: "I will let you taste some of my tea and see if you like it," and ordered one of the eunuchs to bring us some tea, the same as she was drinking. When it came, she put some of the honeysuckle flowers in the cup for us and watched us drink it. It was the most delicious tea I had ever tasted and the putting of flowers in it gave it an extremely delicate flavour.

# CHAPTER FOUR

## A Luncheon With the Empress

WHEN we had finished drinking tea, she told us to go with her into the next room, where the tables had been prepared for lunch, and I wondered if she had any room for lunch, after all that she had just eaten, but I soon found out. As soon as she was inside the room, she ordered the covers to be removed and they were all taken off at one time. Then she took her seat at the head of the table and told us to stand at the foot. She then said: "generally the Emperor takes lunch with me when we have the theatre, but he is shy to-day, as you are all new to him. I hope he will get over it and not be so bashful. You three had better eat with me to-day." Of course, we knew that this was an especial favor, and thanked her by kowtowing before we commenced to eat. This kowtowing, or bowing our heads to the ground, was very tiring at first and made us dizzy, until we got used to it.

When we commenced to eat, Her Majesty ordered the eunuchs to place plates for us and give us silver chopsticks, spoons, etc., and said:

"I am sorry you have to eat standing, but I cannot break the law of our great ancestors. Even the Young Empress cannot sit in my presence. I am sure the foreigners must think we are barbarians to treat our Court ladies in this way and I don't wish them to know anything about our customs. You will see how differently I act in their presence, so that they cannot see my true self."

I was watching her while she was talking to my mother and marvelled to see how she could eat, after having eaten such a quantity of candy, walnuts, etc., while in her bedroom.

Beef was a thing that was tabooed within the precincts of the Palace, as it was considered a great sin to kill and eat animals that were used as beasts of burden. The food consisted mostly of pork, mutton and game, fowls and vegetables. This day we had pork cooked in ten different ways, such as meat balls, sliced cold in two different ways, red and white, the red being cooked with a special kind of sauce made of beans which gives it the red color and has a delicious taste. Chopped pork with chopped bamboo shoots, pork cut in cubes and cooked with cherries and pork cooked with onions and sliced thin. This last dish was Her Majesty's favorite and I must say it was good. Then there was a sort of pancake made of eggs, pork and mushrooms chopped fine and fried, also pork cooked with cabbage and another dish cooked with turnips. The fowl and mutton was cooked in several different ways. In the center of the table was a very large bowl about two feet in diameter of the same yellow porcelain, in which there was a chicken, a duck and some shark fins in a clear soup. Shark fins are considered a great delicacy in China. Besides this there was roast chicken, boneless chicken and roast duck. Ducks and chickens are stuffed with little pine needles to give them a fine flavor and roasted in open air ovens.

There was another dish that Her Majesty was very fond of and that was the skin of roast pork cut into very small slices and fried until it curls up like a rasher of bacon.

As a rule the Manchu people seldom eat rice, but are very fond of bread and this day we had bread, made in a number of different ways, such as baked, steamed, fried, some with sugar and some with salt and pepper, cut in fancy shapes or made in fancy moulds such as dragons, butterflies, flowers, etc., and one kind was made with mincemeat inside. Then we had a number of different kinds of pickles, of which Her Majesty was very fond. Then there was beans and green peas, and peanuts made into cakes and served with sugarcane syrup.

I did not eat very much, as I was too busy watching Her Majesty and listening to what she said, although she told us to eat all we could. In addition to all I have mentioned, we had many different kinds of porridge, some made of sweet corn and some with tiny yellow rice (like bird seed), and Her Majesty said that we must all eat porridge after our meat.

After we had finally finished eating, Her Majesty rose from the table and said: "Come into my bedroom and you will see the Young Empress and the Court ladies eat; they always eat after I am finished." We went with her and I stood near the door between the two rooms and saw the Young Empress and Court ladies come in and stand around the table eating very quietly. They were never allowed to sit down and eat their food.

All this time the theatre had been going on playing some fairy tales, but they were not near as interesting as the first play that we had seen. Her Majesty sat on her long couch in the bedroom and the eunuch brought her some tea and she ordered some brought for us. My reader can imagine how delighted I was to be treated in this way. In China the people think their sovereign is the supreme being and that her word is law. One must never raise their eyes when talking to her. This is a sign of great respect. I thought these extreme favors must be most unusual. I had been told that Her Majesty had a very fierce temper, but seeing her so kind and gracious to us and talking to us in such a motherly way, I thought my informant must be wrong and that she was the sweetest woman in the world.

When Her Majesty had rested a while, she told us that it was time we were returning to the city, as it was getting late. She gave us eight big yellow boxes of fruit and cakes to take home with us. She said to my mother: "Tell Yu Keng (my father) to get better soon and tell him to take the medicine I am sending by you and to rest well. Also give him these eight boxes of fruit and cakes." I thought my father, who had been quite ill since we returned from Paris, would not be much benefited if he ate all those cakes. However, I knew he would appreciate her kind thoughtfulness even if it were detrimental to his health.

As perhaps most of my readers know, it is the custom to kowtow when Her Majesty gives presents and we kowtowed to her when she gave us the fruit and cakes and thanked her for her kindness.

Just as we were leaving, Her Majesty said to my mother that she liked us very much and wanted us to come and be her Court ladies and stay at the Palace. We thought this was another great favor and again thanked her, and she asked us when we could come and told us to bring our clothes and things only, as she would fix everything for us and showed us the house we would live in when we came and told us to come back inside of two days. This house contained three very large rooms and was situated on the right side of her own or private Palace. This Palace Ler Shou Tong (Ever Happy Palace) is situated on the shores of the lake and was Her Majesty's favorite place and where she spent most of her time, reading and resting and when the spirit moved her she would go for a sail on the lake. In this Palace she had quite a number of bedrooms and made use of them all.

When she had finished showing us this house we took leave of Her Majesty, the Young Empress and the Court ladies, and after a long and tiresome ride, reached home exhausted but happy, after the most eventful day of our lives. When we got into the house, we were surprised to find several eunuchs waiting our return. They had brought us each four rolls of Imperial brocade from Her Majesty. Once more we had to bend to custom in thanking her for these gifts. This time, the gift having been sent to the house, we placed the silk on a table in the center of the room and kowtowed to thank Her Majesty and told the eunuchs to tell Her Majesty how grateful we were to her for all her kindness and for the beautiful gifts.

There is another thing that had to be done according to the custom, and that was to give the eunuchs a present or tip, and we had to give each of the eunuchs ten taels for their trouble. We afterwards found out that when eunuchs went anywhere to take presents for Her Majesty, they were required to report to her when they returned how the recipient had thanked her and what had been given them, which she allowed them to keep. She also asked them numerous questions about our house, whether we were pleased with her, etc. These people are extremely fond of talking and after we had returned to the Palace again, they told us what Her Majesty had said about us the first day we were there.

My mother felt very much worried to go to the Palace and leave my father all alone owing to his being in poor health, but we could not disobey Her Majesty's order, so we returned to the Palace three days later.

Our first day there was a busy one for us. When we first arrived we went and thanked Her Majesty for the present that she had sent us. She told us that she was very busy to-day, as she was going to receive a Russian lady, Madame Plancon, wife of the Russian Minister to China, who was bringing a miniature portrait of the Czar and Czarina and family as a present from the Czar to her, the Empress Dowager. She asked me if I could speak Russian. I told her that I could not, but that most Russians spoke French, which seemed to satisfy her. She, however, said: "Why don't you tell me you speak Russian, I won't know or be able to find out," and at the same time was looking at one of the Court ladies. I concluded that someone must be fooling her, for she seemed to appreciate the fact that I had told her the truth. This afterwards proved to be true and one of the Court ladies was dismissed for pretending she could talk foreign languages when she could not speak a word.

Besides this audience there was the theatre and the engagement ceremony of Her Majesty's nephew, Ter Ju. The engagement ceremony, according to the Manchu custom, is performed by two of the Princesses of the Royal family going to the house of the prospective bride, who sits on her bed cross-legged, her eyes closed and awaits their coming. When they arrive at the house, they go to her bedroom and place a symbol called Ru Yee, made of pure jade about one and a half feet long, in her lap and suspend two small bags made of silk and beautifully embroidered, each containing a gold coin, from the buttons of her gown, and place two gold rings on her fingers, on which is carved the characters Ta Hsi (Great Happiness). The meaning of the symbol or sceptre Ru Yee is "May all joy be yours."

During this entire ceremony absolute silence is maintained and immediately they have finished, they return to the Palace and inform Her Majesty that the ceremony has been completed.

# CHAPTER FIVE

## An Audience With the Empress

No one informed us the day before that there was to be an audience to receive the Russian Minister's wife on that very day. We told Her Majesty that we must go and change our clothes in order to receive this lady. The dresses we wore that day were very simply made and short. The reason we wore this kind of costume was that there was no carpet and the bare brick floor had ruined our beautiful red velvet gowns, also the clumsy eunuchs had kept stepping on our trains all the time. We had made up our minds that short dresses for general wear every day would be more practical. Her Majesty said: "Why must you change your clothes? I see you look much better without that tail dragging behind you on the floor. I laughed at the idea of having a tail on one's dresses. I noticed that the first day when you came to the Court." Before we had time to explain to her, she said: "I see, dresses with tails behind must be more dignified than short ones, am I right?" We told her it was so. Then she said: "Go and put on your most beautiful gowns at once." We immediately went and changed. My sister and myself wore our pink crepe de chine gowns, trimmed with Brussels lace and transparent yokes of the same color chiffon. My mother wore her gray crepe de chine embroidered with black roses and a little touch of pale blue satin on her collar and belt. We dressed in a great hurry, as Her Majesty had sent eunuchs to see if we were ready. When she saw us she exclaimed: "Here are three fairies with long tails." Then she asked us: "Is it very tiring to hold half of your dress in your hand when you are walking? The costume is pretty, but I do dislike the tail, there is no sense having a thing like that. I wonder what these foreigners will think of me having you dressed in their costume. I am sure they won't like the idea. My reason is this: I want them to see you in foreign clothes in order to let them understand I know something about the way they dress. I must say that no foreign ladies have yet been presented to me dressed in such lovely gowns as you three have. I don't believe foreigners are as wealthy as the Chinese. I also notice they wear very little jewelry. I was told that I have more jewelry than any sovereign in the world and yet I am getting more all the time."

We were very busy getting ready to receive Mdme. Plancon, who arrived about eleven o'clock and was received in the waiting room of the first courtyard by my sister and from there conducted to the audience hall, Ren Shou Dien, where she was received by Her Majesty, who was sitting on her big throne on the raised dais. The Emperor was present, sitting on Her Majesty's left hand and I stood on her right to interpret for her. Her Majesty was dressed in a yellow transparent satin brocade gown, embroidered with hollyhocks and the Chinese character "Shou" (Long Life) and trimmed with gold braid. She wore her big pearl, which is about the size and shape of an egg, suspended from the button of her dress, also numerous bracelets and rings and gold finger nail protectors. Her hair was dressed in the same style as usual.

When Mdme. Plancon entered the hall, my sister brought her to the steps of the dais and she courtesied to Her Majesty. I then went forward and brought her up onto the dais and Her Majesty shook hands with her and she presented the photograph which she had brought to Her Majesty. Her Majesty made a very pretty speech of acceptance, expressing her appreciation of the gift of their Majesties, the Czar and Czarina. I interpreted this speech in French to Mdme. Plancon, as she could not speak English. After this, Her Majesty told me to take Mdme. Plancon to the Emperor, which I did. He stood up when she came near and shook hands with her and asked after their Majesties' health. This over, Her Majesty stepped down from her throne and took Mdme. Plancon to her own Palace, the one with so many bedrooms, and when they arrived, Her Majesty asked her to sit down, and they talked together for about ten minutes, I interpreting for them, after which I took her to see the Young Empress.

The Manchu law is very strict as regards the mother-in-law and the daughter-in-law, and the Young Empress had been sitting behind the screen at the back of the throne during the audience, and it was there that I found her. From there we went to the banquet hall, where luncheon was served in Manchu style.

Here I must explain the difference between the Chinese way of eating and the Manchu. The Chinese place the bowls of food, one at a time, in the center of the table and everyone eats out of these bowls, sticking their chopsticks in and helping themselves to what they want. The Manchus eat quite differently and are served with individual bowls and dishes, the same as in any other country. Her Majesty was very proud of this and said that it saved time, not to mention being cleaner. The food in the Palace was always very good and clean, especially when we had foreign guests, and of course we had a variety of dishes for such occasions, such as sharkfins, birds' nest pudding, not to mention a great quantity of other things.

Her Majesty had given me the order that morning to have the tables nicely decorated and they did look very nice when we sat down. Besides the usual tableware, we had gold dragon menu holders, little peach-shaped silver saucers filled with almonds and dried watermelon seeds, and knives and forks in addition to chopsticks.

Her Majesty and the Emperor never ate with guests, so Mdme. Plancon was entertained by the Imperial Princess and the Court ladies. When luncheon was half over a eunuch came and told me that Her Majesty wanted to see me at once. The thought flashed through my head that something had gone wrong, or that some of the eunuchs had been making false reports, a bad habit of the Court; and I was much surprised to find her all smiles. She told me what a nice, polite lady Mdme. Plancon was, that she had seen many ladies who had come to the Court, but none with manners like this one, that she was sorry to say that some of the ladies who came did not behave very well. She said: "They seem to think we are only Chinese and do not know anything, and look down upon us. I notice these things very quickly and am surprised to see people who claim to be well educated and civilized acting the way they do. I think we whom they call barbarians are much more civilized and have better manners." She was always very polite to the foreign ladies, no matter how badly they behaved, but after they had gone, she would tell us who was nice and who was not. After she had finished saying this, she gave me a beautiful piece of green jade to give to Madame Plancon. When I gave it to her, she said she wished to thank Her Majesty, and I took her to the Palace again.

When we had finished luncheon, she told me how pleased she was with her reception and the kindness that Her Majesty had shown her, and took her departure, we accompanying her to the courtyard of the Audience Hall, where her chair was waiting.

Her Majesty had made a rule or custom that after all guests had departed, we must go to her and report everything. I suppose she was like all women, a bit of a gossip as well as the rest; it appeared so at any rate. She wanted to know what Mdme. Plancon said, whether she liked the jade and whether she enjoyed her luncheon, etc.

Her Majesty was very well pleased that I had interpreted so well for her and said: "I have never had anyone to interpret for me this way before. Although I don't understand the language, I can see that you speak it fluently. How did you learn? I will never let you go away from me any more. Sometimes the foreign ladies bring their own interpreters, but I can't understand their Chinese and have to guess at what they are saying, especially some of the missionaries Mrs. Conger brings with her. I am very happy to have you and want you to stay with me as long as I live and I will arrange a marriage for you, but won't tell you just now."

I felt very happy at what Her Majesty had said and thought I had made my debut under very favorable auspices, and was very glad that Her Majesty liked me; but this marriage question worried me, for nothing was farther from my mind than this. I afterwards told my mother about it and she told me not to worry, as I could always refuse when the time came.

When we had told Her Majesty all that Mdme. Plancon had said, she told us we could go to our rooms, that as we had risen early that morning and had worked very hard, we must be tired and needed rest, that she would not need us any more that day. We courtesied to her according to the custom when saying good night, and retired.

# CHAPTER SIX

## In Attendance on her Majesty

THE building where we had our rooms, as I have said before, contained four large rooms and a hall, and we three, my mother, sister and myself, each took a room and gave the fourth to our maids. Her Majesty had ordered a eunuch to accompany us and this eunuch told us that Her Majesty had ordered four young eunuchs to attend on us and that if they did not behave, we should tell him. He also said his name was Li, but as there were so many by this name, including the head eunuch, it was very hard to tell them apart.

When we arrived, which took some time, he pointed to a building on our right and said that it was Her Majesty's own Palace and the one which we had just left. I could not understand why it had taken us so long to come, when the Palace was so near, and asked him about it. He told us that our little buildings were at the left side of the Emperor's Palace and that Her Majesty had had the entrance leading from our place to her Palace closed up for certain reasons which he would not tell, but said: "You see this place ought to face East instead of towards the lake." The view on the lake was beautiful and I told him I liked it much better the way it was. He smiled and said: "You will have to learn a lot before you find out this wicked place." I was surprised at what the eunuch said, but did not like to ask him any questions. He also told us that the Emperor's Palace was just behind our place and was a large building similar to Her Majesty's Palace. We looked and could see the trees of his courtyard above the roof. Then he pointed to another building behind the Emperor's, which was larger but lower than the Emperor's Palace, and also had a large courtyard, and said it was the Young Empress's Palace. It had two buildings flanking it on each side and the eunuch told us that the one on the left was the Secondary Wife's bedroom. That there had been an entrance between the two Palaces, but that Lao Fo Yeh (The great old Buddha), as the eunuchs called Her Majesty, had blocked it up so that the Emperor and Empress could not communicate with each other, except through Her Majesty's own Palace. I suppose this was the way she kept watch over them and knew at all times what they were doing. This was all news to me and I did not know what to think of it. I was afraid that this eunuch Li would tell me more of these curious things, so I told him I was tired and would go to my room and rest, and he went away.

When I finally got inside my room and had a chance to look around, I saw that it was very prettily furnished with ebonywood furniture, which was covered with red satin cushions and the windows were hung with red silk curtains. All the bedrooms were just alike. The kong (bed) was made of brick covered with the same kind of wood and ran along the wall under the front window. It had high teaster posts with slats running across on which red curtains were hung. These kongs are very curiously built. They are made of brick and have a hole in the front center in which fire is placed to heat the brick in winter time. During the day a sort of table is placed on top of the kong and removed again at night.

Shortly after we had gone to our rooms, some eunuchs came and brought our dinner, which they placed on a table in the center of the hall. They told us the food had been sent by Her Majesty and that she had ordered them to tell us to make ourselves comfortable. We were so tired that we could not eat very much and were about to retire for the night when this eunuch Li came again and told us that we must be up at five o'clock, not later, so I told my eunuch to knock on my window at five. Immediately after this we went to bed, but did not sleep immediately, as we wanted to talk over the events of the day, which had been many and strange. After we did finally get to bed, it seemed as if we had just fallen asleep when I heard someone knocking on my window. I woke up with a start and asked what the matter was and a eunuch told me it was five o'clock and time to get up.

I immediately got up and opened my window and looked out. The day was just dawning and the sky was a beautiful deep red which was reflected in the lake, which was perfectly calm. The scenery was lovely and in the distance I could see Her Majesty's peony mountain, which was literally covered with these beautiful flowers. I dressed at once and went to Her Majesty's Palace and there met the Young Empress sitting on the veranda. I courtesied to her as a good morning salute. The Emperor's Secondary wife was there also, but we had been ordered not to courtesy to her, as she was considered not to have any standing there. There was also a number of young Court ladies, many of whom I had never seen before. The Young Empress introduced me to them, saying that they were also Court ladies. They were daughters of high Manchu officials and some were very pretty and bright. The Young Empress told me that these ten (there were just ten there) were never allowed to go near Her Majesty, as they were just learning the court etiquette. They were all dressed very nicely in pretty Manchu gowns, the same design as that worn by the Young Empress.

After I had been introduced to these young ladies and talked with them a while, I went inside with the Young Empress and there met Sze Gurgur, fourth daughter of Prince Ching and a young widow twenty-four years of age, Yuen Da Nai Nai, widow of Her Majesty's nephew. Both were busy getting things ready for Her Majesty. The Young Empress told us that we must go at once to Her Majesty's bedroom and assist Her Majesty to dress, so we went at once and courtesied to her and said: "Lao Tsu Tsung Chi Hsiang" (old ancestor, all joy be with you). Her Majesty was still in bed and smiled to us and asked us if we had slept well. We told her the rooms were very comfortable, etc. I thought to myself, we had slept very well for the little time we had, but I had not had half enough. The day before had been very hard for us and we were quite unused to it and it had made us very lame and sore running around so much.

She asked us if we had had any breakfast and we told her not yet. She scolded Li for not having given the order for our breakfast to be brought to our rooms and said: "You must not feel like strangers, order anything you may want." Then she arose and started to dress. She put on her white silk socks first, having slept in her pantaloons as is the custom, and tied them at the ankle with pretty ribbon. I must tell you here that although she always slept in her clothes, she changed them for clean ones every day. Then she put on a pale pink shirt of soft material and over that a short silk gown, that was embroidered with bamboo leaves, as she always wore low heeled shoes in the morning and consequently could not wear her long gowns. After she had dressed she walked over to a window in front of which were two long tables covered with toilet articles of every kind and description.

As she was washing her face and dressing her hair, she said to my mother that she could not bear to have the servant girls, eunuchs, or old women, touch her bed, that they were dirty, so the Court ladies must make it. When she said this she turned to my sister and myself, we were standing a little to one side, and said: "You two must not think for a moment that the Court ladies do servant's work, but you know I am an old woman and could easily be your grandmother and it will do you no harm to work a little for me. When it comes your turn, you can superintend the others and don't have to do the work with your own hands." Then Her Majesty said to me: "Der Ling you are a great help to me in every way and I make you my first lady-in-waiting. You must not work too much for you will have to make all the arrangements for the audiences for foreigners and you will have to interpret for me. I also want you to look after my jewels and don't want you to do rough work

31

at all. Roon Ling (my sister) can choose what she likes to do. I have two more besides you, Sze Gurgur and Yuen Da Nai Nai, making four altogether and you must all work together. It is not necessary to be too polite to them and if they are not nice to you, you let me know." Although I was very happy at receiving this appointment, I knew that according to custom I must refuse it, so I thanked Her Majesty very kindly for the honor she had given me and said that I did not know enough to hold such an important position and would prefer to be just an ordinary Court lady, and that I would learn as quickly as possible to be useful to her. She hardly let me finish what I was saying, when she laughed and said: "Stop! don't say anything like that; you are too modest, which shows you are very clever and not a bit conceited. I am surprised to see what a perfect little Manchu lady you are, knowing even such small etiquette as this, although you have spent many years outside of China." She was very fond of making fun and liked very much to tease, and said that I could try and if she saw that I could not do the work, she would scold me and put someone else in my place. After all this that she had said, I accepted the appointment and went over to her bed to see how it was made, and I found that it was very easy work to do. As this would be one of my duties, I watched while the bed was being fixed. First of all, after Her Majesty had risen, the bedclothes were taken out into the courtyard by the eunuchs and aired, then the bed, which was made of beautifully carved wood, was brushed off with a sort of whiskbroom, and a piece of felt placed over it. Then three thick mattresses made of yellow brocade were placed over the felt. After this came the sheets made of different colored soft silk, and over the whole thing was placed a covering of plain yellow satin embroidered with gold dragons and blue clouds. She had a great many pillows, all beautifully embroidered, which were placed on the bed during the daytime; but had a particular one stuffed with tea leaves on which she slept. It is said that stuffing the pillow on which you sleep with tea leaves is good for the eyes. In addition to all these, she had another very curiously shaped pillow about twelve inches long in the middle of which was a hole about three inches square. It was stuffed with dried flowers, and the idea of the hole was that when she laid on it she could place her ear in this hole and in this way hear any and every sound. I suppose in that way no one could come on her unawares.

Besides this last yellow embroidered cover, there were six covers of different colors, pale mauve, blue, pink, green and violet, and were placed one on top of the other. Over the top of the bed was a frame of wood handsomely carved and from this frame white crepe curtains, beautifully embroidered, hung, and numerous little gauze silk bags filled with scent were suspended from the carved work of the frame. The odor from these bags was very strong and made one feel sick until they became used to it. Her Majesty was also very fond of musk and used it on all occasions.

It took us about fifteen minutes to make the bed, and when I had finished, I turned around and saw that Her Majesty was dressing her hair. I stood beside her Majesty while the eunuch was dressing it and saw that as old as she was, she still had beautiful long hair which was as soft as velvet and raven black. She parted it in the center and brought it low at the back of her ears, and the back braid was brushed up on the top of her head and made it into a tight knot. When she had finished doing this, she was ready to have the Gu'un Dzan (Manchu headdress) placed on and pinned through the knot with two large pins. Her Majesty always dressed her hair first and then washed her face. She was as fussy and particular as a young girl and would give it to the eunuch if he did not get it just to suit her. She had dozens of bottles of all kinds of perfume, also perfumed soap. When she had finished washing her face, she dried it on a soft towel and sprayed it with a kind of glycerine made of honey and flower petals. After that she put some kind of strong scented pink powder on her face.

When she had completed her toilet, she turned to me and said: "It must seem to you quite funny to see an old lady like me taking so much care and pains in dressing and fixing up. Well! I like to dress myself up and to see others dress nicely. It always gives me pleasure to see pretty girls dressed nicely; it makes you want to be young again yourself." I told her that she looked quite young and was still beautiful, and that although we were young we would never dare compare ourselves with her. This pleased her very much, as she was very fond of compliments, and I took great pains that morning to study her and to find out what she liked and what she didn't.

After this Her Majesty took me into another room and showed me where her jewels were kept. This room was covered with shelves on three sides of the room from top to bottom, on which were placed piles of ebony boxes all containing jewels. Small yellow strips were pasted on some of the boxes on which was written the contents. Her Majesty pointed to a row of boxes on the right side of the room and said: "Here is where I keep my favorite everyday jewels, and some day you must go over them and see that they are all there. The rest are all jewels which I wear on special occasions. There are about three thousand boxes in this room and I have a lot more locked up in my safety room, which I will show you when I am not busy." Then she said: "I am sorry you cannot read and write Chinese, otherwise I would give you a list of these things and you could keep a check on them." I was very much surprised at this and wondered who had told her I couldn't. I was anxious to know, but did not dare to ask her, so I told her that although I was not a scholar, I had studied Chinese for some time and could read and write a little, that if she would give me a list I would try and read it. She said: "That is funny, someone told me the first day you were here, I forget now who it was, that you could not read or write your own language at all." While she was saying this, she was looking all around the room and I was sure she knew who it was that had told her, but she would not tell me. Then she said: "When we have time this afternoon, I will go over this list with you. Bring me those five boxes on the first row of shelves." I brought the boxes to her room and placed them on the table. She opened the first one and it contained a most beautiful peony made of coral and jade and each petal trembled like a real flower. This flower was made by stringing the petals which were made of coral on very fine brass wire, also the leaves which were made of pure jade. She took this flower and placed it on the right side of her headdress. Then she opened another box and took from it a magnificent jade butterfly made in the same way. This was an invention of her own and it was done by carving the coral and jade into petals and leaves and boring holes in the lower ends through which brass wire was run. The other two boxes contained bracelets and rings of different patterns. There was a pair of gold bracelets set with pearls, another pair set with jade, with a piece of jade hanging from the end of a small gold chain, etc. The last two contained chains of pearls, the like of which I never saw before, and I fell in love with them at once. Her Majesty took one which was made into a plum blossom string by winding a circle of five pearls around a larger one, then one single pearl, then another circle of five pearls around a large one, and so on, making quite a long chain, which she suspended from one of the buttons of her gown.

At this juncture one of the Court ladies came in carrying several gowns for Her Majesty to select from. She looked at them and said that none of them suited her, to take them back and bring more. I had a look at them and thought they were perfectly lovely, such pretty colors and so beautifully embroidered. In a short while the same Court lady came back carrying more, and from these Her Majesty selected a sea-green one embroidered all over with white storks. She put this gown on and looked at herself in the mirror for a while, then took off her jade butterfly. She said: "You see I am very particular about little details. The jade butterfly is too green and it kills my gown. Put it back in the box and bring me a pearl stork in No. 35 box." I went back to the jewel room and fortunately found No. 35 box and brought it to her. She opened the box and took from it a stork made entirely of pearls set in silver, the bird's bill being made of coral. The pearls making the body of the bird were so cleverly set that the silver could not be seen at all unless one looked at it very closely. It was a most magnificent piece of workmanship and the pearls were of perfect color and shape. Her Majesty took it and placed it in her hair and did look very graceful and pretty. Then she picked out a mauve-colored short jacket, also embroidered with storks, which she put on over her gown. Her handkerchief and shoes were also embroidered with storks and when she was entirely dressed she looked like the stork lady.

Just as she had finished dressing, the Emperor Kwang Hsu came into the bedroom dressed in his official clothes. These clothes were exactly like other official clothes, except that he had no button on his hat and did not wear the peacock feather. He knelt down before Her Majesty and said: "Chin Baba, Chi Hsiang" (dear father, all joy be with you). It may seem curious that the Emperor and all of us should call Her Majesty father, and the reason why this was done was because Her Majesty always wanted to be a man and compelled everyone to address her as if she were actually one. This was only one of her many peculiarities.

I did not know whether to courtesy to the Emperor or not, not having received any orders as to what I should do. However, I thought it better to be too polite than not enough, so I waited until either he or Her Majesty went out of the room, as we were not allowed to salute or courtesy to anyone in her presence. In a little while the Emperor went out and I followed him out into the hall and just as I was in the act of courtesying Her Majesty came out. She looked at me in a very peculiar way, as if she did not approve of what I had done, but said nothing. I felt very uncomfortable and made up my mind that being too polite did not always pay after all.

I then returned to the room again and saw a small eunuch placing several yellow boxes on a table at the left side of the room. Her Majesty seated herself in a large chair, which was called her little throne, and this eunuch opened the boxes, took a yellow envelope from each box and handed them to Her Majesty. She opened these envelopes with an ivory paper knife and read their contents. They were memorials from the heads of the different Boards, or from the Viceroys of the different Provinces. The Emperor had come back and was standing at the side of this table and after she had finished reading, she handed them over to him. While all this was being done I stood at the back of her chair. I watched the Emperor as the different papers were handed to him and noticed that it did not take him very long to finish reading their contents. After he was finished reading the papers, they were placed back in the boxes. During all this time absolute silence was maintained. Just as they had finished the head eunuch came in, knelt down and announced that Her Majesty's chair was ready. She immediately got up and went out of the house, we following her, and I took her arm while she was descending the steps to go to her chair. When she had entered the chair to go to the Audience Hall, the Emperor and Young Empress and we all followed in our usual places, the eunuchs, amahs and servant girls carrying all the things exactly the same as was done the first day I came to the Palace. When we arrived at the Audience Hall, we took our places behind the big screen and the audience commenced. I was very curious to find out just how the audiences were conducted and wanted to listen to what was going on, but the Court ladies would not leave me alone. However, when they were all talking together with my sister, I stole away into a corner where I could sit and rest and listen to the conversation between the different Ministers and Her Majesty. Trust a woman for being inquisitive.

The first part of the audience I could not hear very well, as so many people were whispering and talking at the same time, but by peeping through the carved-work of the screen, I could see a General talking to Her Majesty. I also saw the members of the Grand Council come in headed by Prince Ching, who was the Councillor-in-Chief. After the General had finished, Her Majesty talked with Prince Ching about the appointment of some minor officials, a list of whose names had been handed to her. She looked over this list and spoke about several of the people, but Prince Ching suggested some others, saying: "Although these people whose names have been submitted to Your Majesty should receive appointments, those that I have suggested are better fitted for the positions." Her Majesty said: "All right, I leave it all to you." Then I heard Her Majesty say to the Emperor, "Is that correct?" and he replied, "Yes." This finished the Audience for the morning and the Ministers and Grand Councillors took their leave. We came out from behind the screen to Her Majesty and she said that she wanted to go for a walk to get some fresh air. The servant girls brought her a mirror, placed it on a table, and Her Majesty took off her heavy headdress, leaving the simple knot on the top of her head, which was quite becoming. She wanted to change some of the flower jewels and I opened a box which one of the eunuchs had brought and took out some very dainty flowers made of pearls. I handed her one which she placed at the side of this knot, then she selected a jade dragonfly which she placed on the other side. She said these small flowers were favorites of hers and she liked to wear them when she took off her heavy headdress. I was watching her very closely and wondered what I was going to do with the flowers she had taken off. I had not brought the boxes to put them in, as I did not know she was going to change again after the audience, and felt a little nervous as to what was the right thing to do, or as to what she would say. However, I saw a eunuch come in carrying these boxes and felt much relieved. I quickly placed the things in the boxes where they belonged.

# CHAPTER SEVEN

## Some Incidents of the Court

MY first day with Her Majesty was very trying as I did not know just what she wanted or how she wanted things done, and no one seemed willing to tell me; but by watching very closely I was soon able to grasp the situation. After I had finished putting the things in the boxes I did not know whether to take them back to the jewel room or not, or whether to wait until Her Majesty ordered me, and again I was in a quandary. I saw she was talking to my mother, so I waited a little time and finally made up my mind I would risk it and take them back, which I did. As I was returning I met Her Majesty in the big courtyard. She had just changed her gown again and looked much shorter as she had also changed her shoes for ones with lower heels. This gown was made of heavy sky-blue crepe with no embroidery at all, just trimmed with pale pink ribbons, and she looked very nice in it. When Her Majesty saw me, she asked me: "Where have you been?" I told her that I had just been putting her jewels away. Then she said: "Has anyone told you to put them away as soon as I am finished with them? I forgot to tell you this morning, although I had meant to." I said that no one had told me anything, that I was afraid to have the eunuchs taking such valuable things here and there, that I was sure that she did not want to use them any more, so I thought it would be safer to put them away in the jewel room again. Her Majesty looked at me and said: "I can see that these girls don't tell you anything and I am very glad to see that you have done just the right thing. That is why I thought someone must have told you what to do. Anything you want to know you can ask me, but don't talk to these mean people here." I could see from this that there must be some jealousy among them and decided that I was well able to find my own way, as I knew Her Majesty liked me and would help me out.

Her Majesty walked along a little way, then laughed and said to me: "Don't I look more comfortable now? I am going for a long walk and take lunch on the top of the hill. There is a nice place up there and I am sure you will like it. Come, let us go."

The Emperor had gone back to his own Palace, and the head eunuch had also disappeared. As we were walking along, Her Majesty was talking and smiling as if she had never a care or trouble in the world, or any important questions of state to settle. I thought from what I had seen so far that she had a very sweet disposition. She looked back and said: "Just see how many people are following us." I turned and saw the same crowd that had accompanied Her Majesty earlier in the day to the Audience Hall.

After passing out of the large courtyard on the West side, we came to a large, long veranda running in a zig-zag fashion along the front of the lake, and it was so long that I could not see the end of it. It was very prettily made of solid carved work from one end to the other. Electric lights were hanging from the ceiling at intervals, and when they were lighted at night, made a beautiful sight.

Her Majesty was a very fast walker and we had to step lively to keep up with her. The eunuchs and the servant girls walked on the right side and only one of the eunuchs was allowed to walk behind us, and he was the one who carried Her Majesty's yellow satin stool, which, like her dog, went everywhere she did. This stool she used to rest on when taking a walk. We walked for quite a long while and I began to feel tired, but Her Majesty, as old as she was, was still walking very fast and did not appear to be the least bit tired. She asked me if I liked the Palace and whether I would be satisfied to live with her, etc. I told her that it was a great pleasure for me to serve her, that it had been my dream for years, and now that my dream had come true, I could not help but be satisfied.

We finally arrived at the place where the marble boat was kept, and I was about finished. I never saw such vitality in an old woman in my life as Her Majesty had, and it was no wonder that she had ruled this vast Empire of China so successfully for so many years.

This boat was magnificent, being one mass of carved work, but the inside was all spoiled. Her Majesty showed us all over the boat, and whilst we were looking at the ruin, she said: "Look at those colored glasses in the windows and these beautiful paintings. They were all spoiled by the foreign troops in 1900. I don't intend to have it repaired as I don't want to forget the lesson I have learned and this is a good reminder." After we had been standing there a few minutes, a eunuch who had been carrying the famous satin stool, came forward, and Her Majesty sat down to rest. While we were talking I noticed two large and very fancy-looking boats approaching us, with several smaller ones coming along behind. As they came nearer I saw that they were also very beautifully made, and looked like floating pagodas of beautifully carved natural wood. The windows of the pagodas were hung with red gauze curtains and all was trimmed with silk. Her Majesty said: "There are the boats. We must go over to the west side of the lake and have luncheon." Her Majesty got up and walked to the edge of the lake, two eunuchs supporting her, one at each side. She stepped into the boat and we all followed her example. The inside of the boat was very nicely furnished with carved ebony furniture with blue satin cushions, one with many pots of flowers on both sides of the window. There were two more cabins behind this sitting room. Her Majesty told me to go in to see those two rooms. One little room was a dressing room full of toilet articles. The other one had two couches and several small chairs for Her Majesty to rest whenever she felt tired. Her Majesty sat on her throne and ordered us to sit on the floor. The eunuchs brought in red satin cushions for us to sit upon. To sit on the floor is all right for Chinese clothes, but of course it was out of the question with Paris gowns, and I felt very uncomfortable, but did not like to say so. I wanted to change into Manchu clothes, for I knew they were comfortable and easy to work in, but having received no order from Her Majesty, I did not dare to suggest it. Her Majesty noticed how very uncomfortable we looked sitting on the floor. She said: "You can stand up if you want to and just watch those boats following us." I put my head out of the window and noticed the Young Empress and several other Court ladies were in the other boat. They waved to me, and I waved back. Her Majesty laughed and said to me: "I give you this apple to throw to them." While saying this she took one from the big plates that stood upon the center table. I tried very hard, but the apple did not reach the other boat, but went to the bottom of the lake. Her Majesty laughed and told me to try again, but I failed. Finally, she took one and threw it herself. It went straight to the other boat and hit one of the ladies' head. We all laughed quite heartily. Then I began to enjoy myself. There were several open boats full of eunuchs, and another one of servant girls, amahs and the rest with Her Majesty's luncheon. The lake was beautiful and looked so green in the sun. I told Her Majesty that this color reminded me of the sea. She said: "You have travelled so much, and yet you have not had enough, but are still thinking of the sea. You must not go abroad any more, but stay with me. I want you to enjoy this sailing on this lake instead of the rough sea." I promised her that I would be only too happy to stay with her. I must say the truth, I did enjoy the lovely scenery, the beautiful weather, superb sunshine, with Her Majesty so kind to me and talking to me in such a motherly way made me love her more and more every minute I was there. I was so extremely happy there that even Paris pleasures had gone out of my memory entirely.

At last we arrived at another part of the lake. This was more of a stream, very narrow, just wide enough for one boat to pass. On both sides of the bank were planted drooping willow trees that reminded me of the Chinese Fairy tales I have read. This time I saw the servant girls, amahs, and also eunuchs carrying boxes, walking on both sides of the shore. Only two boats were going then, the Young Empress' and ours. Her Majesty said: "We will arrive at the bottom of the hill in a few minutes." When we came near the shore I saw her yellow chair and several red chairs waiting. We landed and walked to the chairs. I watched Her Majesty get into hers and noticed this was not the same chair she used this morning. This little one was, of course, of yellow, with yellow poles, and two eunuchs carried it, with yellow rope across their shoulders, and four eunuchs supported the poles, one on each corner of the chair. They were just going to raise her chair up when she said: "Yu tai tai (Lady Yu) I give you and your daughters special favor and give you a red chair with red cord that I have given to only a few people." The Young Empress looked at us, which I understood at once was meant for us to kowtow to her, which we did, and waited until the Empress got into hers. Then we went to search for ours. To my surprise our own eunuchs were standing waiting beside our chairs. On the poles I noticed that my name was written and I asked our eunuch the reason. He said that Her Majesty gave the order the night before. It was a lovely ride going to the top of the hill. I saw Her Majesty's chair in front, and the Young Empress'. They looked to me quite dangerous in ascending that way, and the men at the back of the chair had to raise the poles above their heads so as to make the chair the same level in ascending. I was quite nervous and was very much afraid that they might fall off and injure me. Our eunuchs were walking beside our chairs. I said to one of them that I was afraid the chair bearers might slip. He told me to look back of my chair, which I did, and to my surprise they had the poles raised up also above their heads, and I did not feel it at all. He told me that these chair bearers practice for such purposes and that there was no danger at all. It made my heart stop beating looking back and seeing the other Court ladies in their chairs way below mine, the eunuchs and servant girls walking, for fear I might fall off at any time. At last we arrived at the top of the hill. We helped Her Majesty to alight and followed her into the most lovely building I ever saw, the best one in the Summer Palace to my idea (name of this pavilion, Ching Fo Ker). This Palace had only two rooms, with windows on every side. One could see everywhere. Her Majesty used one large one to take her luncheon in and the other as a toilet room. I noticed that wherever we went we found Her Majesty's toilet room. Her Majesty took us around the compound and showed us the lovely flowers planted everywhere. One of the young eunuchs told me that Her Majesty's dainties were ready. That was my first day of real work. I went out and found two large yellow boxes of different kinds of candies and fruits, as I have before mentioned. I carried two plates at a time, and finished in nine times, placing them on a square table near her. She was talking to my mother then about flowers. I noticed that although she was talking, she was watching me at the same time. I placed the plates upon the table very carefully, and already having noticed the day before what were her favorite dishes, and placed these near her. She smiled at me and said: "You have done it very nicely. And how do you know that these are my favorites and have placed them near me? Who told you?" I replied that no one had told me anything and that I had noticed the day before what Lao Tsu Tsung liked (according to the Manchu custom one must address a superior or one's parents in the third person). Her Majesty said: "I can see you use your heart in everything (in China people say heart instead of head) and are not like the crowd I have here; they haven't the brains of a bird." She was soon busy eating, and gave me some candies, and told me to eat right there in her presence. Of course I never forgot to thank her, for I thought I had rather thank her too much than too little. She told me: "Whenever I give you small things you need not kowtow. Just say: 'Hsieh Lao Tsu Tsung Shang' (Thank the old ancestor), that is enough." After a little while she finished eating, and told me to take the dishes away. She said: "To-day is your day, so these things are yours. Take them out and sit down on the veranda and enjoy yourself. You see I could not eat all. There are lots of things left. If you like you can tell your own eunuch to send them to your room." I placed the little dishes back in the boxes and took them to the veranda. There I placed them upon the table and told the Young Empress to eat some. I did not know whether it was right to offer them to her or not and thought I could not do her any harm, even if I tried. She said all right, that she would eat some. I took a piece of candy and had just put it into my mouth when I heard Her Majesty calling my name. I hurried in and found her sitting at her table ready to take her lunch. She said: "What else did Mdme. Plancon say yesterday? Was she really pleased? Do you think they, the foreigners, really like me? I don't think so; on the contrary I know they haven't forgotten the Boxer Rising in Kwang Hsu's 26th year. I don't mind owning up that I like our old ways the best, and I don't see any reason why we should adopt the foreign style. Did any of the foreign ladies ever tell you that I am a fierce-looking old woman?" I was very much surprised that she should call me in and ask me such questions during her meal. She looked quite serious and it seemed to me she was quite annoyed. I assured her that no one ever said anything about Her Majesty but nice things. The foreigners told me how nice she was, and how graceful, etc. This seemed to please her, and she smiled and said: "Of course they have to tell you that, just to make you feel happy by saying that your sovereign is perfect, but I know better. I can't worry too much, but I hate to see China in such a poor condition. Although the people around me seem to comfort me by telling that almost every nation feels very friendly towards China, I don't think that is true. I hope we will be strong some day." While she was saying this I noticed her worried expression. I did not know what to say, but tried to comfort her by saying that that time will come, and we are all looking forward to it. I wanted to advise her on some points, but seeing that she was angry, I thought I had better not make any suggestions that day, but wait until I had another opportunity. I felt sorry for her, and would have given anything in the world to help her by telling what the general opinion of her was so as to let her know the truth, which no one dared to tell her. Something told me to be silent. I kept thinking all the time she was talking to me, and finally made up my mind that the time was not yet ripe for me to make any suggestion. I had grown to love her very much, so I wanted to take care not to offend her; that would probably finish my ambition. I wanted to study her first thoroughly and then try to influence her to reform China.

I stood all the time while she was eating. She got up from the table and handed me her napkin (this napkin was made of a piece of silk a yard square, woven in many colors). One corner was turned in, and a golden butterfly was fastened to it. It had a hook at the back of this butterfly so as to hook on her collar. She said: "I am sure you must be hungry. Go and tell the Young Empress and the rest of the people to come and eat. You can eat anything you want from these tables, so eat all you can." I was very, very hungry. Just imagine, I had been up since 5:00 o'clock and had only a light breakfast, and had walked a great deal. It was almost noon when Her Majesty sat down at her table. She ate so slowly, too. While I stood there talking to her I thought she would never finish. She ate a good meal. The Young Empress stood at the head of the table, and we all stood on either side. We did not like to be forward, so we stood at the other end of the table. The food was very much the same as the first day we were there. Her Majesty came out from the inner room, had just finished washing her face and hands, and had changed into another gown. This one was simple, but very pretty. It was woven with pink and gray raw silks, which gave it a changeable light whenever she moved. She came out and said: "I want to see you people eat; why is it that you are standing at the end of the table, the best dishes are not there? All of you come over here and eat near the Young Empress." So we moved from our end of the table to the other. Her Majesty stood near me, and pointed to a smoked fish and wanted me to try it, as it was her favorite, and said: "Make yourselves at home. You know you have to

43

fight your own battles here with this crowd. Of course you can come and tell me if anyone does not treat you fair." Her Majesty then went out, saying that she would walk a bit. I noticed that some of the court ladies did not look pleased, seeing that Her Majesty paid so much attention to us. I could see they were a little jealous of me, but that did not worry me in the least.

After we got through our luncheon, I followed the Young Empress, for it was all so new to me, and I did not know what I must do – whether to join Her Majesty or not. After seeing that they were jealous of me, I paid strict attention to everything, so as not to make any mistake in doing my work and let them have the satisfaction of laughing at me. I would not give them the chance. I heard Her Majesty talking to the eunuchs who looked after the garden, about some branches which ought to be cut down, saying they were lazy. So we went to her. She said to us: "You see I have to look after everything myself, if not, my flowers would be ruined. I can't depend on them at all. I wonder what they are good for. They ought to look around every day and cut down the dead branches and leaves. They have not been punished for several days and they are looking forward to it." She laughed and said: "I will not disappoint them, but give them all they wish to have." I thought these people must be idiots, looking forward to a whipping, and wondered who would whip them. Her Majesty turned to me and said: "Have you ever witnessed such an operation?" I told her that I had, having seen the convicts being whipped at a Magistrate's Yamen when I was a little girl living at Shansi (on the Yangtsze). She said: "That is nothing. The convicts are not half so wicked as these eunuchs. Of course they deserve a heavier punishment when they are bad." Her Majesty said that I should learn to play dice with her, as she never had enough people to play with, so we went back to the same room where she had taken her lunch. A square table was in the middle of this large room and a little throne of Her Majesty's, facing south (her favorite direction). Her Majesty sat on her throne and said to me: "I will show you how to play this game. Do you think you know enough Chinese to read this map?" I noticed a large map, the same size as the table, and laid upon it, drawn in different colors. In the center of the map was written the direction of the game. It said: "This game is called the 'Eight Fairies Travel across the Sea.' The names are Lu Hsien, Chang Hsien, Li Hsien, Lan Hsien, Hang Hsien, Tsao Hsien and Hain Hsien. These seven were masculine fairies. Hor Hsien was the only lady fairy." This map was the map of the Chinese Empire, and the names of the different provinces were written on the drawing. There were eight pieces of round ivory, about one inch and a half in diameter and a quarter of an inch thick. The names of these fairies were engraved upon them. This game could be played either by eight people or four people, when each person had to take two fairies' places, instead of one. A porcelain bowl was placed in the center of the map, to compare the point by throwing six dice into the bowl. For instance, four people play. One throws these six dice into the bowl and counts the points on them. The highest that one could get was 36, and should 36 be thrown the fairy should go to Hangehow to enjoy the beautiful scenery. This person threw dice for Lu Hsien and had 36 points and placed this ivory piece of Lu Hsien on Hangehow upon the map. The same person has to throw another time for another fairy, so each person throws twice if four people play the game, and once if played by eight. These different points count different provinces. They are counted thus: – Six dice alike. One pair in six dice, to three pairs. The lowest was the double 1, 2, 3. If any unfortunate fairy got this he should go on exile and be left out altogether. Any one of the fairies that travelled round the map to reach the Imperial Palace, the first, was the winner.

I read this to Her Majesty. She seemed to be quite pleased, and said: "I had no idea that you could read so well. This game was my own invention and I taught three Court ladies to play. I had a very hard time teaching them. I also taught them how to read Chinese in order to play the game, but it took them so long to learn anything that I got quite discouraged before I got through with them. I am sure you know how to play it now." I was very much surprised to hear that these Court ladies were as ignorant as this. I thought they must be excellent scholars, so did not dare to show my knowledge of Chinese literature. We began to play the game. Her Majesty was lucky. The two fairies held by her were way ahead of ours. One of the Court ladies said to me: "You will be surprised to see that Lao Tsu Tsung is always the winner." Her Majesty smiled and said to me: "You will never be able to catch my fairies." She said: "You are the first day here to play this game and if any of your fairies beat any of mine I will give you a nice present, so hurry up." I thought I could never get ahead of her fairies, for they were so far ahead of mine, but I tried hard, as Her Majesty told me to call out for the points I wanted. I did, but it came out something so different that it amused her a great deal. I had no idea how long we were playing this game. We counted who came next, and that was one of my fairies, so Her Majesty said to me: "I was sure you could not beat me, as no one could. Seeing that yours are next to mine, I will give you the present just the same." While she was saying this she told a servant girl to bring her some embroidered handkerchiefs. This girl brought several colored ones to her, and she asked me what color I preferred. She handed me a pink one and a pale blue one, all embroidered with purple wisteria, and said: "These two are the best, and I want you to take them." I was just going to thank her by bowing to the ground, but I found that my legs could not move. I tried hard and succeeded finally, with difficulty. Her Majesty laughed very heartily at me and said: "You see you are not accustomed to standing so long and you cannot bend your knees any more." Although my legs were sore I thought I had better not show it, but smiled and told her that it was nothing, only my legs were a little stiff, that was all. She said: "You must go and sit on the veranda and rest a minute." I was only too glad to sit down, so I went to the veranda and found the Young Empress sitting there with several Court ladies. The Young Empress said: "You must be tired standing so long. Come and sit near me." My legs were very stiff and my back was tired. Of course Her Majesty did not know how uncomfortable we were while she was sitting on her cozy throne. Foreign attire is out of the question for the Imperial Palace of Peking. I had hoped that Her Majesty would tell us to change into our Manchu gowns. I noticed that she asked many questions every day about foreign costumes, and she said: "The foreign costume is not any prettier than ours and I should say they must be quite uncomfortable round one's waist. I wouldn't be squeezed that way for anything." Although she was saying such things she did not suggest that we should give them up, so we had to wait patiently for her orders. The Young Empress took her watch out of her pocket, and said to me: "This game has lasted just two hours." I said to her that it seemed to me longer than that. While we were talking I saw our own eunuchs bringing four round boxes, made of thin board, carried at each end of bamboo poles. They put them down near where we sat, and one of them brought me a cup of tea. When my mother and sister came the same eunuch brought another two cups, and there were several Court ladies talking with us. This eunuch did not give them any. I noticed at the other end of this long veranda there were another two boxes, exactly the same as these, and a big tall eunuch made tea and brought it to the Young Empress in a yellow porcelain cup, with a silver saucer and a silver top cover. He did not give any to the others.

I was puzzled when one of the Court ladies sitting next to me said: "Would you mind telling Wang (our head eunuch) to give me a cup of your tea, just to save me the trouble to go and get it from the small room at the end of this long veranda?" I gave her such a surprised look, for I did not know that this was our tea, but I thought I'd just tell Wang to bring her a cup, and find out afterwards the reason, for I would give anything in the world rather than appear ignorant before those people. While we were talking Her Majesty came out. Before she reached the veranda I got up and told the Young Empress that Her Majesty was coming. I saw her first because I sat facing her back hall. Her Majesty said to us all: "It is almost three o'clock now, and I am going to rest a while. Let us leave here." We all stood in a line for her to enter her chair, and then we went to ours. It was quite a fast ride and we got out of our chairs before arriving at the courtyard of her own Palace. We walked ahead of her chair and formed into another line for her to alight. She walked to her bedroom and we all followed. A eunuch brought her a cup of hot water and another brought a bowl of sugar. She took her golden spoon and took two teaspoonfuls of sugar and put it into her cup of hot water, and drank it very slowly. She said: "You know before one goes to sleep or ever lies down, sugar water will quiet one's nerves. I always take it, and find it very good indeed." She took the flowers off from her headdress and I fixed them back in their boxes at once, and placed them in the jewel-room. When I came out of this jewel-room she was in bed already, and said to us: "You all go and rest a while. I don't need you now."

# CHAPTER EIGHT

## The Court Ladies

WE retired from her room, but I noticed that two of the Court ladies did not come out with us. One of them said to me: "I am glad that I can rest a bit to-day, for I have been sitting three afternoons in succession." At first I did not know what she meant. Then she said: "Oh, your turn has not come yet. We don't know whether you received the order or not. You know two of us must stay with Her Majesty during her afternoon siesta, to watch the eunuchs and the servant girls." I thought that was the funniest thing I had ever heard of, and wondered how many people would be in her room. The Young Empress said: "We had better go at once and rest ourselves, otherwise Her Majesty will be up again before we get the chance." Of course I had not the least idea how long she slept. So we went back to our rooms. I did not realize how tired I was until I sat down in my room. I felt finished and awfully sleepy at the same time, for I was not used to getting up at 5 o'clock. Everything was so new to me. As I sat there my thoughts wandered to Paris, and I thought how strange it was that I used to go to bed at 5 o'clock after the dances, and here I had to get up at such a time. All the surroundings seemed new to me, seeing the eunuchs running here and there waiting on us, as if they were chambermaids. I told them that I didn't need them any more. I wanted them to go out of the room so that I could lie down a bit. They brought us tea and different kinds of candies, and asked what else was wanted. I was just going to change into a comfortable dress, when the eunuch came in and informed me that "Yo ker lila" (visitors have come), and two Court ladies came, and another girl of about seventeen came in. I had seen her that very morning when I came to the Palace, busy working, but I was not introduced to her. These two girls said: "We have come to see you and also to find out if you are comfortable." I thought they were kind to come and see me that way, but I did not like their faces. They introduced this mean-looking girl to me and told me her name was Chun Shou (Graceful Long Life). She did not look as if her life would last long, being so thin and delicate. She looked sick and worn out to me. I did not know who she was. She courtesied to me and I returned to her, in a sort of half way. (I will explain about the courtesy.)

(To Her Majesty, the Emperor and the Young Empress, we went down and bent our knees, while we stood upright to the people of lower rank than ourselves. In this case one must always wait while the inferior

48

courtesies first, and bend the knees a little bit in return. This was the way I returned Chun Shou's courtesy to me.) The two girls then said "Chun Shou's father is only a small official, so she has not much standing at the Court. She is not exactly a Court lady, but she is not a servant girl either." I almost laughed right out, to hear such a funny statement, and wondered what she must be. I saw her sitting down with the Court ladies that very morning, so of course I asked her to sit down, too. These two Court ladies asked me if I felt tired, and how I liked the Empress Dowager. I told them that Her Majesty was the most lovely lady I had ever seen, and that I already loved her very much, although I had only been there a few days. They looked at Chun Shou and exchanged smiles. They did that in such a peculiar way that it annoyed me. They asked: "Do you think you would like to live in this place, and how long do you intend to stay?" I said I would love to stay long, and would do my best to wait on Her Majesty, and be useful to her, for she had been so kind towards us in the short time we had been there, and besides, it was my duty to serve my sovereign and country. They laughed and said: "We pity you, and are sorry for you. You must not expect any appreciation here, no matter how hard you work. If you are really going to do as you have said just now, you will be disliked by everybody."

I did not know what they were talking about, or what their conversation referred to. I thought this was so strange that I had better put a stop to it, so I immediately changed the subject. I asked them who dressed their hair, and who made their shoes for them, as they had asked me. They answered my questions by saying that their maids did everything for them. Chun Shou said to these two girls: "Tell her everything about this Palace, and I am sure she will change her mind when she actually sees things for herself." I didn't like this Chun Shou, and her face didn't impress me. She was a little bit of a thing, tiny head with thin lips. When she laughed one could only hear the noise she made; no expression was on her face at all. I was just going to say something to them, so as not to give them the opportunity of gossiping, but found they were too cunning. They noticed that I tried every way to stop them, so they said: "Now let us tell you everything. No one else will know. We like you very much and we want to give you some warning, so as to be able to protect yourself whenever you are in trouble." I told them that I would take great care to do my work and didn't think that I would ever get into trouble. They laughed and said: "That makes no difference. Her Majesty will find fault." I could not believe these things that they said, and intended to tell them that I refused to hear such statements, but I thought I had better listen to what they had to say first and not to offend them, for I never believed in making enemies. I then told them that it would be impossible for so sweet and kind-hearted a person like Lao Tsu Tsung (the old ancestor) to find fault with such helpless girls as we were, for we were her people, and she could do anything she liked with us. They said: "You don't know, and have no idea how wicked this place is; such torture and suffering one could not imagine. We are sure that you think you must be happy to be with the great Empress Dowager, and proud to be her Court Lady. Your day hasn't come yet, for you all are new to her. Yes, she is extremely kind to you just now, but wait until she gets tired of you and then see what she will do. We have had enough, and know what the Court life is. Of course you must have heard that Li Lien Ying (the head eunuch) rules this Palace behind Lao Tsu Tsung's back. We are all afraid of him. He pretends that he cannot influence Lao Tsu Tsung, but we always know the result after a long conversation consulting how to punish anyone. If any of us do anything wrong, we always go to him and beg him to help us out. Then he says he has no power to influence Her Majesty, and also that he dare not tell her much, for she would scold him. We hate all the eunuchs, they are such bad people. We can see very plainly they are awfully polite to you because they can see that you are in favor. To receive such rudeness from them, constantly, as we do, is unbearable.

"Lao Tsu Tsung is very changeable. She may like one person to-day, to-morrow she hates this same person worse than poison. She has moods, and has no appreciation whatsoever. Even Chu Tzu, the Young Empress (Chu Tzu means Mistress, that is to say she was mistress of us all, for the Manchus were considered by the sovereign as slaves) is afraid of Li Lien Ying, and has to be very nice to him. In fact, we all have to be polite to him." They talked so long that I thought they would never finish. About this time Wang came in and brought tea for us. Suddenly I heard people howling in the distance, so I asked Wang what was the matter. The girls were listening also and a eunuch came flying in and told us Lao Fo Yeh chin la (The Great Buddha wakes up). The girls got up and said we must all go to see her, so they went. I was not at all pleased with their visit, and wished they hadn't come, especially as they told me such horrible things. It made me quite sad to listen to the awful way they talked about Her Majesty. I loved her the first day I was there, and made up my mind to forget everything they had told me.

I was cross also because I didn't have time to change my clothes, and had to go up to Her Majesty at once. I went into her bedroom, and found her sitting upon the bed cross-legged, with a small table placed on the bed in front of her. She smiled and asked: "Have you had a good rest? Did you sleep at all?" I said that I was not sleepy, and could not sleep in the daytime. She said: "When you are old like me, you will be able to sleep at any time. Just now you are young, and fond of play. I think you must have been on the hills to gather flowers, or walked too much, for you look tired." I could only say "Yes." The two Court ladies who had just been talking nonsense about Her Majesty came in, to assist in handing her the toilet articles. I looked at them, and felt ashamed for them to face her, after having said so many disagreeable things. Her Majesty washed her face and combed her hair, and a servant girl brought her fresh flowers, of white jasmine and roses. Her Majesty stuck them in her hair and said to me: "I am always fond of fresh flowers – better than jade and pearls. I love to see the little plants grow, and I water them myself. I have been so busy ever since you came that I haven't been able to visit my plants. Tell them to get the dinner ready and I will take a walk afterwards." I came out of her room and gave the eunuch the order. As usual we brought little dainties to her. By this time Her Majesty was dressed and was sitting in the large hall, playing solitaire with her dominoes. The eunuch laid the tables as usual, and Her Majesty stopped play, and commenced to eat. She asked me: "How do you like this kind of life?" I told her that I very much enjoyed being with her. She said: "What kind of a place is this wonderful Paris I have heard so much about? Did you enjoy yourself while you were there, and do you wish to go back again? It must be hard for you people to leave China for three or four years, and I suppose you were all pleased when you received the order to come back, after your father's term was finished."

The only thing I could say was "Yes," because it wouldn't be nice to tell her that I was awfully sorry to leave Paris. She said: "I think we have everything in China, only the life is different. What is dancing? Someone told me that two people hold hands and jump all over the room. If that is the case I don't see any pleasure in it at all. Do you have to jump up and down with men? They told me that old women, with white hair, dance, too." I explained to her about the balls given by the President, and all the private dances, and also all about the masquerade balls, etc. Her Majesty said: "I don't like this masquerade ball because you don't know whom you are dancing with if they are wearing a mask." I explained to her how carefully the people issued their invitations, and that anyone who behaved badly could never enter into high society. Her Majesty said: "I would like to see how you jump, can you show me a little?" I went in search of my sister, and found her busy talking to the Young Empress. I told her that Her Majesty wished to see how people dance, and that we must show her. The Young Empress and all the

51

Court ladies heard this, and all said that they also wished to see. My sister said that she had noticed a large gramophone in Her Majesty's bedroom, and that perhaps we could find some music. I thought that was a good idea, and went to ask her for the gramophone. She said: "Oh, must you jump with music?" I almost laughed when she said that, and told her it was much nicer with music, as otherwise one could not keep in time. She ordered the eunuchs to have the gramophone brought to the hall, and said: "You jump while I take my dinner." We looked over a lot of records, but they were all Chinese songs, but at last we found a waltz, so we started to dance. We could see that a lot of people were looking at us, who perhaps thought that we were crazy. When we had finished we found Her Majesty laughing at us. She said: "I could never do that. Are you not dizzy turning round and round? I suppose your legs must be very tired also. It is very pretty, and just like the girls used to do centuries ago in China. I know that it is difficult and one ought to have any amount of grace to do it, but I don't think it would look nice to see a man dancing with a girl like that. I object to the hand around the girl's waist; I like to see the girls dance together. It would never do for China for a girl to get too close to a man. I know the foreigners don't seem to think about that at all. It shows that they are broader minded than us. Is it true that the foreigners don't respect their parents at all-that they could beat their parents and drive them out of the house?" I told her that it was not so, and that someone had given her wrong ideas about foreigners. Then she said: "I know that perhaps sometimes one among the commonest class do that, and that people are apt to take it wrong, and conclude that all foreigners treat their parents that way. Now I see just the same thing done by the common people in China." I wondered who had told her such nonsense and made her believe it.

After we had taken our dinner it was just half-past five, and Her Majesty said she would take a walk along the long veranda, so we followed her. She showed me her flowers, and said that she had planted them herself. Whenever Her Majesty went anywhere there was always a lot of attendants following her, exactly the same as when she went to the morning audiences. When we reached the end of this long veranda, which took us a quarter of an hour to walk, Her Majesty ordered her stool to be brought into one of the summer houses. These summer houses were built of nothing but bamboo, all the furniture being made of different shaped bamboo. Her Majesty sat down, and one of the eunuchs brought tea and honeysuckle flowers. She ordered the eunuchs to give us tea also. Her Majesty said: "This is my simple way of enjoying life. I love to see the country scenery. There are a great many pretty places which I will show you and I am sure that after you have seen them you will not like foreign countries any more. There is no scenery in the world which can beat the Chinese. Some returned Ministers from abroad said to me that the trees and mountains in foreign countries looked ugly and savage. Is that true?" I concluded right away that someone had wished to please her by saying things about foreigners, so I told her that I had been in almost every country, and had found lovely scenery, but of course it was different from China. While we were talking Her Majesty said that she felt chilly and asked: "Are you cold? You see you have your own eunuchs, they are all standing around, and have nothing to do. Next time tell them to carry your wraps along with you. I think that foreign clothes must be quite uncomfortable either too warm or too cold. I don't see how you can eat, having your waist squeezed that way." Her Majesty got up and we all went on walking slowly towards her own Palace. She sat down on her favorite little throne in the hall and started to play solitaire. We came out on the veranda, and the Young Empress said to us: "You must be tired, for I know you are not used to doing such hard work all day long without stopping. You had better wear Manchu clothes, because they are comfortable and easy to work in. Look at your long train; you have to take it up in your hands while walking."

I told her that I would be only too pleased to change the clothes, but that not having received an order from Her Majesty I could not make any suggestions. The Young Empress said: "No, don't ask anything, and I am sure Her Majesty will tell you to change by and by. Just now she wishes to see your Paris gowns, because she wants to know how foreign ladies dress on different occasions. She thought that some of the ladies came to the Garden Party dressed in woolen clothes. We thought that foreign ladies were not so extravagant as we are until we met Mdme. Plancon the other day. Do you remember what Her Majesty said to you? 'That Mdme. Plancon was so different from many ladies she had met, and also dressed differently.'" It was a chiffon dress, with hand paintings, which Mdme. Plancon wore, which pleased Her Majesty very much. While I was talking with the Young Empress all the electric lights turned up, so I went to Her Majesty to see if she needed anything. She said: "Let us play a game of dice before I go to bed." We began to play the same thing as we had done in the afternoon. Her Majesty won another game, this time it took only an hour to finish the game. Her Majesty said to me: "Why can't you win once?" I knew she wanted to tease, so I said that my luck was bad. She laughed and said: "To-morrow you try to put your stocking on wrong side out; that is a sure sign of winning." I told her that I would, and I knew that pleased her.

During the short time I was there I kept studying her most of the while. I could see nothing would make her happier than for me to obey her orders. Her Majesty said that she felt tired, and that we must bring her milk. She said to me: "I want you to burn incense sticks and bow to the ground every night to the Buddha in the next room before I go to bed. I hope you are not a Christian, for if you are I can never feel as if you are mine at all. Do tell me that you are not." I did not expect that question at all, and I must say that it was a very difficult question to answer. For my own protection I had to say that I had nothing to do with the Christians. I felt guilty at having deceived her that way, but it was absolutely necessary, and there was no other way out of it. I knew that I had to answer her question at once, because it would never do for her to see any hesitation, which would arouse her suspicions. Although my face showed nothing, my heart stopped beating for a while. I felt ashamed to have fooled her. The earliest training I had was never to be ashamed to tell the truth. When Her Majesty heard me say that I was not a Christian, she smiled and said: "I admire you; although you have had so much to do with foreigners, yet you did not adopt their religion. On the contrary, you still keep to your own. Be strong and keep it as long as you live. You have no idea how glad I am now, for I suspected you must believe in the foreign God. Even if you don't want to, they can make you believe it. Now I am ready for bed."

We helped her to undress, and I, as usual, put away her jewels, and noticed she wore only one pair of jade bracelets to sleep. She changed into her bed clothes and lay down between the silk covers and said to us: "You can go now." We courtesied to her and withdrew from her bedroom. Out in the hall there was on the cold stone floor six eunuchs. They were the watchmen and must not sleep at all during the night. In her bedroom were two eunuchs, two servant girls, two old women servants and sometimes two Court ladies. These people also must not sleep. The two girls massaged her legs every night, and the two women were there to watch the girls, the two eunuchs to watch the two old women, and the two Court ladies to watch them all, in case they did any mischief. They all took turns, and that was the reason why sometimes two Court ladies must sit overnight when it happened that the eunuchs were not reliable. Her Majesty trusted the Court ladies the most. I was never more surprised in my life than when one of these six eunuchs told me in the hall, for I had asked what they were all doing there.

Later on one of the Court ladies said to me that it was customary for them to take turns to attend at Her Majesty's bedchamber in the morning to wake her up, and that I should take my turn the next morning and my sister the following morning. While saying this she smiled in a most peculiar way. I did not understand at the time, but found out later. I asked her what I should do to wake Her Majesty, and she said: "There is no particular way, you will have to use your own judgment; but be careful not to make her angry. It was my turn this morning. I knew that she was very tired, having had a very trying time the day before, so I had to make a little more noise than usual when waking her. She was very angry and scolded me dreadfully when she arose, as it was rather late. This very often happens when Her Majesty gets up late, as she always says that we do not make enough noise to wake her. However, I don't think she will do this to you, just now, as you are new here; but wait until you have been here a few months." What this Court lady said to me worried me quite considerably; but from what I had seen of Her Majesty so far, I could not believe that she would be angry with anyone who was doing her duty properly.

# CHAPTER NINE

## The Emperor Kwang Hsu

THE next day I arose earlier than usual and dressed in a great hurry, as I feared I might be late. When I got to Her Majesty's Palace there were a few Court ladies there sitting on the veranda. They smiled and asked me to sit down with them as it was still too early, being only five o'clock. I had been told to wake Her Majesty at five thirty. The Young Empress came up a few minutes later and we all courtesied and wished her "good morning." After talking with us a few minutes, she asked if Her Majesty was awake and which one of us was on duty that day. When I informed her that it was my turn, she immediately ordered me to go to Her Majesty's room at once. I went very quietly and found some servant girls standing about and one Court lady, who was sitting on the floor. She had been on duty all night. When she saw me she got up and whispered to me, that now that I had come, she would go and change her clothes and brush up a bit, and for me not to leave the room until Her Majesty was awake. After this Court lady had gone, I went near to the bed and said: "Lao Tsu Tsung, it is half-past five." She was sleeping with her face toward the wall, and without looking to see who had called her, she said: "Go away and leave me alone. I did not tell you to call me at half-past five. Call me at six," and immediately went off to sleep again. I waited until six and called her again. She woke and said: "This is dreadful. What a nuisance you are." After she had said this, she looked around and saw me standing by the bed. "Oh! it is you, is it? Who told you to come and wake me?" I replied: "One of the Court ladies told me that it was my turn to be on duty in Lao Tsu Tsung's bedchamber." "That is funny. How dare they give orders without receiving instructions from me first? They know that this part of their duty is not very pleasant and have put it off on you because they know you are new here." I made no reply to this. I got along as best I could that day and found it no easy matter, as Her Majesty was very exacting in everything. However, the next time I managed to divert her attention to things new or interesting in order to take her mind off of what she was doing, and in this way had much less trouble getting her out of bed.

My reader can't imagine how very glad we were to get back to our rooms, and it was just 10:30 P. M. I was very tired and sleepy, so I undressed and went to bed at once. I think that as soon as my head touched the pillow I was asleep.

The following day there was the same thing, the usual audience in the morning, of course busy all the time, which went on for fifteen days before I realized it. I began to take great interest in the Court life, and liked it better every day. Her Majesty was very sweet and kind to us always, and took us to see the different places in the Summer Palace. We went to see Her Majesty's farm, situated on the west side of the lake, and had to cross over a high bridge to get there. This bridge is called Tu Tai Chiao (Jade Girdle Bridge). Her Majesty often took us under this bridge in a boat, or we walked round on the border. She seemed very fond of sitting on the top of this bridge on her stool and taking her tea, in fact this was one of her favorite places. She used to go and see her farm once every four or five days, and it always pleased her if she could take some vegetables and rice or corn from her own farm. She cooked these things herself in one of the courtyards. I thought that was good fun, and also turned up my sleeves to help her cook. We brought fresh eggs also from the farm and Her Majesty taught us how to cook them with black tea leaves.

Her Majesty's cooking stoves were very peculiar. They were made of brass, lined with bricks. They could be moved anywhere, for they had no chimneys. Her Majesty told me to boil the eggs first until they were hard, and to crack them but to keep the shells on, and add half a cup of black tea, salt and spices. Her Majesty said: "I like the country life. It seems more natural than the Court life. I am always glad to see young people having fun, and not such grand dames when we are by ourselves. Although I am not young any more, I am still very fond of play." Her Majesty would taste first what we had been cooking, and would give us all to taste. She asked: "Do you not think this food has more flavor than that prepared by the cooks?" We all said it was fine. So we spent the long days at the Court having good fun.

I saw Emperor Kwang Hsu every morning, and whenever I had the time he would always ask some words in English. I was surprised to learn that he knew quite a bit of spelling, too. I found him extremely interesting. He had very expressive eyes. He was entirely a different person when he was alone with us. He would laugh and tease, but as soon as he was in the presence of Her Majesty he would look serious, and as if he were worried to death. At times he looked stupid. I was told by a great many people who were presented to him at the different audiences that he did not look intelligent, and that he would never talk. I knew better, for I used to see him every day. I was at the Court long enough to study him, and found him to be one of the most intelligent men in China. He was a capital diplomat and had wonderful brains, only he had no opportunities. Now a great many people have asked me the same question, if our Emperor Kwang Hsu had any courage or brains. Of course outsiders have no idea how strict the law is, and the way we have to respect our parents. He was compelled to give up a great many things on account of the law. I have had many long talks with him and found him a wise man, with any amount of patience. His life was not a happy one; ever since his childhood his health was poor. He told me that he never had studied literature very much, but it came natural to him. He was a born musician and could play any instrument without studying. He loved the piano, and was always after me to teach him. There were several beautiful grand pianos at the Audience Hall. He had very good taste for foreign music, too. I taught him some easy waltzes and he kept the time beautifully. I found him a good companion and a good friend, and he confided in me and told me his troubles and sorrows. We talked a great deal about western civilization, and I was surprised to learn he was so well informed in everything. He used to tell me, time after time, his ambitions for the welfare of his country. He loved his people and would have done anything to help them whenever there was famine or flood. I noticed that he felt for them. I know that some eunuchs gave false reports about his character, – that he was cruel, etc. I had heard the same thing before I went to the Palace. He was kind to the eunuchs, but there was always that distinction between the master and the servants. He would never allow the eunuchs to speak to him unless they were spoken to, and never listened to any kind of gossip. I lived there long enough, and I know just what kind of cruel people those eunuchs were. They had no respect for their master. They came from the lowest class of people from the country, had no education, no morals, no feeling for anything, not even between themselves. The outside world has heard so many things against His Majesty, the Emperor Kwang Hsu's character, but I assure my readers that these things were told by the eunuchs to their families, and of course they always stretched it out as far as possible in order to make the conversation interesting. The majority of the people living in Peking get all kinds of information through them. I have witnessed the same thing many a time during my stay at the Palace.

One day during the time of Her Majesty's afternoon rest we heard a dreadful noise. It sounded just like the firing off of fire-crackers. Such a noise was quite unusual in the Palace for such things are not allowed to be brought into the Palace grounds. Of course Her Majesty woke up. In a few seconds time everyone became excited and were running to and fro as if the building was on fire. Her Majesty was giving orders and telling the eunuchs to be quiet, but no one listened to her and kept yelling and running around like crazy people, all talking at the same time. Her Majesty was furious and ordered us to bring the yellow bag to her. (I must explain about this bag. It was made of ordinary yellow cloth and contained bamboo sticks of all sorts and sizes and are made to beat the eunuchs, servant girls and old women servants with.) This bag was carried everywhere Her Majesty went, to be handy in case of emergency. Everyone of us knew where this bag was kept. We took all the sticks from the bag and Her Majesty ordered us to go to the courtyard and beat the eunuchs. It was such a funny sight to see all the Court ladies and servant girls each with a stick trying to separate the excited crowd. On my part I thought I was having good fun so I laughed and found the rest were laughing too. Her Majesty was standing on the veranda watching us but she was too far away to see well and with all that noise, we knew she could not hear us laughing. We tried our best to separate the crowd, but were laughing so much we did not have enough strength to hurt any of them. All of a sudden all the eunuchs became quiet and stopped talking, for one of them saw the head eunuch, Li Lien Ying, followed by all his attendants coming towards them. Everyone of them became frightened and stood there like statues. We stopped laughing, too, and turned back each with a stick in our hand, walking toward Her Majesty. Li Lien Ying was having a nap, too, and had heard the noise and had come to enquire what the trouble was and to report it to Her Majesty. It seemed one of the young eunuchs caught a crow. (The eunuchs hated crows, as they are considered an unlucky bird. The people in China called eunuchs crows because they were very disagreeable. That was the reason why the eunuchs hated them so.) They always set traps to catch them and then tied a huge fire-cracker to their legs, set fire to the cracker and then set the unfortunate birds free. Naturally the poor birds would be glad to fly away and by the time the powder exploded would be high up in the air and the poor bird would be blown to pieces. It seemed this was not the first time the eunuchs had played this cruel trick. I was told it always delighted them so much to see blood and torture. They always invited others to drink some wine with them to celebrate an occasion such as this. This cruel deed was always done outside of the wall of the Audience Hall but that day the crow flew towards Her Majesty's own Palace while she was sleeping and the powder exploded while the bird was passing the courtyard. After the head eunuch had told Her Majesty what had happened, she was very angry and ordered that this young eunuch be brought in and receive punishment in her presence. I noticed one of the head eunuch's attendants push the culprit out from the crowd. The head eunuch immediately gave orders to lay this man on the ground and two eunuchs stood on each side of him and beat him on his legs with two heavy bamboo sticks one at a time. The victim never uttered a word while this was going on. The head eunuch counted until this man had received one hundred blows, then he gave orders to stop. Then he knelt in front of Her Majesty waiting for her orders and at the same time kowtowed on the ground until his head made a noise on the stone steps, asking to be punished for his carelessness and neglect of duty. Her Majesty said that it was not his fault and ordered him to take the offender away. During all this time the offender was still on the ground, and did not dare to move. Two eunuchs each took hold of a foot and dragged him out of the courtyard. We were all afraid even to breathe aloud for fear Her Majesty would say that we were pretending to be frightened at witnessing this punishment, at the same time when it was over we would go and gossip about how cruel she was. No one was surprised at what had happened, as we were accustomed to seeing it almost every day and were quite used to it. I used to pity them, but I changed my mind very soon after I had arrived.

The first person I saw punished was a servant girl, she had made a mistake about Her Majesty's socks and had brought two which were not mates, Her Majesty finding that out, ordered another servant girl to slap her face ten times on each cheek. This girl did not slap hard enough, so Her Majesty said they were all good friends and would not obey her orders, so she told the one who had been slapped to slap the other. I thought that was too funny for anything and wanted to laugh the worst way, but of course did not dare. That night I asked those two girls how they felt slapping each other that way. The reason why I asked them was because they were laughing and joking as usual immediately they were out of Her Majesty's bedchamber. They told me that was nothing; that they were quite used to it and never bothered themselves about such small things. I in turn soon became used to it, and was as callous as they were.

Now regarding the servant girls, they are a much better class of people than the eunuchs. They are the daughters of Manchu soldiers, and must stay ten years at the Palace to wait upon Her Majesty, and then they are free to marry. One got married after my first month at the Court. Her Majesty gave her a small sum of money, five hundred taels. This girl was so attached to Her Majesty that it was very hard for her to leave the Court. She was an extremely clever girl. Her name was Chiu Yuen (Autumn's Cloud). Her Majesty named her that because she was so very delicate looking and slight. I liked her very much during the short time that we were together. She told me not to listen to anyone's gossip at the Court, also that Her Majesty had told her she was very fond of me.

On the twenty-second day of the third moon she left the Palace, and we were all sorry to lose her. Her Majesty did not realize how much she missed her until after she had gone. For a few days we had nothing but troubles. It seemed as if everything went wrong. Her Majesty was not at all satisfied without Chiu Yuen. The rest of the servant girls were scared, and tried their best to please Her Majesty, but they had not the ability, so we had to help and do a part of their work so as not to make Her Majesty nervous. Unfortunately, she stopped us, and said: "You have enough to do of your own work, and I do not want you to help the servants. You don't please me a bit that way." She could see that I was not accustomed to her ways, for she had spoken severely, so she smiled and said to me: "I know you are good to help them so as not to make me angry, but these servants are very cunning. It isn't that they cannot do their work. They know very well that I always select the clever ones to wait on me in my bedroom and they don't like that, so they pretend to be stupid and make me angry so that I will send them to do the common work. The eunuchs are worse. They are all afraid to take Chiu Yuen's place. Now I have found them out, and I will only keep the stupid ones to wait on me from now." I almost laughed when I noticed that they all looked serious for a moment. I thought these people must be really stupid, and not lazy, but I had dealings with them every day and found them out all right. The eunuchs don't seem to have any brains at all. They are such queer people and have no feelings. They have the same mood all day long – I should say they are in a cruel mood. Whenever Her Majesty gave an order they always said "Jer" (Yes) and as soon as they got to our waiting room they would say to each other: "What was the order? I have forgotten all about it." Then they used to come to one of us who had happened to be present when the order was given: "Please tell us what the order was. I did not listen while Her Majesty was talking." We used to laugh and make fun of them. We knew they were afraid to ask Her Majesty, and of course we had to tell them. One of the eunuch writers had to keep writing down the orders that had been given during the day, for Her Majesty wanted to keep records of everything. There were twenty eunuchs who were educated and they were excellent scholars. These had to answer any questions which Her Majesty happened to ask them about Chinese literature, while she had a good knowledge of it herself. I noticed that it pleased her a great deal if anyone could not answer a question, or knew less than she did. She took delight in laughing at them. Her Majesty was also very fond of teasing. She knew that the Court ladies did not know very much about literature, so she used to try it on us. We had to say something whether it was appropriate to her questions or not, and that would make her laugh. I was told that Her Majesty did not like anyone to be too clever, and yet she could not bear stupid people, so I was rather nervous, and did not know how to act for the first three weeks I was there, but it did not take me very long to study her. She certainly admired clever girls, but she did not like those who would show their cleverness too much. How I won her heart was this way. Whenever I was with her I used to fix my whole attention on her and watched her very closely (not staring, for she hated that) and always carried out her orders properly. I noticed another thing, and that was that whenever she wanted anything to be brought to her, such as cigarettes, handkerchief, etc., she would only look at the article and then look at anyone who happened to be there at the time. (There was always a table in the room, on which everything she needed for the day was placed.) I got so used to her habits that after a short time I knew just what she wanted by looking at her eyes, and I was very seldom mistaken. This pleased her a great deal. She was strong-minded, and would always act the way she thought was right, and had perfect confidence in herself. At times I have seen her looking very sad. She had strong emotions, but her will was stronger. She could control herself beautifully, and yet she liked people to sympathize with her – only by actions, not by words, for she did not like anyone to know her thoughts. I am sure my readers will think how hard it was to be the Court lady of Her Majesty, the Empress Dowager of China, but on the contrary I enjoyed myself very much, as she was so interesting, and I found that she was not at all difficult to please.

The first day of the fourth moon Her Majesty was worried over the lack of rain. She prayed every day after the audience for ten days, without any result. Every one of us kept very quiet. Her Majesty did not even give any orders that day, and spoke to no one. I noticed that the eunuchs were scared, so we went without our luncheon. I worked so hard that morning, and was so hungry – in fact all the Court ladies were. I felt sorry for Her Majesty. Finally she told me I could go, as she wanted to rest a while, so we came back to our own quarters. I questioned our own eunuch Wang as to why Her Majesty was worrying about rain, for we were having lovely weather then, day after day. He told me that Lao Fo Yeh (Old Buddha) was worried for the poor farmers, as all their crops were dead without rain for so long. Wang also reminded me that it had not rained once since I came to live at the Palace. I did not realize that it was so long as two months and seven days, and on the other hand it seemed to me longer than that, for the life was very nice and pleasant, and Her Majesty was very kind to me, as if she had known me for years already. Her Majesty took very little food at dinner that night. There was not a sound anywhere, and everyone kept quiet. The Young Empress told us to eat as fast as we could, which puzzled me. When we came back to our waiting room, the Young Empress said to me that Her Majesty was very much worried for the poor farmers and that she would pray for rain, and stop eating meat for two or three days. That same night, before Her Majesty retired, she gave orders that no pigs were to be slaughtered within the gates of Peking. The reason of this was that by sacrificing ourselves by not eating meat the Gods would have pity on us and send rain. She also gave orders that everyone should bathe the body and wash out the mouth in order that we might be cleansed from all impurities and be ready to fast and pray to the Gods. Also that the Emperor should go to the temple inside the Forbidden City, to perform a ceremony of sacrifice (called Chin Tan). He was not to eat meat or hold converse with anyone, and to pray to the Gods to be merciful and send rain to the poor farmers. His Majesty, the Emperor Kwang Hsu, wore a piece of jade tablet about three inches square, engraved "Chai Chieh" (the meaning being just like Chin Tan-not to eat meat but to pray three times a day), both in Manchu and Chinese, and all the eunuchs who went with the Emperor wore the same kind of tablets. The idea was that this jade tablet was to remind one to be serious in performing the ceremonies.

The next morning Her Majesty got up very early and ordered me not to bring any jewels for her. She dressed herself in great haste. Her breakfast was very simple that day, just milk and steamed bread. Our own breakfast was cabbage and rice cooked together, with a little salt. It was tasteless. Her Majesty did not talk to us at all, except when giving orders, and so, of course, we kept silent. Her Majesty wore a pale gray gown, made very plain, with no embroidery or trimmings of any kind. She wore gray shoes to match, not to mention her gray handkerchief. We followed her into the hall where a eunuch knelt with a large branch of willow tree. Her Majesty picked a little bunch of leaves and stuck it on her head. The Young Empress did the same, and told us to follow her example. Emperor Kwang Hsu took a branch and stuck it on his hat. After that Her Majesty ordered the eunuchs and the servant girls to do the same thing. It was a funny sight, and everyone did look queer with a bunch of leaves on the head. The head eunuch came and knelt in front of Her Majesty and said that everything was prepared for the ceremony in the little pavilion in front of her own palace. She told us that she preferred to walk, as she was going to pray. It took us only a few minutes to cross the courtyard. When we arrived at this pavilion I noticed a large square table was placed in the center of the room. A few large sheets of yellow paper and a jade slab, containing some vermilion powder instead of ink, with two little brushes to write with. At each side of the table stood a pair of large porcelain vases, with two large branches of willow. Of course no one was allowed to speak, but I was curious and wanted to find out why everyone had to wear the willow leaves on the head. Her Majesty's yellow satin cushion was placed in front of this table. She stood there and took a piece of sandalwood and placed it in the incense burner filled with live charcoal. The Young Empress whispered to me to go over and help Her Majesty to burn them. I placed several pieces in until she told me that was enough. Then Her Majesty knelt on her cushion, the Young Empress knelt behind her, and we all knelt in a row behind the Young Empress, and commenced to pray. The Young Empress taught us that very morning how to say the prayer: "We worship the Heavens, and beg all the Buddhas to take pity on us and save the poor farmers from starving. We are willing to sacrifice for them. Pray Heaven send us rain." We repeated the same prayer three times, and bowed three times – nine times in all. After that Her Majesty went to her usual morning audience. It was much earlier than usual that morning for the Court was returning to the Forbidden City at noon. His Majesty, the Emperor Kwang Hsu, was to pray at the Forbidden City and Her Majesty always wanted to accompany him wherever he went. It was nine o'clock in the morning when the audience was over. She ordered me not to bring any jewels for her to the Forbidden City this time, for she would not need them at all. I went to the jewel-room and locked everything up, and placed the keys in a yellow envelope, sealed it, and placed the envelope among the others, and gave them to a eunuch who takes care of these things. We packed all her favorite things. Her gowns were the most important things to pack, she had so many and it was impossible to take all. I noticed that the Court lady who was looking after her gowns was the busiest amongst us. She had to select gowns enough to last four or five days. She told me that she had selected about fifty different ones. I told her that Lao Tsu Tsung might stay at the Forbidden City four or five days, and that she would not need so many gowns. She said it was safer to bring many, for one was not sure what would be Her Majesty's idea for the day. Packing at the Court was very simple. Eunuchs brought many yellow trays, which are made of wood, painted yellow, about five feet by four feet and one foot deep. We placed a large yellow silk scarf in the tray, then the gowns, and covered them with a thick yellow cloth. Everything was packed the same way. It took us about two hours to pack fifty-six trays. These things always started off first, carried by the eunuchs. His Majesty, the Emperor Kwang Hsu, the Young Empress and all the Court ladies, had to kneel on the ground for Her Majesty's sedan chair to pass the Palace Gate, then we went in search of our own chairs. The procession as usual was pretty, soldiers marching in front of her chair, four young Princes riding on horseback on each side of her, and from forty to fifty eunuchs also on horseback behind her, all dressed in their official robes. The Emperor's chair and the Young Empress' chair were of the same color as Her Majesty's. The Secondary wife of the Emperor had a deep yellow chair. The chairs of the Court ladies were red, and were carried by four chair bearers, instead of eight like their Majesties. Our own eunuchs also rode on horseback, behind us. We rode a long time, it seemed to me, before I noticed the Emperor's chair begin to descend from the stone-paved road, and we all followed him. I could see that Her Majesty's chair was still going straight on, and we took a nearer route to reach Wan Shou Si (The long life temple), to await Her Majesty's arrival. We alighted from our chairs and started at once to prepare Her Majesty's tea and her little dishes. I went to help her to alight, and supported her right arm to mount the steps. Her Majesty sat on Her Throne, and we placed a table in front of her and my sister brought her tea. (The custom was, that if she went anywhere, or during the festivals, we must bring to her everything, instead of the eunuchs.) We placed all the dainties in front of her, and then we went to rest. Her Majesty always stopped at this temple on the way from the Summer Palace to the Forbidden City.

# CHAPTER TEN

## The Young Empress

I THOUGHT of so many things while I was riding in my chair. It was a glorious day. I felt sorry for Her Majesty, for she was very quiet that day. Generally she was happy, and made everyone laugh with her. I thought about the branches of willow, too, but could not understand the meaning. I came out of the hall while Her Majesty was dining with the Emperor, and found the Young Empress sitting in a small room on the left side of the courtyard, with several Court ladies. When they saw me they made signs for me to go there. I found them all drinking tea, and the Young Empress said to me, "I am sure you must be tired and hungry. Come and sit near me and have a cup of tea." I thanked her and sat down beside her and we talked of what we saw on the roads and how we had enjoyed our long ride. She said: "We have still an hour's ride before we reach the Forbidden City." She also talked about the ceremony we had performed that morning and said that we must all pray earnestly for rain. I could not wait any longer, so I asked her what those branches of willow meant. She smiled and told me that willow could bring water, as the Buddhist religion believes, and that it was an old custom of the Court wearing willow leaves, when praying for rain. She also told me that we must perform the same ceremony every morning until the rain came.

We heard Her Majesty talking in the courtyard, and knew that she had finished her luncheon, so we went in with the Young Empress, and ate what was left, as usual. I found the food very nice indeed, although it seemed rather funny without having meat. We came out into the courtyard and saw that Her Majesty was walking up and down. She said to us: "My legs are so stiff, riding in the chair. I must walk a little before we leave here. Are you all tired?" We told her that we were not tired, so she ordered us to walk with her. It looked very funny to see us walking round and round, Her Majesty in front, and we following her. Her Majesty turned and smiled at us, and said: "We are just like horses taking their rounds at a stable." It reminded me of a circus. Li Lien Ying came and knelt down, and said that it was time for Her Majesty to depart, in order to reach the Forbidden City at the lucky hour she had selected, so we left Wan Shou Si. All the chairs went very fast, and after an hour's ride we came near the Palace Gate. We followed the Emperor's chair, taking a shorter route, and noticed the gate was wide open. His Majesty, the Emperor, and the Young Empress' chairs went

66

in, but we had to alight and walk in. There were small chairs waiting for us. (As I explained before these little chairs were carried by eunuchs, with a rope across their shoulders.) We came to the courtyard of the Audience Hall where the Emperor and the Empress were waiting for us. As usual His Majesty knelt in front. Behind him was the Young Empress, and we knelt in a row behind her, waiting to welcome Her Majesty to her Palace. She went to her room where the eunuchs had placed everything in order long before her arrival. We held the ceremony that afternoon and evening. After Her Majesty had retired we came back to our rooms and found that everything was in order, our eunuchs had made up our beds already. It was very nice to have them, for we could not do our own work at all. I was so tired and my limbs were stiff. I immediately went to sleep and did not realize how long I had slept until I heard someone knocking at my window. I got up and pulled the blind away. I noticed that the sky looked dull and thought it was clouded. I felt happy, and thought it might rain, and so relieve Her Majesty. I got dressed in great haste, but much to my disappointment I saw the sunshine on the opposite windows.

The Palace in the Forbidden City was so old, and built in such a queer way. The courtyards were small, and the verandas very broad. All the rooms were dark. No electric light. We had to use candle light. One could not see the sky except by going into the courtyard and looking up. I found that I had risen before the sun was up, and I was not quite awake yet, and thought the sky was clouded. I went to Her Majesty's own Palace and found the Young Empress already there. She was always the first and always looked so tidy I often wondered how early she had to get up. She told me that I was not late, although Her Majesty was awake but not up yet. I went into her bedroom and made my usual morning courtesy to her. The first thing she asked me was about the weather. I had to tell her the truth – that there was no sign of rain. Her Majesty got up, dressed, and had her breakfast as usual, and told us there would be no audience that morning. The Emperor went to the Temple, sacrificing, and there was nothing important to attend to. We prayed for three days in succession, but no rain came. I found that Her Majesty was truly discouraged, and ordered each of us to pray twenty times a day. We marked a spot with vermilion powder and a little water on big yellow sheets of paper each time we prayed.

On the sixth day of the fourth moon the sky was clouded. I ran to Her Majesty's bedroom that morning to tell her the news, but found that someone had told her already. She smiled, and said to me: "You are not the first one to give me the good news. I know everyone of you wanted to be the first to tell me. I feel very tired today, and wish to lie down a little longer. You can go, and I will send for you when I am ready to get up." When I went to search for the Young Empress I found all the Court ladies there also. They all asked me if I had noticed the rain. We came out of the waiting room and found that the courtyard was wet, and after a while it rained very fast. Her Majesty got up, and we prayed as usual. Fortunately the rain did not stop, but came pouring down all that day.

Her Majesty played solitaire with the dominoes, and I stood at the back of her chair watching her. I saw that the Young Empress and all the girls were standing on the veranda. Her Majesty saw them, too, and said to me: "Go and tell them to wait in the waiting room. Can't they see that the veranda is wet?" I went to them, but before I had the opportunity of telling them anything the Young Empress told me that the waiting room was wet, and that the water had gone in. As I said before, this building was very old, and there were no drains at all. Her Majesty's own Palace was high; it had twelve steps, while our waiting room, which was on the left side of her Palace, was built right on the ground, with no raised foundation at all. While I was talking on the veranda just for a few minutes, I got quite wet. Her Majesty knocked at her glass window and told us to go in. Now I must explain that none of us, not even the Young Empress could enter Her Majesty's Palace without her orders except we had work to do there, or were on duty. Her Majesty was very happy that day. She laughed and said that we looked as if we had just been pulled out of the lake. The Young Empress had on a pale blue gown, and the red tassel on her headdress was dripping red water all over her gown. She smiled and said to us: "Look at those girls; their gowns are all spoiled." While we were talking, Her Majesty gave us orders for us to change our clothes.

After they had gone, I went back to Her Majesty. She looked at me and said: "You are wet also, only your clothes do not show." I had on a cashmere dress which was made very plain. She touched my arm and said: "How wet you are. You had better change, and put on a thick dress. I think foreign clothes must be very uncomfortable; the waist is too small and it seems to me out of proportion to the rest of the body. I am sure that you will look much prettier in our Manchu gown. I want you to change and put your Parisian clothes away as souvenirs. I only wanted to know how foreign ladies dressed and now I have seen enough. The Dragon Boat Festival will be here next month and I will make some pretty gowns for you." I thanked her by kowtowing to the ground and told her that I would be only too pleased to change into Manchu clothes, but having lived so many years abroad, and having always worn foreign clothes, I had not had any made. We were planning to change into Manchu gowns before coming to the Court, but we had received orders that Lao Tsu Tsung wished to see us in foreign clothes. I was very glad when I received that order as there were several reasons why I wanted to wear Manchu gowns. First, the Court ladies at the beginning treated us as outsiders. Secondly, I knew that Her Majesty did not like them, and besides, we were very uncomfortable living at the Palace in Peking, and made up our minds that we must wear Manchu clothes, which were made for it. We had so much work to do, and having to stand most of the time one absolutely needed loose garments. Her Majesty ordered one of the eunuchs to bring one of her dresses for me to try on, so I went back to my own room, and took off my wet clothes and changed. I tried on her gown, but it was too loose for me. The length was quite all right and so were the sleeves. Her Majesty told one of the eunuch writers to write down my measurements in order to have a gown made for me, and said she was sure it would fit me. She did the same thing for my mother and sister, and ordered our gowns to be made at once. I knew she was pleased, as she told me what color would suit me the best. She said that I should always wear pink and pale blue, for they suited, and were her favorite colors, too. She also talked about our headdress, and ordered some made the same as worn by the other Court ladies. She said to me: "I know you can wear my shoes, for I tried yours on the first day you came, don't you remember? I must select a lucky day for you to become a Manchu once more," she said this with a smile, "and no more foreign clothes after that." She took her special book for lucky days and hours, and studied it a little while, then she said the eighteenth of that month was the best. Li Lien Ying, the head eunuch knew how to please Her Majesty, and said he would give orders to have everything ready for us at that time. Her Majesty told us the way we must have our hair dressed, and what kind of flowers we should wear, in fact she was very happy arranging to make us into Manchus. A short while after she dismissed us for the day. It rained for three days without stopping. The last day the Emperor came back, and all ceremonies ceased. Her Majesty never liked to stay in the Forbidden City, and I was not a bit surprised, as I hated the place. We had to use candles to dress by, in the morning, as the rooms were in absolute darkness even in the middle of the afternoon. It rained so much that finally Her Majesty said she would return to the Summer Palace the next day, whether it was raining or not, and we were all very glad to go.

We returned to the Summer Palace on the seventh. It was a dull day, but no rain. We packed everything in just the same way we had done when we came, and stopped at Wan Shou Si and had our luncheon.

That day we commenced to eat meat again. I noticed that Her Majesty enjoyed her meal very much. She asked me if I liked the food without meat, and I told her that everything was nicely done and that I enjoyed the food very much, although without meat. She told me that she could not eat that kind of food and enjoy it, and that if it were not necessary to make sacrifice she would not have abstained.

The first garden party of the year was given by the Empress Dowager to the ladies of the Diplomatic Corps, in the fourth moon. This year Her Majesty desired to deviate a little from previous custom, and issued orders that stalls should be arranged in the garden, on a similar principal to a bazaar, on which were to be displayed curios, embroidered work, flowers, etc., etc. These were to be given as presents to the guests. The guests were: Mrs. Conger, wife of the American Minister, Mrs. Williams, wife of Chinese Secretary of the American Legation, Madame and Mademoiselle de Carcer, wife and daughter of the Spanish Minister, Madame Uchida, wife of the Japanese Minister, and a few ladies of the Japanese Legation, Madame Almeida, wife of the Portuguese Charge d' Affaires, Madame Cannes, wife of the Secretary of the French Legation, the wives of several French Officers, Lady Susan Townley, wife of the First Secretary of the British Legation, two ladies from the German Legation, wives of German Officers, and wives of a few Customs Officials. On this occasion Her Majesty selected a most beautiful gown of peacock blue, embroidered all over with phoenix. The embroidery was raised and each phoenix had a string of pearls two inches long sewed into its mouth. Whenever Her Majesty stirred, these strings of tiny pearls moved forwards and backwards and it made a very pretty effect. Of course, she wore her jade phoenix on her hair as usual and shoes and handkerchief embroidered with the same pattern. My mother wore a lavender silk gown, trimmed with silver braid, her hat was of the same shade with plumes to match. My sister and myself wore pale blue Chinese silk gowns with insertion and medallions of Irish crochet and trimmed with tiny velvet bands. We wore blue hats with large pink roses. All the Court ladies dressed in their most picturesque gowns and it was a very pretty sight to see the procession walking to the Audience Hall.

Her Majesty was in her happiest mood that morning and said to us: "I wonder how I would look in foreign clothes; my waist is very small, but wearing this kind of loose gown it would not show. I don't think I would need to squeeze myself so tight, either, but I don't think there is anything in the world prettier than our Manchu gowns."

First the guests were received in audience by Their Majesties. They were accompanied by the Doyen, Baron Czikann, Minister for Austria, and an interpreter from each Legation. On entering the Audience Hall all the guests stood in line and the Doyen presented a short address to Their Majesties. This was translated to Prince Ching, who, in turn, communicated it to the Emperor. The Emperor made a suitable reply in Chinese which was translated by the Doyen's interpreter. Then the Doyen mounted the steps of the dais and shook hands with Their Majesties, the rest of the guests being presented in turn. I was standing at the right hand of the Empress Dowager and as each guest came forward, called out their names, and the Legation which they represented. Her Majesty had a few words for everyone, and when she saw a new face she would ask how long they had been in China; whether they liked it, etc., etc. All these conversations I interpreted for Her Majesty. As the guests finished paying their respects they passed along and remained standing in the Hall until everybody had been presented.

The interpreters, who did not take part in this ceremony but had remained standing in the Hall until it was over, were then conducted by Prince Ching to another part of the Palace, where refreshments were provided for them. After they had gone out Their Majesties descended from the dais and mixed with the guests.

The formal ceremony now being concluded, chairs were brought in and everybody made themselves comfortable. Tea was brought in by the eunuchs and after a few minutes' conversation, we all adjourned to the refreshment room, with the exception of the Empress Dowager, the Emperor, the Young Empress and the Secondary wife. In the absence of Her Majesty, the Imperial Princess (The Empress Dowager's adopted daughter) officiated as hostess, Mrs. Conger sitting at her right and Madame de Carcer, wife of the Spanish Minister, on her left. The food was all Chinese, but knives and forks were provided for the use of the guests. During the luncheon the Imperial Princess stood up and spoke a few words of welcome, which I translated into English and French. After the luncheon was over we adjourned to the garden where Their Majesties were awaiting us. A brass band was playing European airs.

Her Majesty led the way around the gardens, passing the various stalls on the way, where the ladies would stop and admire the different articles, which were later presented to them as souvenirs of the occasion. On arriving at a teahouse which had been erected in the gardens, everybody rested and partook of tea. Their Majesties then wished everybody good-bye and the guests were then conducted to their chairs and took their departure.

As usual, we reported to Her Majesty everything that had taken place and how the guests had enjoyed themselves. She said: "How is it that these foreign ladies have such large feet? Their shoes are like boats and the funny way they walk I cannot say I admire. I haven't yet seen one foreigner with pretty hands. Although they have white skins, their faces are covered with white hair. Do you think they are beautiful?" I replied that I had seen some American beauties when I was abroad. Her Majesty said: "No matter how beautiful they are they have ugly eyes. I can't bear that blue color, they remind me of a cat." After a few more remarks, she ordered us to retire, saying that we must be tired. We were rather used up and glad of an opportunity to rest, so made our courtesies and retired.

We had been at the Palace more than two months, and I had had no opportunity to see my father at all, who was quite ill at that time. We did not know whether we could ask leave of absence from the Court. I received letters from my father every day, telling me to have courage, and to do my duty. My mother asked the Young Empress if it would be correct to ask Her Majesty for permission to go home for a day or two. The Young Empress told us that it would be quite all right to do that, but she thought it would be better if we could wait until after the eighth, for there would be a feast on that day. The eighth day of the fourth moon every year is the ceremony of eating green peas. According to the Buddhist religion there is a hereafter which divides or grades, according to the life that is lived on earth, that is to say, those who live good lives go to Heaven when they die and those who are bad go to a bad place to suffer. On this occasion Her Majesty sent to the people she liked, each a plate containing eight peas, and we had to eat them. The Young Empress told me that if I presented a plate of peas to Her Majesty it would please her, which I did. This meant: "May we meet in the hereafter" (Chi Yuen Dou). Her Majesty was very happy that day. We went to the west side of the lake and had our luncheon there. Her Majesty talked to us about the first day we came to the Court, and then said to mother: "I wonder if Yu Keng is any better. When will he be able to come to the Court? I haven't seen him since he returned from France." (My father had asked three months leave of absence from the Court on account of his poor health.) My mother answered and said that he was feeling better, but that his legs were still very weak, and he could not walk much. Her Majesty then said to us: "Oh, I have forgotten to tell you that if you wish to go home, you can ask permission. I have been so busy lately, and forgot to remind you." We thanked her and told her that we would like to go home and see how my father was, so she gave orders that we should leave the Court the next day. Then she asked me how long I would like to stay at home, and of course I knew the custom, and told her that I was waiting for her orders: "Would two or three days be enough?" We told her that it suited us beautifully. I was so surprised when she mentioned it to us, and wondered if anyone had told her of our intentions, or if Her Majesty was a mind reader.

When she retired that afternoon I went to see the Young Empress, who was always very nice and kind, and asked me to sit near her. Her eunuch brought me a cup of tea. Her rooms were furnished exactly the same as Her Majesty's, but everything looked extremely dainty, and showed very good taste. We talked about the life at the Palace for a long time, and she told me that she was very fond of us, and so was Her Majesty. I told her that Her Majesty had mentioned to us about going home for two or three days and that I was surprised to see how thoughtful she was. She said that someone had reminded Her Majesty to let us go home, for we had been at the Court for more than two months. I found out afterwards that it was the head eunuch Li who had heard that we were anxious to go. The Young Empress said to me: "I want to teach you to be wise, that is, you are ordered to leave the Court to-morrow, but Her Majesty did not mention any particular hour. You must not talk about it to anyone, and don't show that you are excited to go home. Don't dress as if you are going out to-morrow, but be natural and do your work as if you don't care about going at all. Don't you remind her, in case she forgets to tell you to go, and come back on the second day, which is the custom. It will show that you are anxious to see Her Majesty, so you come back one day earlier than the appointed time." I was so happy to get this information and asked her if it would be all right to bring Her Majesty some presents when we returned to the Court. She said that was just the proper thing to do. The next day we did the same work, and went to the Audience Hall with Her Majesty, as usual. After the audience was over Her Majesty ordered her luncheon to be served at the country teahouse. This teahouse was built in country style, and right on top of her peony mountain, with bamboo and straw, and all the furniture was made of bamboo also. They were beautifully made, and the frames of the windows were carved into a line of characters – Shou (long life), and butterflies, with pink silk curtain hangings. At the rear of this exquisite little building was a bamboo shade, with railings all around, hung with red silk lanterns. The seats were built against the railings, so that one could sit on them comfortably. This was supposed to be used by the Court ladies as their waiting room. We played dice with Her Majesty when luncheon was over. We played a very long time, and I won the game that day. Her Majesty laughed and said to me: "You have luck to-day. I think you are so happy to go home that your fairies have helped you to win the game." As I mentioned before, this game was called "Eight Fairies Going across the Sea." "I think it is time for you to go now." While saying this she turned and asked one of the eunuchs what the time was, and he answered that it was half-past two. We kowtowed to Her Majesty, and stood waiting for more orders. Then she said: "I am sorry to see you go although I know you are coming back within two or three days. I know I shall miss you." To my mother she said: "Tell Yu Keng to take care of his health and get well soon. I have ordered four eunuchs to accompany you, and am sending some of my own rice for him." We had to kowtow again in thanking Her Majesty for her kindness and finally she said: "Nemen tzowba" (you can go now).

We withdrew, and found the Young Empress on the veranda. We courtesied to her, and said good-bye to the Court ladies and came to our rooms to get ready to start. Our eunuchs were very good, and had everything packed up ready for us. We gave ten taels to each of our eunuchs, for that was the custom, and gave four taels to each chair bearer of the Palace. When we arrived at the Palace Gate our own chairs were waiting for us. We said good-bye to our eunuchs. Strange to say they seemed attached to us and told us to come back soon. The four eunuchs ordered by Her Majesty to see us home were there, and as soon as we got into our chairs I saw them riding on horseback beside us. It seemed to me just like a dream the two months I had spent at the Court, and I must say I felt very sorry to leave Her Majesty, but at the same time I wanted very much to see my father. We got home after a two hours' ride, and found him looking much better, and one can imagine how happy he was to see us. The four eunuchs came into our parlor, and placed the yellow bag of rice on the table. My father thanked Her Majesty by kowtowing to the ground. We gave these eunuchs each a little present, and they departed.

I told my father about my life at the Palace, and how very kind Her Majesty was to me. He asked me if I could influence Her Majesty to reform some day, and hoped he would live to see it. Somehow or other I had the idea that I could and promised him that I would try my best.

Her Majesty sent two eunuchs to see us the next morning, and also sent us food and fruits. They told us that Her Majesty missed us, and had told them to ask if we missed her. We told these eunuchs that we were returning to the Court the next day. We stayed at home only two days and a great many people came to see us, and kept us busy all the time. My father suggested that we should start from the house at about 3:00 A. M., so as to get to the Summer Palace before Her Majesty was up. We left our house at 3:00 A. M. in total darkness, just like we had two months before. What a change. I thought I was the happiest girl in the world. I was told by many people, especially by the Young Empress, that Her Majesty was extremely fond of me. I had also heard that she did not care for young people at all. Although I was happy, I noticed that some of the Court ladies did not like me, and they made me uncomfortable on many occasions by not telling me just the way Her Majesty wanted the work to be done. They smiled to each other whenever Her Majesty was saying to my mother that she liked me, and that I was always careful in doing anything that pleased her. I knew I was going to see those people again. However, I made up my mind to fight my battles alone. I only wished to be useful to Her Majesty, and would not take any notice of them.

It was a little after five o'clock when we reached the Summer Palace. Our own eunuchs were very happy to see us again and told us that Her Majesty was not up yet and that we had time to go to our rooms, where they had some breakfast prepared for us. We went to see the Young Empress first, and found she was ready to go to Her Majesty's Palace. She was also very glad to see us, and told us that our Manchu costumes were all ready, and that she had seen them and they were perfectly lovely. We were very hungry, and enjoyed our breakfast immensely. After that we went to see Her Majesty. She was awake, so we went into her bedroom. We greeted her the same way that we did every morning, and kowtowed to her and thanked her for all the things she had sent us while we were at home. She sat up on the bed, smiled, and said: "Are you glad to come back? I know everyone who comes to me and stays for a while does not like to go away from here any more. I am glad to see you (to my mother). How is Yu Keng?" My mother told her that my father was much better. She asked us what we did for those two days, staying at home. She also wanted to know whether we still remembered which day she had chosen for us to change into our Manchu costume. We told her we knew the date, and were looking forward to it. The eunuchs brought in three large yellow trays, full of beautiful gowns, shoes, white silk socks, handkerchiefs, bags for nuts, in fact the whole set, including the gu'un dzan (Manchu headdress). We kowtowed to her, and told her we were very much pleased with everything she had given us. Her Majesty told the eunuchs to bring everything out for us to see. She said to us: "You see I give you one full official dress, one set of

Chao Chu (amber heads), two embroidered gowns, four ordinary gowns for everyday wear, and two gowns for Chi Chen wear (the anniversary of the death of an Emperor or Empress), one sky blue, the other mauve, with very little trimming. I also have a lot of underwear for you." I was excited and told Her Majesty that I would like to commence to dress up at once. She smiled, and said: "You must wait until the day comes, the lucky day I have selected for you. You must try to fix your hair first, which is the most difficult thing to do. Ask the Young Empress to teach you." Although she told me to wait, I knew she was pleased to see that I showed so much enthusiasm. She asked me the first day when we came to the Court why my hair was so curly. I showed her that I curled it with paper, and she teased me ever afterwards. She also said that I could not pull my hair straight in time to wear Manchu clothes, that everyone would laugh at me, and how ugly I would look. That night one Court lady came over to me while I was sitting on the veranda and said: "I wonder if you will look nice in Manchu dress?" I told her I only wanted to look natural. "You have lived so many years abroad we consider you are a foreigner to us." I told her that as long as Her Majesty considered I was one of her own, I would be satisfied and that she need not worry herself about me. I knew they were jealous of us, so I went in search of the Young Empress and left this girl alone. We were talking with the Young Empress in the waiting room, and this girl came in and sat near me, smiling to herself most of the time. One of the servant girls was fixing some fresh flowers for Her Majesty. She looked at her and asked her why she was smiling. The Young Empress saw, and asked her the same question. She would not answer, but kept on smiling all the time. At this moment a eunuch came and said that Her Majesty wanted me. I afterwards tried to find out what she had told the Young Empress but could not. Several days passed very quietly. Her Majesty was happy, and so was I. One day the Young Empress reminded us that we should make all preparations in order to be able to dress ourselves properly on the eighteenth, as the time was getting short – only two days left. That night, after Her Majesty had retired, I went to my own room and fixed my headdress on and went to see the Young Empress. She said that I looked very nice, and that she was sure Her Majesty would like me better in Manchu costume. I told her that I used to wear Manchu dress when I was a little girl, before we went to Europe, and of course I knew how to put it on. I also told her that I could not understand why these girls looked upon me as a foreigner. She said that they only showed their ignorance, and that they were jealous of me and I should not pay any attention to them at all.

# CHAPTER ELEVEN

## Our Costumes

THE next day we got up earlier than usual and dressed ourselves in our new gowns. I could not believe my own eyes, and asked several times whether that was myself or not. I found that I looked all right, although I hadn't been wearing this sort of costume for so long. They seemed to think that we would look awkward. Our own eunuchs were delighted to see us dressed that way. The Young Empress came in while passing our rooms on her way to the Empress Dowager's Palace, and waited for us to go with her. When we arrived at the waiting room a lot of people came in and looked at us, and talked so much about us, that it made me feel rather shy. Everyone told us that we looked much better that way than in foreign clothes, except the Emperor Kwang Hsu. He said to me: "I think your Parisian gowns are far prettier than this." I smiled and said nothing. He shook his head at me, and went into Her Majesty's bedroom. Li Lien Ying came and saw us, and was very much excited and told me to go and see Her Majesty at once. I told him that everyone was looking at us, as if we were curios. He said: "You don't know how nice you look now, and I wish that you would not wear foreign clothes at all." Her Majesty laughed so loud when she saw us that it made me uncomfortable, for I was afraid we looked unnatural to her. She said: "I cannot believe you are the same girls. Just look at yourselves in this looking-glass." She pointed to a large mirror in her room. "See how you have changed. I feel that you belong to me now. I must have some more gowns made for you." Then Li Lien Ying said that the twenty-fourth would be the first day of the Summer. On that day everyone would begin to wear jade hairpins instead of gold, and we had none. Her Majesty said to Li: "I am very glad you told me that. I must give them each a jade hairpin after having asked them to change into Manchu dress." Li went away and came back with a box of hairpins of pure green jade. Her Majesty took a beautiful one and handed it to my mother and told her that that pin had been worn by three Empresses. She took two very nice ones, and gave one to me and one to my sister. She told us that these two were a pair, and that the other Empress Dowager (the East Empress Dowager) used to wear one, and that the other was worn by herself when she was young. I felt ashamed that Her Majesty had given us so many presents and I had done nothing for her in any way. However, we thanked her most sincerely, and showed our appreciation. She said: "I look upon you as my own people, and the gowns I have made for you are the very best. I have also decided to let

77

you wear the full Court dress, the same as one of the Princesses. You are my Court lady, so you are equally ranked here." Li stood there behind her and made a sign to us to kowtow to her. I cannot remember how many times I kowtowed that day. The headdress was very heavy, and I was not quite used to it; I was afraid it might fall off. Her Majesty also said that she would make our rank known to the Court on her seventieth birthday. I will explain this. On every decade from the time of her birth Her Majesty used to give special favors to anyone she liked, or to anyone who had done something for her, and had been useful to her. She could promote anyone at any time, but on these occasions it was something special. The Young Empress congratulated us, and said that Her Majesty was looking for a young Prince to marry me. She was also very fond of teasing. I wrote to my father about all the favors that had been given to me. He wrote me he hoped that I deserved them all, and that I must do all I could to be useful and loyal to Her Majesty as long as she lived.

I was very happy. Life was perfectly lovely at the Palace. Her Majesty was always nice and kind. I noticed the difference in the way she had treated us since (as she said) we had become Manchus once more. One day Her Majesty asked me while we were sailing on the lake in the moonlight, if I wanted to go to Europe any more. It was a superb night, and several boats were sailing behind us. In one boat several eunuchs were playing a kind of sweet music on the flute and an instrument very much like the mandolin, called Yeuh Chin (small harp, like the shape of the moon), with Her Majesty singing very softly to herself. I told her I was satisfied to be with her, and did not wish to go anywhere at all. She said that I must learn to sing poetry and that she would teach me every day. I told her that my father had made me study all kinds of poetry and I had composed some myself. She looked surprised and said: "Why didn't you tell me that before? I love poems. You must read to me sometimes. I have many books here containing poems of different dynasties." I told her that my knowledge of Chinese literature was very limited, and I dared not let her see how little I knew. I had only studied eight years. Her Majesty told me that the Young Empress and herself were the only ones who were familiar with Chinese literature at the Court. She told me that she tried to teach the Court ladies to read and write some time ago, but having found them so lazy she gave them up. My father told me to be very careful not to show them what I could do until I was asked, so I kept it to myself. After they found this out, some of the Court ladies were very disagreeable to me, and this went on day after day.

Except for this unpleasantness the fourth moon passed very agreeably. The first day of the fifth moon was a busy day for us all, as from the first to the fifth of the fifth moon was the festival of five poisonous insects, which I will explain later – also called the Dragon Boat Festival. All the Viceroys, Governors and high officials, besides the Imperial Family, Court ladies and eunuchs, all offer Her Majesty beautiful presents. I never saw such a lot of things as came into the Palace during this festival. Each person who sent in presents must accompany them with a sheet of yellow paper, and at the right lower corner the sender's name must be written and also the word Kuai Jin, meaning to present their gifts kneeling, also to write what the presents were. The eunuchs took big yellow trays to bring them in. During these five days everyone was busy, especially the eunuchs. I could not count just how many people sent presents to Her Majesty. The presents were of every kind, such as things for the household; silks and jewelry of all kinds and description. A large part of the presents were foreign goods of the ordinary kind. I also saw lovely carved thrones and embroideries. Her Majesty ordered them to be put away, and the foreign things to be kept in her Palace, for those were new to her.

The third day of the fifth moon was the day for just the people of the Palace to make presents. It was a most beautiful sight to see. We were busy all night making preparations, and had to go and help the Young Empress. The next morning we placed our presents in the big courtyard in these big yellow trays. The Young Empress had her trays in the first row. The presents from the Young Empress to the Empress Dowager were made by her own hands. There were ten pairs of shoes, silk embroidered handkerchiefs, little bags for betel nuts, and bags for tobacco, all exquisitely done. The Secondary wife of the Emperor Kwang Hsu presented about the same to Her Majesty. The Court ladies' presents were all different, as we could ask permission to go out shopping before the Feast. We could not go out together, for one or two of us must be there at all times, and it was very exciting to tell each other what we had bought. We ourselves did not ask permission to go out of the Palace, for we had our presents ready long before. Everyone seemed to be talking about presents, whether Her Majesty would like them or not. My mother, my sister and myself had written to Paris to get some lovely French brocades, one set of furniture, French Empire style. We had learned Her Majesty's taste already during our short stay there, so including those presents we also gave her fans, perfumes, soaps and some other French novelties. Her Majesty always looked over everything, and noticed some of the presents were of very poor quality, and wanted to know the sender's name. The eunuchs and servant girls also made her good and useful presents. Her Majesty would select the articles she liked the best, and order the rest to be put away, and she might never see them again. I must say that Her Majesty liked and admired some foreign things very much, she especially loved the French fancy brocades, for she was making new gowns almost every day. She was also pleased with soaps and powder that would beautify the skin. She always thanked us in a very nice way and said how very thoughtful we were in selecting beautiful articles for her. Her Majesty would also say something nice to the eunuchs and girls, and that made everyone feel pleased.

The fourth day of the fifth moon was the day that Her Majesty gave presents to us all, the different Princes, high officials, servant girls and eunuchs. Her memory was something extraordinary, for she could remember every one of the presents that had been given to her the day before, and the names of the givers also. That was a busy day for us. Her Majesty gave people presents according to the way they gave her. We had yellow sheets of paper and wrote out the names of those to whom she wished to give. That day Her Majesty was very angry with one of the wives of a certain Prince because her presents were the poorest. Her Majesty told me to keep that tray in her room and said she would go over them and see what they were. I knew she was not pleased, for she had a telltale face. She told us to measure the silks and ribbons in that tray, and leave it in the hall. The ribbons were all of different lengths, all too short to trim a gown, and the dress materials were not of good quality. Her Majesty said to me: "Now you look for yourself. Are these good presents? I know very well all these things were given to them by other people and they of course would select the best for themselves, and give me what was left. They know they are obliged to send me something. I am surprised to see how careless they are. Probably they thought as I receive so many presents I would not notice. They are mistaken, for I notice the poorest the first, in fact I can remember everything. I can see those who gave me things in order to please me, and those who gave because they were obliged to. I will return them the same way." She gave the Court ladies each a beautiful embroidered gown and a few hundred taels, the same to the Young Empress and the Secondary wife. The presents which she gave us were a little different, consisting of two embroidered gowns, several simple ones, jackets and sleeveless jackets, shoes, and flowers for the Manchu headdress. She said that we had not so many gowns, and instead of giving us the money, she had things made for us. Besides that, she gave me a pair of very pretty earrings, but none to my sister, for she noticed that I had a pair of ordinary gold earrings, while my sister had a pair set with pearls and jade. Her Majesty said to my mother: "Yu Tai Tai. I can see you love one daughter better than the other. Roonling has such pretty earrings and poor Derling has none." Before my mother could answer her she had turned to me while I was standing at the back of her chair: "I will have a nice pair made for you. You are mine now." My mother told her that I did not like to wear heavy earrings. Her Majesty laughed and said: "Never mind, she is mine now, and I will give her everything she needs. You have nothing to do with her." The earrings she gave me were very heavy. Her Majesty said that if I would wear them every day I would get used to them, and so it proved that after some time I thought nothing of it.

Now about this Feast. It is also called the Dragon Boat Feast. The fifth of the fifth moon at noon was the most poisonous hour for the poisonous insects, and reptiles such as frogs, lizards, snakes, hide themselves in the mud, for that hour they are paralyzed. Some medical men search for them at that hour and place them in jars, and when they are dried, sometime use them as medicine. Her Majesty told me this, so that day I went all over everywhere and dug into the ground, but found nothing. The usual custom was that at noon Her Majesty took a small cup filled with spirits of wine, and added a kind of yellow powder (something like sulphur). She took a small brush and dipped it into the cup and made a few spots of this yellow paint under our nostrils and ears. This was to prevent any insects from crawling on us during the coming summer. The reason why it was also called the Dragon Boat Festival was because at the time of the Chou Dynasty the country was divided into several parts. Each place had a ruler. The Emperor Chou had a Prime Minister named Chi Yuan, who advised him to make alliance with the other six countries, but the Emperor refused, and Chi Yuan thought that the country would be taken by others in the near future. He could not influence the Emperor, so he made up his mind to commit suicide and jumped into the river, taking a large piece of stone with him. This happened on the fifth day of the fifth moon, so the year afterwards, the Emperor got into a Dragon boat to worship his soul, and throw rice cakes, called Tzu Tsi, into the river. On that day the people have celebrated this feast ever since. At the Palace the theatre played first this history, which was very interesting, and also played the insects trying to hide themselves before the most poisonous hour arrived. On that day we all wore tiger shoes, the front part of which was made of a tiger's head, with little tigers made of yellow silk to wear on the headdress. These tigers were only for the children to wear, and signified that they would be as strong as a tiger, but Her Majesty wanted us to wear them also. The wives of the Manchu officials came to the Court, and when they saw us they laughed at us. We told them it was by Her Majesty's orders.

A register recording the birthdays of all the Court ladies was kept by the head eunuch, and a few days before my own birthday came around, the tenth day of the fifth moon, he informed me that the custom of the Court was to make a present to Her Majesty and said that the present should take the form of fruit, cakes, etc., so I ordered eight boxes of different kinds.

Early in the morning I put on full Court dress, and made myself look as nice as possible and went to wish Her Majesty good morning. When she had finished dressing, the eunuchs brought in the presents and, kneeling, I presented them to Her Majesty, bowing to the ground nine times. She thanked me and wished me a happy birthday. She then made me a present of a pair of sandalwood bracelets, beautifully carved, also a few rolls of brocade silk. She also informed me that she had ordered some macaroni in honor of my birthday. This macaroni is called (Chang Shou Me'en) long life macaroni. This was the custom. I again bowed and thanked her for her kindness and thoughtfulness. After bowing to the Young Empress and receiving in return two pairs of shoes and several embroidered neckties, I returned to my room, where I found presents from all the Court ladies.

Altogether I had a very happy birthday.

I can never forget the fifteenth day of the fifth moon as long as I live, for that was a bad day for everyone. As usual we went to Her Majesty's bedroom quite early that morning. She could not get up and complained that her back ached so much. We rubbed her back, in turns, and finally she got up, though a little late. She was not satisfied. The Emperor came in and knelt down to wish her good morning, but she scarcely took any notice of him. I noticed that when the Emperor saw that Her Majesty was not well, he said very little to her. The eunuch who dressed her hair every morning was ill, and had ordered another one to help her. Her Majesty told us to watch him very closely to see that he did not pull her hair off. She could not bear to see even one or two hairs fall out. This eunuch was not used to trickery, for instance, in case the hair was falling off, he could not hide it like the other one did. This poor man did not know what to do with any that came out. He was frightened, and Her Majesty, seeing him through the mirror, asked him whether he had pulled her hair out. He said that he had. This made her furious, and she told him to replace it. I almost laughed, but the eunuch was very much frightened and started to cry. Her Majesty ordered him to leave the room, and said she would punish him later. We helped her to fix up her hair. I must say it was not an easy job, for she had very long hair and it was difficult to comb.

She went to the morning audience, as usual, and after that she told the head eunuch what had happened. This Li was indeed a bad and cruel man, and said: "Why not beat him to death?" Immediately she ordered Li to take this man to his own quarters to receive punishment. Then Her Majesty said the food was bad, and ordered the cooks to be punished also. They told me that whenever Her Majesty was angry everything went wrong, so I was not surprised that so many things happened that day. Her Majesty said that we all looked too vain with our hair too low down at the back of the head. (This Manchu headdress is placed right in the center of one's head and the back part is called the swallow's tail, and must reach the bottom part of one's collar.) We had our hair done up the same way every day, and she had previously never said a word about it. She looked at us, and said: "Now I am going to the audience, and don't need you all here. Go back to your rooms and fix your hair all over again. If I ever see you all like that again I am going to cut your hair off." I was never more surprised in my life when I heard her speak so sharply to us. I don't know whether I was spoken to or not, but I thought it well to be wise, and I answered I would. We were all ready to go and Her Majesty stood there watching us. When we were about five or six feet away we heard her scolding Chun Shou (the girl who was neither a Court lady nor a servant). Her Majesty said she was pretending she was all right, and Her Majesty ordered her to go also. When we were walking towards our own place, some of them laughed at Chun Shou, which made her angry. When Her Majesty was angry with anyone, she would say that we were all doing something on purpose to make her angry. I must say that everyone of us was scared, and wondered who would have dared to do that. On the contrary, we tried our best to please her in every way.

But that day she was furious all day and I tried to stay away from her. I noticed some of the eunuchs went to her to ask questions concerning important matters, but she would not look at them, but kept on reading her book. To tell the truth, I felt miserable that day. At the beginning I thought all the eunuchs were faithful servants, but seeing them every day, I got to know them. It did not do them any harm to be punished once in a while.

The Young Empress told me to go in and wait on Her Majesty as usual.

She said that probably if I would suggest playing dice with her, she might forget her troubles. At first I did not want to go, for I was afraid that she might say something to me, but seeing that the poor Young Empress spoke to me so nicely, I told her I would try. When I entered Her Majesty's sitting room I found her reading a book. She looked at me and said: "Come over here, I would like to tell you something. You know these people at the Palace are no good and I don't like them at all. I don't want them to poison your ears by telling you how wicked I am. Don't talk to them. You must not fix your hair too low down at the back of your head. I was not angry with you this morning. I know you are different. Don't let them influence you. I want you to be on my side, and do as I tell you." Her Majesty spoke very kindly to me, and her face changed also – not at all the same face she had that morning. Of course I promised her that I would be only too happy to do all I could to please her. She spoke to me just like a good mother would speak to a dear child. I changed my opinion and thought that perhaps after all she was right, but I had often heard from the officials that one cannot be good to a eunuch, as he would do all he could to injure you without any reason whatsoever.

I noticed that day they all seemed to be more careful in doing their work. I was told that when once Her Majesty got angry, she would never finish. On the contrary, she talked to me very nicely, just as if there had been no troubles at all. She was not difficult to wait upon, only one had to watch her moods. I thought how fascinating she was, and I had already forgotten that she had been angry. She seemed to have guessed what I was thinking, and said: "I can make people hate me worse than poison, and can also make them love me. I have that power." I thought she was right there.

# CHAPTER TWELVE

## The Empress and Mrs. Conger

ON the twenty-sixth day of the fifth moon, during the morning audience, Prince Ching told Her Majesty that Mrs. Conger, the wife of the American Minister to Peking, had asked for a private audience, and would Her Majesty please mention a day. She told him not to give any answer until the next day, just to give her time to think it over. I was sitting behind the large screen, listening, but the other Court ladies made too much noise, so Her Majesty ordered them not to say a word during audience. I was very glad myself, because I could listen to some of the interesting conversations between the Empress Dowager and her Ministers. After the audience, Her Majesty ordered her lunch to be served on the top of the hill at Pai Yuen Dien (Spreading Cloud Pavilion). She said that she preferred to walk, so we followed her very slowly. To get to this place we had to mount two hundred and seventy-two steps, besides ten minutes' climbing over rough stones. She did not seem to mind the climbing part at all. It was the funniest thing to see two little eunuchs on either side, to support her arms, trying to keep pace with her. I noticed that she was very much preoccupied, and did not speak to any of us. When we arrived at our destination we were very tired and quite exhausted. Her Majesty, who was a good walker herself, laughed at us. She was always very much pleased when she excelled in games of skill or endurance. She said: "You see I am old, and can walk much faster than you young people. You are all no use. What is the matter with you?" Her Majesty was very fond of receiving compliments. I had been there long enough to know and had learned to say things which would please her. She also hated anyone to pay her compliments at the wrong moment, so one had to be very careful even in paying her compliments.

This "spreading cloud" pavilion was a beautiful Palace. It had an open space in front of the building, just like one of the courtyards, with pink and white oleanders all over the place. There was a porcelain table and several porcelain stools. Her Majesty sat on her own yellow satin stool and was drinking her tea in silence. It was very windy that day, although the sky was blue with warm sunshine. Her Majesty sat there just for a few minutes, and then said it was too windy and went into the building. I was more than glad to go in, too, and whispered to the Young Empress that I thought the wind might blow off my headdress. The eunuchs brought the luncheon and placed everything upon the

85

table. The Young Empress made a sign for us to follow her, which we did. When we came to the back veranda we sat down on the window seats. I will explain about these seats. All the windows were built low at the Palace, and on the veranda there was something like a bench built along the window, about a foot wide. There were no chairs to be seen excepting Her Majesty's thrones. The Young Empress asked me whether I had noticed that Her Majesty had something on her mind. I told her that perhaps she was thinking about the private audience which Prince Ching had mentioned that morning. She said that I had guessed right, and asked: "Do you know anything about this audience? When will it take place?" I said that Her Majesty had not yet given her answer.

By this time Her Majesty had finished eating and was walking up and down the room, watching us eating. She came over to my mother and said: "I am just wondering why Mrs. Conger asks for a private audience. Perhaps she has something to say to me. I would like to know just what it is so I can prepare an answer." My mother said that probably Mrs. Conger had someone visiting her who wished to be presented to Her Majesty. "No, it can't be that, because they must give the list of names of those who wish to come to the Palace. I don't mind the formal audiences, but I don't think that I should have private ones at all. I don't like to be questioned, as you all know. The foreigners are, of course, very nice and polite, according to their own way, but they cannot compare with us, so far as etiquette is concerned. I may be conservative in saying that I admire our custom and will not change it as long as I live. You see our people are taught to be polite from their earliest childhood, and just look back at the oldest teachings and compare them with the new. People seem to like the latter best. I mean that the new idea is to be Christians, to chop up their Ancestral Tablets and burn them. I know many families here who have broken up because of the missionaries, who are always influencing the young people to believe their religion. Now I tell you why I feel uneasy about this audience is because we are too polite to refuse anyone who asks any favors in person. The foreigners don't seem to understand that. I'll tell you what I will do. Whenever they ask me anything, I'll simply tell them that I am not my own boss, but have to consult with my Ministers; that although I am the Empress Dowager of China, I must also obey the law. To tell the truth, I like Madame Uchida (wife of the Japanese Minister to Peking) very much. She is always very nice and doesn't ask any silly questions. Of course the Japanese are very much like ourselves, not at all forward. Last year, before you came to the Court, a missionary lady came with Mrs. Conger, and suggested that I should establish a school for girls at the Palace. I did not like to offend her, and said that I would take it into consideration. Now, just imagine it for a moment. Wouldn't it be foolish to have a school at the Palace; besides, where am I going to get so many girls to study? I have enough to do as it is. I don't want all the children of the Imperial family studying at my Palace."

Her Majesty laughed while she was telling us this, and everyone else laughed, too. She said: "I am sure you will laugh. Mrs. Conger is a very nice lady. America is always very friendly towards China, and I appreciate their nice behavior at the Palace during the twenty-sixth year of Kwang Hsu (1900), but I cannot say that I love the missionaries, too. Li Lien Ying told me that these missionaries here give the Chinese a certain medicine, and that after that they wish to become Christians, and then they would pretend to tell the Chinese to think it over very carefully, for they would never force anyone to believe their religion against their own will. Missionaries also take the poor Chinese children and gouge their eyes out, and use them as a kind of medicine." I told her that that was not true; that I had met a great many missionaries, and that they were very kind-hearted and willing to do anything to help the poor Chinese. I also told her what they had done for the poor orphans – given them a home, food and clothing; that sometimes they went into the interior and found the blind children who might be useless to their parents, and when they get them they have to support them. I know several cases like that. These country people offer their deformed children to the missionaries, as they are too poor to feed and take care of them. I told her about their schools, and how they helped the poor people. Her Majesty then laughed, and said: "Of course I believe what you say, but why don't these missionaries stay in their own country and be useful to their own people?" I thought it would be of no use for me to talk too much, but at the same time I would like her to know of the dreadful times some of the missionaries had in China. Some time ago, two of them were murdered at Wu Shuih, in June, 1892 (a little below Hankow), the church being burnt down by the mob. My father was appointed by Viceroy Chang Chih Tung to investigate the matter. After much trouble he caught three of the murderers and, according to the Chinese law, they were put to death by hanging in wooden cages, and the Government paid an indemnity to the families of the murdered missionaries. The year after, 1893, a Catholic church was burnt down at Mar Cheng, on the Yangtse, near Ichang. The mob said they saw many blind children at the church, who were made to work after having their eyes gouged out. The Prefect of Ichang Province said it was true that missionaries did get the Chinese childrens' eyes for making medicine, so my father suggested having those blind children brought into the Yamen and ask them. The Prefect was a most wicked man, and was very anti-foreign also. He gave the poor children plenty of food, and taught them to say that the missionaries did gouge their eyes out, but when they were brought in the next day they said that the missionaries treated them very kindly and gave them a nice home, good food and clothing. They said they were blind long before they became Catholics, and also said that the Prefect had taught them to say that the missionaries were cruel to them, which was not true. The blind children begged to go back to the school and said that they were very happy there.

Her Majesty said: "That may be all right for them to help the poor and relieve their suffering. For instance, like our great Buddha Ju Lai, who fed the hungry birds with his own flesh. I would love them if they would leave my people alone. Let us believe our own religion. Do you know how the Boxer rising began? Why, the Chinese Christians were to blame. The Boxers were treated badly by them, and wanted revenge. Of course that is always the trouble with the low class of people. They went too far, and at the same time thought to make themselves rich by setting fire to every house in Peking. It made no difference whose house. They wanted to burn so long as they could get money. These Chinese Christians are the worst people in China. They rob the poor country people of their land and property, and the missionaries, of course, always protect them, in order to get a share themselves. Whenever a Chinese Christian is taken to the Magistrate's Yamen, he is not supposed to kneel down on the ground and obey the Chinese law, as others do, and is always very rude to his own Government Officials. Then these missionaries do the best they can to protect him, whether he is wrong or not, and believe everything he says and make the magistrate set the prisoner free. Do you remember that your father established rules in the twenty-fourth year of Kwang Hsu, how the Chinese officials should treat the Bishops whenever they had dealings with each other? I know the common class of people become Christians – also those who are in trouble – but I don't believe that any of the high officials are Christians." Her Majesty looked around and whispered: "Kang Yue Wai (the reformer in 1898) tried to make the Emperor believe that religion. No one shall believe as long as I live. I must say that I admire the foreigners in some ways. For instance, their navies and armies, and engineers, but as regards civilization I should say that China is the first country by all means. I know that many people believe that the Government had connections with the Boxers, but that is not true. As soon as we found out the trouble we issued several Edicts, and ordered the soldiers to drive them out, but they had gone too far already. I made up my mind not to go out of the Palace at all. I am an old woman, and did not care whether I died or not, but Prince Tuang and Duke Lan suggested that we should go at once. They also suggested that we should go in disguise, which made me very angry, and I refused. After the return of the Court to Peking, I was told that many people believed that I did go in disguise, and said that I was dressed in one of my servant's clothes, and rode in a broken cart drawn by a mule, and that this old woman servant of mine was dressed as the Empress Dowager, and rode in my sedan chair. I wonder who made that story up? Of course everyone believed it, and such a story would get to the foreigners in Peking without any trouble.

"Now to come back to the question of the Boxer Rising. How badly I was treated by my own servants. No one seemed anxious to go with me, and a great many ran away before the Court had any idea of leaving the Capital at all, and those who stayed would not work, but stood around and waited to see what was going to happen. I made up my mind to ask and see how many would be willing to go, so I said to everyone: 'If you servants are willing to go with me, you can do so, and those who are not willing, can leave me.' I was very much surprised to find that there were very few standing around listening. Only seventeen eunuchs, two old women servants and one servant girl, that was Sho Chu. Those people said they would go with me, no matter what happened. I had 3,000 eunuchs, but they were nearly all gone before I had the chance of counting them. Some of the wicked ones were even rude to me, and threw my valuable vases on the stone floor, and smashed them. They knew that I could not punish them at that important moment, for we were leaving. I cried very much and prayed for our Great Ancestors' Souls to protect us. Everyone knelt with me and prayed. The Young Empress was the only one of my family who went with me. A certain relative of mine, whom I was very fond of, and gave her everything she asked, refused to go with me. I knew that the reason she would not go was because she thought the foreign soldiers would catch up the runaway Court, and kill everyone.

"After we had been gone about seven days, I sent one eunuch back, to find out who was still in Peking. She asked this eunuch whether there were any foreign soldiers chasing us, and whether I was killed. Soon after the Japanese soldiers took her Palace, and drove her out. She thought she was going to die anyway, and as I was not yet assassinated, she might catch up with the Court, and go with us. I could not understand how she traveled so fast. One evening we were staying at a little country house, when she came in with her husband, a nice man.

89

She was telling me how much she had missed me, and how very anxious she had been all that time to know whether I was safe or not, and cried. I refused to listen to what she was saying and told her plainly that I did not believe a word. From that time she was finished for me. I had a very hard time, traveling in a sedan chair, from early morning, before the sun rose, until dark and in the evening had to stop at some country place. I am sure you would pity me, old as I am, that I should have had to suffer in that way.

"The Emperor went all the way in a cart, drawn by a mule, also the Empress. I went along, and was praying to our Great Ancestors for protection, but the Emperor was very quiet, and never opened his mouth. One day something happened. It rained so much and some of the chair carriers ran away. Some of the mules died suddenly. It was very hot, and the rain was pouring down on our heads. Five small eunuchs ran away also, because we were obliged to punish them the night before on account of their bad behavior to the Magistrate, who did all he could to make me comfortable, but of course food was scarce. I heard these eunuchs quarreling with the Magistrate, who bowed to the ground, begging them to keep quiet, and promised them everything. I was of course very angry. Traveling under such circumstances one ought to be satisfied that one was provided for.

"It took us more than a month before we reached Shi An. I cannot tell you how fatigued I was, and was of course worrying very much, which made me quite ill for almost three months. So long as I live I cannot forget it.

"We returned to Peking early in the twenty-eighth year of Kwang Hsu and I had another dreadful feeling when I saw my own Palace again. Oh! it was quite changed; a great many valuable ornaments broken or stolen. All the valuable things at the Sea Palace had been taken away, and someone had broken the fingers of my white jade Buddha, to whom I used to worship every day. Several foreigners sat on my throne and had their photos taken. When I was at the Shi An I was just like being sent into exile, although the Viceroy's Yamen was prepared for us, but the building was very old, damp and unhealthy. The Emperor became ill. It would take a long time to tell you everything; I thought I had enough trouble, but this last was the worst. When I have time, I will tell you more about it. I want you to know the absolute truth.

"Now let us come back to the question of Mrs. Conger's private audience. There must be something special, but I hope that she will not ask for anything, for I hate to refuse her. Can you guess what it is?" I told Her Majesty that there could not be anything special; besides, Mrs. Conger considered herself to be a person who knew Chinese etiquette very well, and I didn't believe she would ask for anything at all. Her Majesty said: "The only objection I have is that Mrs. Conger always brings one of the missionaries as her interpreter, when I have your mother, your sister and yourself, which I think should be sufficient. I don't think it is right for her to do that; besides, I cannot understand their Chinese very well. I like to see the ladies of the Diplomatic body sometimes, but not the missionaries. I will stop that when the opportunity comes."

The next morning Prince Ching told Her Majesty that the American Admiral, and Mrs. Evans, and suite wished to be presented to her. The American Minister asked two private audiences. He said he had made a mistake by telling her that Mrs. Conger had asked an audience for herself, the day before.

After the regular morning audience was over Her Majesty laughed and said: "Didn't I tell you yesterday that there must be a reason for asking an audience? I rather would like to meet the American Admiral and his wife." Turning to us she said: "Be sure and fix everything up pretty, change everything in my bedroom, so as not to show them our daily life." We all said "Jur" (yes), but we knew it was going to be a hard task to turn the Palace upside down.

It was just the night before the appointed audience. We started to work taking off the pink silk curtains from every window, and changing them for sky blue (the color she hated); then we changed the cushions on the chairs to the same color. While we were watching the eunuchs doing the work, several of them came into the room, carrying a large tray full of clocks. By this time her Majesty had come into the room, and ordered us to remove all her white and green jade Buddhas and take some of the jade ornaments away, for those things were sacred, and no foreigners should see them, so we replaced them with these clocks, instead. We also took away the three embroidered door curtains, and changed them for ordinary blue satin ones. I must explain that these three curtains were sacred, too. They were embroidered to represent five hundred Buddhist deities, on old gold satin, and had been used by Emperor Tou Kwang. Her Majesty believed that by hanging these curtains at her door they would guard against evil spirits entering her room. The order was that one of us should remember to place them back again when the audience was over. We fixed every piece of furniture in her bedroom.

Her toilet table was the most important thing. She would not let anyone see it-not even the wives of the Officials who came in, so of course we had to put it in a safe place, and lock it up. We changed her bed from pink color into blue. All her furniture was made of sandalwood, also carvings on her bed. This sandalwood, before it was made into furniture, was placed in different temples, to be sanctified, so of course no foreigner could see it. As we could not take this carving from her bed, we covered it up with embroidered hangings. While we were working Her Majesty came in and told us not to hurry in her bedroom, because the audience the next day would only be for Admiral Robley Evans and his staff, and they would not visit the private rooms. The audience for Mrs. Evans and the other ladies would be the day after. She said it was important to see that the Audience Hall was fixed up properly. She said: "Place the only carpet we have here in the hall. I don't like carpets anyway, but it cannot be helped."

After we had finished, Her Majesty started to tell us what to wear for the ladies' audience. She said to me: "You need not come to the throne to-morrow, there will only be gentlemen. I will get one of the Ministers from Wai-Wu-Pu (Bureau of Foreign Affairs). I don't want you to talk to so many strange men. It is not the Manchu custom. These people are all strangers. They might go back to America and tell everybody what you look like." At the same time Her Majesty gave orders for the Imperial Yellow Gown to be brought in next day, for the gentleman's audience. She said that she must dress in her official robe for this occasion. This robe was made of yellow satin, embroidered with gold dragons. She wore a necklace composed of one hundred and eight pearls, which formed part of this official dress. She said: "I don't like to wear this official robe. It is not pretty, but I am afraid I will have to." She said to all of us: "You need not dress especially."

The next morning Her Majesty got up early, and was busier than ever. It seemed to me that whenever we had an audience we always had so much trouble. Something was sure to go wrong and make Her Majesty angry. She said: "I want to look nice, and be amiable, but these people always make me angry. I know the American Admiral will go home and tell his people about me, and I don't want him to have a wrong impression." It took her almost two hours to dress her hair, and by that time it was too late for her usual morning audience, so she proposed holding that after the foreigners had gone away. She looked at herself in the looking-glass, with her Imperial robe on, and told me that she did not like it, and asked me whether I thought the foreigners would know that it was an official robe. "I look too ugly in yellow. It makes my face look the same color as my robe," she said. I suggested that as it was only a private audience, if she wished to dress differently, it would not matter at all. She seemed delighted, and I was afraid lest I had not made a proper suggestion, but anyway I was too busy to worry. Her Majesty ordered that her different gowns should be brought in, and after looking them over she selected one embroidered all over with the character "Shou" (long life), covered with precious stones and pearls, on pale green satin. She tried it on, and said that it was becoming to her, so she ordered me to go to the jewel-room and get flowers to match for her hair. On one side of the headdress was the character (shou) and on the other side was a bat (the bat in China is considered to be lucky). Of course her shoes, handkerchiefs and everything else were embroidered in the same way. After she was dressed, she smiled and said: "I look all right now. We had better go to the audience hall and wait for them, and at the same time we can play a game of dice." Then to us all she said: "All of you will stay at the back of the screen during the audience. You can see all right, but I don't wish that you should be seen." The eunuchs had laid the map down on the table and were just going to commence playing dice, when one of the high rank eunuchs came into the Hall and, kneeling down, said that the American Admiral had arrived at the Palace Gate, together with the American Minister – ten or twelve people altogether. Her Majesty smiled and said to me: "I thought it was just going to be the American Minister and the Admiral, and one or two of his staff. Who can the rest of the people be? However, never mind, I will receive them anyway." We helped her to mount her throne upon the dais, fixed her clothes, and handed her the paper containing the speech she was to give. Then we went back of the screen, with the Young Empress. It was so very quiet, not a sound anywhere, that we could hear the boots of the visitors as they walked over the stones in the courtyard. We were peeping from behind the screen, and could see several of the Princes mounting the steps, conducting these people to the Hall. The Admiral and the American Minister came in, and stood in a line. They bowed three times to the Empress Dowager. The Emperor was also on his throne, sitting at her left hand. His throne was very small, just like an ordinary chair. Her Majesty's speech was simply to welcome the Admiral to China. They then came up to the dais and shook hands with their Majesties, ascending on one side, and retiring down the other. Prince Ching took them into another Palace building, where they had lunch, and the audience was over. It was very simple and formal.

After the audience was over Her Majesty said that she could hear us laughing behind the screen, and that maybe the people would talk about it, and did not like it at all. I told her that it was not myself who laughed. She said: "The next time when I have men in audience you need not come into the Audience Hall at all. Of course it is different when I have my own people at the morning audiences."

Her Majesty did not go to her bedroom that afternoon. She said she wanted to wait until these people had gone and hear what they had to say. After a couple of hours Prince Ching came in and reported that they had lunched, and that they were very pleased to have seen Her Majesty, and had gone away. I must here explain that the Admiral had entered by the left gate of the Palace. The middle gate was only used for Their Majesties, with one exception, viz.: in the case of anyone presenting credentials. Then they entered by the center gate. The Admiral left by the same gate he had entered. Her Majesty asked Prince Ching whether he had showed them around the Palace buildings or not (this was in the Summer Palace), and what they had thought about it. Did they say anything, and were they pleased or not. She said to Prince Ching: "You can go now, and make the necessary preparations for the ladies' audience next day." That same evening Her Majesty said to us: "You must all dress alike to-morrow, and wear your prettiest clothes. These foreign ladies who are coming to the Palace may never see us again, and if we don't show them what we have now, we will not have another opportunity." She ordered us all, including the Young Empress, to wear pale blue, also the Secondary wife of the Emperor. She said to me: "If the ladies ask who the Secondary wife is, you can tell them; but if they don't ask, I don't want you to introduce her to them at all. I have to be very careful. These people at the Palace here are not used to seeing so many people and they might not have nice manners, and the foreigners will laugh at them." Then she said to us again: "I always give presents when ladies come to the Court, but don't know whether I will give this time or not, for at the last audience I did not give anything at all." Addressing me, she said: "You can prepare some pieces of jade, in case I need them. Put them in a nice box and have them all ready. Don't bring them to me until I ask for them." She said: "We have talked enough now, and you can all go to rest." We courtesied good night. I was only too glad to go to my own room.

The next morning everything went on very nicely and there was no trouble at all. Her Majesty was well satisfied, for we had all taken great care in fixing ourselves up. She said to me: "You never put enough paint on your face. People might take you for a widow. You will have to paint your lips, as that is the custom. I don't need you yet, so go back and put some more paint on." So I went back to my room and painted myself just like the rest of them, but I could not help laughing at seeing myself so changed. By the time I got to her room again, she said: "Now you look all right. If you think that powder is expensive, I will buy some for you." She said that with a laugh, for she always liked to tease me.

By the time Her Majesty had finished her toilet, one of the ladies brought a number of gowns for her to select one from. She said she would wear pale blue that day. She looked over twenty or thirty gowns, but found nothing which suited her, so she gave orders for some more to be brought in. Finally she chose a blue gown embroidered with one hundred butterflies, and wore a purple sleeveless jacket, which was also embroidered with butterflies. At the bottom of this gown were pearl tassels. She wore her largest pearls, one of which was almost as large as an egg, and was her favorite jewel. She only wore this on special occasions. She wore two jade butterflies on each side of her headdress. Her bracelets and rings were also all designed in butterflies, in fact everything matched. Among her beautiful jewels, she always wore some kind of fresh flowers. White jessamine was her favorite flower. The Young Empress and the Court ladies were not allowed to wear fresh flowers at all unless given to them by Her Majesty as a special favor. We could wear pearls and jade, etc., but she said that the fresh flowers were for her, her idea being that we were too young, and might spoil fresh flowers if we wore them. After she was dressed we went into the Audience Hall. She ordered her cards to be brought in as she wanted to play solitaire. She talked all the time she was playing, and said that we must all be very nice and polite to the American ladies, and show them everywhere. She said: "It doesn't matter now, for we have everything changed." She said: "I want to laugh myself. What is the use of changing everything? They will imagine we are always like this. By and bye, if they question you about anything, just tell them that it is not so, and that we change everything at each audience, just to give them a bit of surprise. You must tell it some day, otherwise no one will know it at all, and the trouble would not be worth the while." It was a private audience for ladies, and Her Majesty did not use the big throne, but was sitting on her little throne at the left side of the Audience Hall, where she received her own Ministers every morning; the Emperor was standing. A eunuch came in, the same as the day before, and announced that the ladies had arrived at the Palace Gate, nine in all. Her Majesty sent some of the Court ladies to meet them in the courtyard, and bring them to the Audience Hall, which they did. I was standing at the right side of Her Majesty's chair, and could see them mounting the steps. Her Majesty whispered to me, and asked: "Which one is Mrs. Evans?" As I had never seen the lady, I answered that I could not tell, but when they got nearer I saw a lady walking with the American Minister's wife, and concluded that she must be Mrs. Evans, and told Her Majesty. As they got nearer, Her Majesty said: "Again that missionary lady with Mrs. Conger. I think she must like to see me. She comes every time. I will tell her I am very glad to see her always, and see if she understands what I mean."

Mrs. Conger shook hands with Her Majesty and presented Mrs. Evans and also the wives of the American officers. I was watching Her Majesty and saw that she was very nice and amiable, with such a pleasant smile – so different from her everyday manner. She told them she was delighted to see them. Her Majesty ordered the eunuchs to have chairs brought in for the ladies, and at the same time other eunuchs brought in tea. Her Majesty asked Mrs. Evans whether she liked China; what she thought of Peking; how long she had been there; how long she was going to stay, and where she was staying. I was so accustomed to Her Majesty's questions that I knew exactly what she would ask. Mrs. Conger told her interpreter to tell Her Majesty that she had not seen her for such a long time, and enquired about Her Majesty's health. Her Majesty said to me: "You tell Mrs. Conger that I am in good health and that I am delighted to see her. It is a pity that I cannot hold an audience more frequently, otherwise I could see more of her." She continued: "The Imperial Princess (her adopted daughter-daughter of Prince Kung) will accompany them to lunch." This ended the audience.

Lunch was served at the back of her own Palace building (Yang Yuen Hsuen – the place where the clouds gather to rest). This room was specially furnished as a banqueting room where refreshments could be served. All the Court ladies went to the lunch, except Her Majesty, the Young Empress and the Secondary wife. It had taken me two hours to fix the table for the luncheon. Her Majesty ordered that a white foreign tablecloth should be used, as it looked cleaner. The eunuch gardeners had decorated the table with fresh flowers, and Her Majesty gave instructions as to how the seats were to be placed. She said: "Mrs. Evans is the guest of honor. Although Mrs. Conger is the wife of the American Minister, she is more of a resident, so Mrs. Evans must have the principal seat." She also told me to arrange to seat everybody according to their respective ranks. The Imperial Princess and Princess Shun (Her Majesty's niece, sister of the Young Empress) were hostesses, and were to sit opposite each other. We placed golden menu holders and little gold plates for almonds and watermelon seeds; the rest all silver ware, including chopsticks. Her Majesty ordered that foreign knives and forks should be provided also. The food was served in Manchu style, and was composed of twenty-four courses, besides sweetmeats – candies and fruits. Her Majesty instructed us that only the best champagne was to be served. She said: "I know that foreign ladies love to drink."

I think I was the only one who was really happy to meet these ladies, more so than the rest of the Court ladies, the reason being that Her Majesty lectured them too severely, telling them how to behave, so that they had grown to hate the very mention of a foreign audience. While we were eating, a eunuch came in and told me that Her Majesty was waiting at her private Palace, and that I should bring these ladies there after the lunch was over. So when we had finished we entered her own Palace and found her waiting there for us. She got up and told me to ask Mrs. Evans whether she had had anything to eat – that the food was not very good. (This is a custom with the Chinese when entertaining, always to underrate the food.) She said that she would like to show Mrs. Evans her private apartments, so that she could form some idea of the way we lived, so she took Mrs. Evans to one of her bedrooms. She invited Mrs. Evans and Mrs. Conger to sit down, and the eunuchs brought in tea, as usual. Her Majesty asked Mrs. Evans to stay a little while in Peking, and to visit the different temples. She said: "Our country, although very old, has not such fine buildings as there are in America. I suppose you will find everything very strange. I am rather too old now, otherwise I would like to travel around the world. I have read much about different countries, but of course there is nothing like visiting the different places and seeing them yourself. However, one cannot tell. I may be able to go after all, by and bye, but I am afraid to leave my own country. By the time I returned I should not know the place any more, I'm afraid. Here everything seems to depend on me. Our Emperor is quite young."

She then turned and ordered us to take these ladies to visit the different buildings of the Palace, also the famous temple of the King of Dragons. This is on a little island in the center of the lake of the Summer Palace. Mrs. Conger said that she had something to ask Her Majesty, and told the Missionary lady to proceed. While Mrs. Conger was speaking to this lady Her Majesty became rather impatient as she wanted to know what they were talking about, so she asked me. It was very hard for me to listen to both of the ladies and to Her Majesty at the same time. The only words I heard were: "The portrait," so I guessed the rest. Before I had a chance to tell Her Majesty this Missionary lady said: "Mrs. Conger has come with the special object of asking permission to have Her Majesty's portrait painted by an American lady artist, Miss

Carl, as she is desirous of sending it to the St. Louis Exhibition, in order that the American people may form some idea of what a beautiful lady the Empress Dowager of China is." Miss Carl is the sister of Mr. F. Carl who was for so many years Commissioner of Customs in Chefoo.

Her Majesty looked surprised, for she had been listening very carefully whilst this lady was talking. She did not like to say that she did not quite understand, so she turned to me, as had been previously arranged, – a sign for me to interpret. I did not, however, do so immediately, so Mrs. Conger told her missionary friend to repeat the request in case Her Majesty had not quite understood it. Her Majesty then said to me: "I cannot quite understand what this lady says. I think perhaps you can tell me better." So I explained everything, but I knew that Her Majesty did not know what a portrait was like, as, up to that time she had never even had a photograph taken of herself.

I must here explain that in China a portrait is only painted after death, in memorium of the deceased, in order that the following generations may worship the deceased. I noticed that Her Majesty was somewhat shocked when the request was made known to her. I did not want Her Majesty to appear ignorant before these foreign ladies, so I pulled her sleeve and told her that I would explain everything to her later. She replied: "Explain a little to me now." This was spoken in the Court language, which the visitors were unable to understand, it being somewhat different from the ordinary Chinese language. This enabled Her Majesty to form some idea of the conversation, so she thanked Mrs. Conger for her kind thought, and promised to give her answer later. She said to me: "Tell Mrs. Conger that I cannot decide anything alone, as she is probably aware that I have to consult with my Ministers before deciding anything of an important character. Tell her that I have to be very careful not to do anything which would give my people an opportunity to criticize my actions. I have to adhere to the rules and customs of my ancestors." I noticed that Her Majesty did not seem inclined to discuss the subject further at the moment.

Just then the head eunuch came in and, kneeling down, informed Her Majesty that the boats for the ladies were ready to take them across the lake, to see the temple. This action on the part of the eunuch was owing to his having received a signal from one of the Court ladies, which implied that Her Majesty was getting tired of the conversation, and wished to change the subject. I must explain that on every occasion when a foreign audience was taking place, one of the Court ladies was always told off to watch Her Majesty, and whenever she appeared to be displeased or tired of any particular subject under discussion, she, the Court lady, would give the signal to the head eunuch, who would break in upon the conversation in the above manner, and thus save the situation from becoming embarrassing. So Her Majesty said good-bye to the ladies, as she thought it would be too late for them to have to return to say good-bye, besides which it would give them more time to see the various sights.

The ladies then proceeded to the island in the Empress Dowager's pleasure boat known as the Imperial barge, previously described, and visited the temple. This temple is built on top of a small rock, in the center of which is a natural cave, and it was generally supposed that no human being had ever been inside of this cave. The Empress Dowager believed the popular superstition that this hole was the home of the King of Dragons – from which the temple derives its name.

# CHAPTER THIRTEEN

## The Empress's Portrait

AFTER staying a little while at the temple, we returned to the Palace, and the ladies said goodbye and took chairs to the Palace gate, where their own chairs were waiting for them. I then went to report to Her Majesty in the usual way what had been said by the visitors; whether they had expressed themselves as being pleased with the reception they had received. Her Majesty said: "I like Mrs. Evans. I think she is a very good woman. It seems to me that her manners are quite different from those of the other American ladies whom I have met. I like to meet people who are polite." Then, referring to the subject of the portrait Her Majesty said: "I wonder why Mrs. Conger has this idea. Now please explain to me what painting a portrait really is." When I explained that it would be necessary for her to sit for several hours each day she was excited, and afraid she would never have the patience to see it through. She asked me what she must do during the sitting, so I explained that she would simply have to pose for the portrait, sitting in one position all the time She said: "I shall be an old woman by the time the portrait is finished." I told her that I had had my own portrait painted during my stay in Paris, by the same artist Mrs. Conger had proposed should paint her own portrait (Miss Carl). She immediately told me to fetch the portrait of myself so that she could examine it and see what it was like, so I gave the order right away to a eunuch who was standing by to go to my house and bring it. Her Majesty said: "I do not understand why I must sit for the portrait Couldn't someone else do it for me." I explained to her that as it was her own portrait, and not that of somebody else, they wished to paint, it would be necessary for her to sit herself. She then enquired whether it would be necessary for her to wear the same dress at each sitting, also the same jewels and ornaments. I replied that it would be necessary to do so on each occasion. Her Majesty then explained that in China it was only necessary for an artist to see his subject once, after which he could start right away and finish the portrait in a very short time, and thought that a really first-class foreign artist should be able to do the same. Of course I explained the difference between foreign portrait painting and Chinese, and told her that when she had seen it she would see the difference and understand the reason for so many sittings. She said: "I wonder what kind of a person this lady artist is. Does she speak Chinese?" I said that I knew Miss Carl very well, and that she was a very nice lady, but that she didn't speak Chinese. She said: "If her brother has been in the Customs service for so long, how is it that she doesn't speak Chinese also?" I told her that Miss Carl had been away from China for a long time; that in fact she had only been in China for a very short time altogether, most of her work being in Europe and America. Her Majesty said: "I am glad she doesn't understand Chinese. The only objection about this portrait painting is that I have to have a foreigner at the Palace all the time. With my own people gossiping they might tell her things which I don't want anyone to know." I told her that would be impossible as Miss Carl did not understand Chinese at all, neither did any of the people at Court understand English, with the exception of ourselves (my mother, sister and myself). Her Majesty answered: "You must not rely too much on that, as after spending a short time at the Court they will soon learn to understand each other." Continuing, she said: "By the way, how long will it take before this portrait is finished?" I told her that it depended entirely upon how often she sat, and how long each time. I didn't like to tell her exactly how long it would take, as I was afraid she might consider it too much bother, so I said that when the artist arrived I would tell her to get along and finish the portrait as quickly as possible.

Her Majesty said: "I don't see how I can very well refuse Mrs. Conger's request. Of course I told her, as you know, that I would have to consult with my Ministers, just to give me time to think the matter over. If you know all about this artist lady, and think she is quite all right to come here to the Palace, of course she may come, and I will tell Prince Ching to reply to Mrs. Conger to that effect. First of all we must talk over what we are going to do, for to have a foreign lady staying in the Palace is out of the question altogether. As a rule I always spend the summer at my Summer Palace, and it is so far from the city that I don't think she will be able to go to and from the Palace every day, on account of the distance. Now, where can we put her? Someone will have to watch her all the time. This is such a difficult matter that I hardly know what to decide upon. How would you like to look after her? Do you think you could manage it in such a way that no one at the Palace will have a chance to talk with her during the daytime, but who is going to stay and watch her during the night?" Her Majesty walked up and down the room thinking it over for quite a while. Finally she smiled and said: "I have it. We can treat her as a prisoner without her knowing it, but it will all depend on your mother, your sister and yourself to act for me in this matter. Each of you will have to play your part very carefully, and I mine also. I will give orders to have the Palace Garden of Prince Chung (the Emperor Kwang Hsu's father) fixed up for Miss Carl during her stay here."

This Palace garden is quite close to Her Majesty's own Palace, about ten minutes' drive. It is not in the Palace ground, but is quite a separate Palace outside the Summer Palace.

Continuing, Her Majesty said: "Now, you will have to come with her every morning and return to stay with her every night. I think this is the safest way out of the difficulty, but be careful with regard to all correspondence which she may either receive or send away. The only thing about it is that it will give you a lot of extra work, but you know how particular I am over things of this kind, and it will save a lot of trouble in the end. There is another thing you will have to be very careful about, and that is to watch that Miss Carl has no chance to talk with the Emperor. The reason why I say this is because, as you know, the Emperor is of a shy disposition, and might say something which would offend her. I will appoint four extra eunuchs to be in attendance during the sittings for the portrait, so that they will be on hand in case anything is wanted." Her Majesty then said: "I noticed that Mrs. Conger was watching you when you pulled my sleeve. I wonder what she thought of it. You needn't care, anyway. Let her think anything she likes. I understood what you meant if Mrs. Conger didn't, and that is all that is necessary." I told her that perhaps Mrs. Conger thought I wanted to advise her to refuse this request, but Her Majesty said: "What does that matter? If it hadn't been that you know the artist yourself I would not have consented in any case. It is not the painting of the portrait that I mind, but it might give rise to serious results."

The next morning I received a letter from Mrs. Conger begging me not to prejudice Her Majesty against Miss Carl in any way. I translated this to Her Majesty, and it made her furious. She said: "No one has any right to write to you in such a way. How dare she suggest that you would say anything against Miss Carl? Didn't I tell you she was watching you when you pulled my sleeve? When you reply to that letter tell her whatever you like, but answer in the same way she writes herself, or, better still, you write and inform her that it is not customary for any Court lady to try and influence Her Majesty in this country, and that in addition, you are not so mean as to say anything against anybody. If you don't like to say that, just say that as Miss Carl is a personal friend of yours you certainly would never think of saying anything against her."

I therefore replied to Mrs. Conger's letter in the ordinary way, making it as formal as possible.

Her Majesty then talked of nothing but the portrait during the whole of that afternoon. By and bye she said: "I hope that Mrs. Conger will not send a missionary lady with Miss Carl to keep her company during her stay at the Palace. If she does I will certainly refuse to sit. The next morning the eunuch arrived with my portrait, and everyone at the Court had a good look at it before I took it to show to Her Majesty. Some of them were of the opinion that it was very much like me, while the others thought the painting a very poor one. When I informed Her Majesty of the arrival of the portrait she ordered that it should be brought into her bedroom immediately. She scrutinized it very carefully for a while, even touching the painting in her curiosity. Finally she burst out laughing and said: "What a funny painting this is, it looks as though it had been painted with oil." (Of course it was an oil painting.) "Such rough work I never saw in all my life. The picture itself is marvellously like you, and I do not hesitate to say that none of our Chinese painters could get the expression which appears on this picture. What a funny dress you are wearing in this picture. Why are your arms and neck all bare? I have heard that foreign ladies wear their dresses without sleeves and without collars, but I had no idea that it was so bad and ugly as the dress you are wearing here. I cannot imagine how you could do it. I should have thought you would have been ashamed to expose yourself in that manner. Don't wear any more such dresses, please. It has quite shocked me. What a funny kind of civilization this is to be sure. Is this dress only worn on certain occasions, or is it worn any time, even when gentlemen are present?" I explained to her that it was the usual evening dress for ladies and was worn at dinners, balls, receptions, etc. Her Majesty laughed and exclaimed: "This is getting worse and worse. Everything seems to go backwards in foreign countries. Here we don't even expose our wrists when in the company of gentlemen, but foreigners seem to have quite different ideas on the subject. The Emperor is always talking about reform, but if this is a sample we had much better remain as we are. Tell me, have you yet changed your opinion with regard to foreign customs? Don't you think that our own customs are much nicer?" Of course I was obliged to say "yes" seeing that she herself was so prejudiced. She again examined the portrait and said: "Why is it that one side of your face is painted white and the other black? This is not natural – your face is not black. Half of your neck is painted black, too. How is it?" I explained that it was simply the shading and was painted exactly as the artist saw me from the position in which she was sitting. Her Majesty then enquired: "Do you think that this Artist lady will paint my picture to look black also? It is going to America, and I don't want the people over there to imagine that half of my face is white and half black." I didn't like to tell her the truth, that her portrait would in all probability be painted the same as mine, so I promised Her Majesty that I would tell the artist exactly how she wished to be painted. She then asked me if I knew when the artist proposed commencing the portrait. I told her that the artist was still in Shanghai, but that Mrs. Conger had already written to her to come up to Peking, to make the necessary preparations. One week later I received a letter from Miss Carl informing me that she proposed coming up to Peking at once, and that she would be delighted if Her Majesty would allow her to paint this portrait. I translated the letter to Her Majesty, who said: "I am very glad that you know this lady personally. It will make it much easier for me. You know there may be some things which I may want to tell Miss Carl, but which I don't want Mrs. Conger to know. I mean that there might be certain things which I shall have to say to Miss Carl, which, if Mrs. Conger heard of them, would give her the impression that I was very difficult to please. You understand what I mean. As this lady is a friend of yours, you will of course be able to tell her things in such a manner as not to offend her, and I may tell you again that if it were not that she is a personal friend of your own I would not have her here at all, as it is quite contrary to our custom."

On the third day of the second-fifth moon Prince Ching informed Her Majesty that the artist had arrived at Peking and was staying with Mrs. Conger and wished to know Her Majesty's pleasure in regard to commencing the portrait. Now I must explain that the Chinese year varies as to the number of moons it contains. For example, one year contains the ordinary twelve months or moons. The following year may contain thirteen moons. Then the two years following that may contain twelve moons only, and thirteen moons the next year, and so on. At the time of the proposed visit of the artist the Chinese year contained thirteen moons, there being two fifth moons in that year. When Prince Ching asked Her Majesty to name the day on which Miss Carl should commence her work, she replied: "I will give her my answer to-morrow. I must first consult my book, as I don't want to start this portrait on an unlucky day." So the next day, after her usual morning audience Her Majesty consulted this book for quite a time. Finally she said to me: "According to my book the next lucky day will not occur for another ten days or so," and handed me the book to look myself. Eventually she picked out the twentieth day of the second-fifth moon as the most lucky day for beginning the work. Next she had to consult the book again in order to fix on the exact hour, finally fixing on 7 o'clock in the evening. I was very much worried when she told me that, as by that time it would be quite dark, so I explained to Her Majesty as nicely as I could that it would be impossible for Miss Carl to work at that hour of the day. Her Majesty replied: "Well, we have electric lights here. Surely that would be sufficient light for her." Then I had to explain that it would not be possible to get such good results by means of artificial light as if it were painted during the daytime. You see I was anxious to get her to change the hour, as I was sure that Miss Carl would refuse to paint by means of electric light. Her Majesty replied: "What a bother. I can paint pictures myself in any kind of light, and she ought to be able to do the same." After much discussion it was finally settled that 10 o'clock on the morning of the twentieth day of the second-fifth moon should be the time for Miss Carl to commence to paint this portrait, and I can assure you that I felt very much relieved when it was all settled. When the eunuch brought in my portrait, he also brought in several photographs which I had had taken during my stay in Paris, but I decided not to show them to Her Majesty in case she should decide to have a photograph taken instead of having this portrait painted, as it would be much quicker and save her the trouble of sitting each day. However, as Her Majesty was passing on the veranda in front of my bedroom the next morning she stepped into the room just to have a look around and, as she put it, to see whether I kept everything clean, and in good order. This was the first time she had visited me in my own room, and I was naturally very much embarrassed, as she very rarely visited the rooms of her Court ladies. I could not keep her standing, and I could not ask her to sit down in any of my own chairs, as it is the Chinese custom that the Emperor and Empress should only sit down in their own special chairs, which are usually carried by an attendant wherever they go. I therefore was on the point of giving an order for her own stool to be brought in, when Her Majesty stopped me and said that she would sit on one of the chairs in the room, and so bring me good luck. So she sat down in an easy chair. A eunuch brought in her tea, which I handed to her myself instead of letting the eunuch wait upon her. This of course was Court etiquette, and was also a sign of respect

After she had finished her tea, she got up and went around the room, examining everything, opening up all my bureau drawers and boxes in order to see whether I kept my things in proper order. Happening to glance into one corner of the room she exclaimed: "What are those pictures on the table over there," and walked across to examine them. As soon as she picked them up, she exclaimed in much surprise: "Why, they are all photographs of yourself, and are very much better than the picture you had painted. They are more like you. Why didn't you show them to me before?" I hardly knew what to answer, and when she saw that I was very much embarrassed by her question, she immediately started talking about something else. She often acted in this manner when she saw that any of us were not quite prepared for any of her questions, but she would be sure to reopen the subject at some future time, when we were expected to give a direct answer.

After examining the photographs for sometime, which by the way, were all taken in European dress, Her Majesty said: "Now these are good photographs; much better than the portrait you had painted. Still I have given my promise, and I suppose I shall have to keep it. However, if I do have my photograph taken, it will not interfere at all with the painting of the portrait. The only trouble is I cannot ask an ordinary professional photographer to the Palace. It would hardly be the thing."

My mother thereupon explained to Her Majesty that if she desired to have her photograph taken, one of my brothers, who had studied photography for some considerable time, would be able to do all that was necessary.

I would like to explain that I had two brothers at Court at that time, who held appointments under the Empress Dowager. One was in charge of all the electrical installation at the Summer Palace, and the other, her private steam launch. It was the custom for all the sons of the Manchu officials to hold certain positions at the Court for two or three years. They were perfectly free to walk about the grounds of the Palace, and saw Her Majesty daily. Her Majesty was always very kind to these young men, and chatted with them in quite a motherly way. These young fellows had to come to the Palace each morning very early, but as no man was allowed to stay all night in the Palace they of course had to leave when they had finished their duties for the day.

When Her Majesty heard what my mother said, she was very much surprised, and asked why she had never been told that my brother was learned in photography. My mother replied that she had no idea that Her Majesty wished to have a photograph taken, and had not dared to suggest such a thing herself. Her Majesty laughed, and said: "You may suggest anything you like, as I want to try anything that is new to me, especially as outsiders can know nothing about it." She gave orders to send for my brother at once. On his arrival Her Majesty said to him: "I hear that you are a photographer. I am going to give you something to do." My brother was kneeling, as was the custom of the Court, whilst Her Majesty was addressing him. Everybody, with the exception of the Court ladies, had to kneel when she was speaking to them. Even the Emperor himself was no exception to this rule. Of course the Court ladies, being constantly in attendance, were allowed not to kneel, as Her Majesty was talking to us all the time, and it was her orders that we should not do so, as it would be wasting a lot of time.

Her Majesty asked my brother when he would be able to come and take her photograph, and what kind of weather was necessary. My brother said that he would go back to Peking that night, to fetch his camera, and that he could take the photograph at any time she desired, as the weather would not affect the work. So Her Majesty decided to have her photograph taken the next morning. She said: "I want to have one taken first of all in my chair, when going to the audience, and you can take some others afterwards." She also asked my brother how long she would have to sit, and was surprised to learn that only a few seconds would suffice. Next she enquired how long it would be before it was finished, so that she could see it. My brother answered that if it were taken in the morning it could be finished late the same afternoon. Her Majesty said that was delightful, and expressed a wish to watch him do the work. She told my brother that he might select any room in the Palace to work in, and ordered a eunuch to make the necessary preparations.

The next day was a beautiful day, and at eight o'clock my brother was waiting in the courtyard with several cameras. Her Majesty went to the courtyard and examined each of them. She said: "How funny it is that you can take a person's picture with a thing like that." After the method of taking the photograph had been fully explained to her, she commanded one of the eunuchs to stand in front of the camera so that she might look through the focusing glass, to see what it was like. Her Majesty exclaimed: "Why is it your head is upside down? Are you standing on your head or feet?" So we explained when the photo was taken it would not look that way. She was delighted with the result of her observations, and said that it was marvellous. Finally she told me to go and stand there, as she wanted to have a look at me through this glass also. She then exchanged places with me, and desired that I should look through the glass and see if I could make out what she was doing. She waved her hand in front of the camera, and on my telling her of it, she was pleased.

She then entered her chair, and ordered the bearers to proceed. My brother took another photograph of Her Majesty in the procession as she passed the camera. After she had passed the camera she turned and asked my brother: "Did you take a picture?" and on my brother answering that he had, Her Majesty said: "Why didn't you tell me? I was looking too serious. Next time when you are going to take one, let me know so that I may try and look pleasant."

I knew that Her Majesty was very much pleased. While we were at the back of the screen during the audience, I noticed that she seemed anxious to get it over, in order to have some more photographs taken. It only took about twenty minutes to get that particular audience over, which was very rare.

After the people had gone, we came from behind the screen and Her Majesty said: "Let us go and have some more pictures taken while the weather is fine." So she walked the courtyard of the Audience Hall, where my brother had a camera ready, and had another photograph taken. She said that she would like to have some taken sitting on her throne, exactly as though she were holding an audience. It took us only a few minutes to have everything prepared in the courtyard. The screen was placed behind the throne, and her footstool was also placed ready for her, and she ordered one of the Court ladies to go and bring several gowns for her to select from. At the same time I went and brought some of her favorite jewelry. She ordered the two gowns which she had worn at the audiences when she received Admiral Evans and Mrs. Evans, to be brought in, and also the same jewels as she had worn on those respective occasions. She had two photographs taken in these costumes, one in each dress. Next she wanted one taken in a plain gown, without any embroidery. She then ordered my brother to go and finish the pictures which had already been taken, as she was anxious to see what they were like. She said to my brother: "You wait a minute, I want to go with you and see how you work on them." Of course, I had not considered it necessary to explain to Her Majesty the process of developing the pictures, the dark room, etc., so I explained to her as well as I could the whole thing. Her Majesty replied: "It doesn't matter. I want to go and see the room, no matter what kind of a room it is." So we all adjourned to the dark room in order to see my brother work on the photographs. We placed a chair so that Her Majesty could sit down. She said to my brother: "You must forget that I am here, and go along with your work just as usual." She watched for a while, and was very pleased when she saw that the plates were developing so quickly. My brother held up the plate to the red light, to enable her to see more distinctly. Her Majesty said: "It is not very clear. I can see that it is myself all right, but why is it that my face and hands are dark?" We explained to her that when the picture was printed on paper, these dark spots would show white, and the white parts would be dark. She said: "Well, one is never too old to learn. This is something really new to me.

I am not sorry that I suggested having my photograph taken, and only hope that I shall like the portrait painting as well." She said to my brother: "Don't finish these photographs until after I have had my afternoon rest. I want to see you do it." When she got up at about half-past three, it did not take her long to dress herself, as was her usual custom, and she went immediately to where my brother had the papers and everything prepared. He then showed Her Majesty how the printing was done. There was plenty of light, as it was summer time, and as it was only four o'clock in the afternoon, the sun was still high. Her Majesty watched for two hours while my brother was printing, and was delighted to see each picture come out quite plainly. She held the first one in her hands so long while examining the others, that when she came to look at it again, she found that it had turned quite black. She could not understand this at all, and exclaimed: "Why has this gone black? Is it bad luck?" We explained to her that it must be washed after printing, otherwise a strong light would cause the picture to fade, as this one had done. She said: "How very interesting, and what a lot of work there is."

After the printing process had been finished, my brother placed the pictures in a chemical bath, as usual, finally washing them in clean water. This caused Her Majesty even more surprise when she saw how clear the pictures came out, and caused her to exclaim: "How extraordinary. Everything is quite true to life." When they were finally completed, she took the whole of them to her own room and sat down on her little throne, and gazed at them for a long time. She even took her mirror in order to compare her reflection with the photographs just taken.

All this time my brother was standing in the courtyard awaiting Her Majesty's further commands. Suddenly she recollected this fact, and said: "Why, I had forgotten all about your brother. The poor fellow must be still standing waiting to know what I want next. You go and tell him – no, I had better go and speak to him myself. He has worked so hard all the day, that I want to say something to make him feel happy." She ordered my brother to print ten copies of each of the photographs, and to leave all his cameras at the Palace, in order that he could proceed with the work the next day.

The following ten days it rained continually, which made Her Majesty very impatient, as it was impossible to take any more photographs until the weather improved. Her Majesty wanted to have some taken in the Throne Room, but this room was too dark, the upper windows being pasted over with thick paper, only the lower windows allowing the light to enter. My brother tried several times, but failed to get a good picture.

During this rainy period the Court was moved to the Sea Palace, as the Emperor was to sacrifice at the Temple of Earth. This was a yearly ceremony and was carried out on similar lines to all other annual ceremonies. On account of the rain Her Majesty ordered that boats should be brought alongside the west shore of the Summer Palace. On entering the boats, Her Majesty, accompanied by the Court, proceeded to the Western Gate of the city, and on arrival at the last bridge, disembarked. Chairs were awaiting us and we rode to the gate of the Sea Palace. There we again entered the boats and proceeded across the lake, a distance of about a mile. While crossing the lake Her Majesty noticed a lot of lotus plants which were in full bloom. She said: "We are going to stay at least three days here. I hope the weather will be fine, as I should like to have some photographs taken in the open boats on the lake. I have also another; good idea, and that is, I want to have one taken as 'Kuan Yin' (Goddess of Mersy). The two chief eunuchs will be dressed as attendants. The necessary gowns were made some time ago, and I occasionally put them on. Whenever I have been angry, or worried over anything, by dressing up as the Goddess of Mercy it helps me to calm myself, and so play the part I represent. I can assure you that it does help me a great deal, as it makes me remember that I am looked upon as being all-merciful. By having a photograph taken of myself dressed in this costume, I shall be able to see myself as I ought to be at all times."

When we arrived at the private Palace the rain ceased. We walked to her bedroom, although the ground was still in bad condition. One of Her Majesty's peculiarities was a desire to go out in the rain and walk about. She would not even use an umbrella unless it was raining very heavily. The eunuchs always carried our umbrellas, but if Her Majesty did not use her umbrella, of course we could not very well use ours. The same thing applied in everything. If Her Majesty wanted to walk, we had to walk also, and if she decided to ride in her chair, we had to get into our chairs and ride as well. The only exception to this rule was when Her Majesty, being tired walking, ordered her stool to rest on. We were not allowed to sit in her presence, but had to stand all the time. Her Majesty liked her Sea Palace better than her Palace in the Forbidden City. It was far prettier, and had the effect of making her good tempered.

Her Majesty ordered us to retire early that day, as we were all very tired after the trip, and said that in the event of it being fine the next day, she would have the proposed photographs taken. However, much to Her Majesty's disappointment, it rained incessantly for the next three days, so it was decided to stay a few days longer. On the last day of our stay it cleared up sufficiently to enable the photographs to be taken, after which we all returned to the Summer Palace.

The day after our arrival at the Summer Palace Her Majesty said that we had better prepare everything for the audience to receive the lady artist (Miss Carl). She told the chief eunuch to issue orders to all the other eunuchs not to speak to Miss Carl, but simply be polite as occasion required. We Court ladies received similar orders. Also, that we were not to address Her Majesty while Miss Carl was present. The Emperor received similar instructions. Her Majesty gave orders to have the Gardens of Prince Chung's Palace ready. She then said to us: "I trust you three to look after this lady artist. I have already given orders for food to be supplied by the Wai Wu Pu. The only thing that I have been worried about is that I have no foreign food here for Miss Carl." She ordered us to have our stove taken over to Prince Chung's Palace in case Miss Carl desired something cooked. She said: "I know it will be very hard for you to take her to the Palace each morning and return with her at night, besides having to watch her all day long, but I know you do not mind. You are doing all this for me." After a while she smiled, and said: "How selfish of me. I order you to bring all your things to this place, but what is your father going to do? The best thing will be to ask your father to come and live in the same place. The country air might benefit him." We kowtowed and thanked Her Majesty, as this was a special favor, no official nor anyone else having been allowed to live in Prince Chung's Palace previously. We all were very pleased – I could now see my father every day. Hitherto we had only been able to see him about once a month, and then only by asking special leave.

The next day Her Majesty sent us to Prince Chung's Palace to make all necessary arrangements for Miss Carl's stay.

This Palace of Prince Chung's was a magnificent place. All the smaller dwellings were quite separate from each other, not in one large building, as was the custom. There was a small lake in the grounds, and lovely little paths to walk along, exactly like the Empress Dowager's Summer Palace, but, of course, on a much smaller scale. We selected one of these small dwellings, or summer houses, for the use of Miss Carl during her stay, and had it fitted up nicely, to make her as comfortable as possible. We ourselves were to occupy the next house to Miss Carl, in order that we might always be on hand, and at the same time keep a good eye on her. We returned to the Summer Palace the same evening, and told Her Majesty just how everything had been arranged. She said: "I want you all to be very careful not to let this lady know that you are watching her." She seemed very anxious about this, repeating these instructions for several days prior to Miss Carl's arrival.

I felt very much relieved when the day before the audience arrived, and everything was finally fixed to Her Majesty's satisfaction. She ordered us to retire early that evening, as she wanted to rest and look well the next morning. When morning came we hurried over everything, even the usual morning audience, so that we could be ready when Miss Carl arrived.

While I was standing behind the screen, as usual, a eunuch came and told me that Mrs. Conger, the artist, and another lady had arrived, and that they were now in the waiting room. By that time the audience was about finished. The chief eunuch came in and told Her Majesty that the foreign ladies had arrived and were waiting in another room. Her Majesty said to us: "I think I will go to the courtyard and meet them there." Of course, at all private audiences Her Majesty received the people in the Throne Room, but as Miss Carl was more of a guest, she did not think it necessary to go through the usual formal reception.

While we were descending the steps we saw the ladies entering the gate of the courtyard. I pointed out Miss Carl to Her Majesty, and noticed that she eyed Miss Carl very keenly. When we arrived in the courtyard, Mrs. Conger came forward and greeted Her Majesty and then presented Miss Carl. Her Majesty's first impression of Miss Carl was a good one, as Miss Carl was smiling very pleasantly, and Her Majesty, who always liked to see a pleasant smile, exclaimed to me in an undertone: "She seems to be a very pleasant person," to which I replied that I was very glad she thought so, as I was very anxious about the impression Miss Carl would make on Her Majesty. Her Majesty watched Miss Carl and myself as we greeted each other, and I could see that she was satisfied. She told me afterwards that she had noticed Miss Carl appeared very glad to see me again, and said: "We will handle her pretty easily, I think." Her Majesty then went to her own private Palace, and we all followed. On our arrival, Miss Carl told me that she had brought her own canvas. This was a piece about six feet by four feet. I had told Miss Carl a little previously that Her Majesty refused to sit for a very small portrait and that she would like a life-size one. When Her Majesty saw the canvas she appeared to be very much disappointed, as in her opinion even that was not large enough. We placed the tables ready for Miss Carl, and Her Majesty asked her to choose the position in which she wished to paint. I knew that Miss Carl would have great difficulty in choosing a good position on account of the windows being built so low, there being very little light except low down near the ground. However, Miss Carl finally placed the canvas near the door of the room. Her Majesty told Mrs. Conger and the rest to sit down for a while as she wanted to change into another gown. I followed her into her bedroom. The first question Her Majesty asked was how old I thought Miss Carl was, as she herself could not guess her age, her hair being extremely light, in fact almost white. I could hardly refrain from laughing outright on hearing this, and told Her Majesty that Miss Carl's hair was naturally of a light color. Her Majesty said that she had often seen ladies with golden hair, but never one with white hair, excepting old ladies. She said: "I think that she is very nice, however, and hope she will paint a good portrait."

Turning to one of the Court ladies, she ordered her to fetch a yellow gown as although, as she put it, she did not like yellow, she thought it would be the best color for a portrait. She selected one from a number which the Court lady brought, embroidered all over with purple wisteria. Her shoes and handkerchiefs matched. She also wore a blue silk scarf, embroidered with the character "Shou" (long life). Each character had a pearl in the center. She wore a pair of jade bracelets and also jade nail protectors. In addition she wore jade butterflies and a tassel on one side of her headdress, and, as usual, fresh flowers on the other side. Her Majesty certainly did look beautiful on that occasion.

By the time she came out from her room Miss Carl had everything prepared. When she saw how Her Majesty was dressed, she exclaimed: "How beautiful Her Majesty looks in this dress," which remark I interpreted to Her Majesty, and it pleased her very much.

She seated herself on her throne, ready to pose for the picture. She just sat down in an ordinary easy position, placing one hand on a cushion. Miss Carl explained: "That is an excellent position, as it is so natural. Please do not move." I told Her Majesty what Miss Carl said, and she asked me whether she looked all right, or not. If not, she would change her position. I assured her that she looked very grand in that position. However, she asked the opinion of the Young Empress and some of the Court ladies, who all agreed that she could not look better. I could see that they never looked at Her Majesty at all, they were too much interested in what Miss Carl was doing.

When Miss Carl commenced to make the rough sketch of Her Majesty everyone watched with open mouth, as they had never seen anything done so easily and so naturally. The Young Empress whispered to me: "Although I don't know anything about portrait painting, still I can see that she is a good artist. She has never seen any of our clothes and headdresses, and she has copied them exactly. Just imagine one of our Chinese artists trying to paint a foreign lady, what a mess he would make of it."

After the sketch was finished Her Majesty was delighted and thought it was wonderful for Miss Carl to have made it so quickly and so accurately. I explained that this was a rough sketch and that when Miss Carl commenced painting, she would soon see the difference. Her Majesty told me to ask Miss Carl whether she was tired and would like to rest; also to tell her that she was very busy all the day, and would only be able to give her a few minutes' sitting each day. We then took Miss Carl to luncheon, together with Mrs. Conger, and after luncheon we accompanied Her Majesty to the theatre.

After Mrs. Conger had departed I took Miss Carl to my room to rest. As soon as we arrived there, Her Majesty sent a eunuch to call me to her bedroom. Her Majesty said: "I don't want this lady to paint during my afternoon rest. She can rest at the same time. As soon as I am up you can bring her here to paint. I am glad that it looks like turning out better than I had anticipated." I therefore told Miss Carl Her Majesty's wishes in this respect and that she could paint for a little while, if she chose to, after Her Majesty had had her rest. Miss Carl was so interested in Her Majesty, she told me she didn't want to rest at all, but that she would like to go on with the painting right away. Of course, I did not like to tell her anything the first day, as it might upset her, and did not say that this was a command from Her Majesty. After a lot of maneuvering I got her to give up the idea of continuing straight off, without offending her. I took her out on the veranda as the eunuch was preparing the table for Her Majesty's dinner in the room we were then occupying. The Young Empress kept Miss Carl busy talking, I acting as interpreter. Soon one of the eunuchs came and informed us that Her Majesty had finished dinner, and would we please come and take ours. On entering the room I was very much surprised to see that chairs had been placed there, as this had never been done previously, everybody, with the exception of Her Majesty, taking their meals standing. The Young Empress was also very much surprised and asked me whether I knew anything about it. I said that perhaps it was on account of Miss Carl being there. The Young Empress told me to go over and ask Her

Majesty, as she was afraid to sit down without receiving orders to do so. Her Majesty whispered to me: "I don't want Miss Carl to think we are barbarians, and treat the Young Empress and the Court ladies in that manner. Of course, she does not understand our Court etiquette and might form a wrong impression, so you can all sit down without coming over to thank me, but be natural, as though you were accustomed to sitting down to dinner every day."

After Her Majesty had washed her hands she came over to our table. Of course we all stood up. Her Majesty told me to ask Miss Carl whether she liked the food, and was pleased when Miss Carl answered that she liked the food better than her own kind. That relieved Her Majesty.

After dinner was over I told Miss Carl to say good-bye to Her Majesty. We courtesied to her, also to the Young Empress, and said good night to the Court ladies. We then took Miss Carl to the Palace of Prince Chung. It took us about ten minutes' ride in the carts. We showed Miss Carl her bedroom, and were pleased to leave her and get to our own rooms, for a good night's rest.

The next morning we took Miss Carl to the Palace, and arrived there during the morning audience. Of course Miss Carl, being a foreigner, could not enter the Throne Room, so we sat down on the back veranda of the Audience Hall and waited until it was over. This, of course, prevented my being in attendance each morning, as usual, and was a great disappointment to me, as I was unable to keep in touch with what was taking place. Moreover, during the time I had been at Court, my one object had been to endeavor to interest Her Majesty in Western customs and civilization. I believed that to a great extent Her Majesty was becoming interested in these things, and would refer the subjects of our conversations to her Ministers, for their opinions. For instance, I had shown her photographs taken of a Naval Review at which I was present in France. Her Majesty seemed to be impressed, and said that she would certainly like to be able to make a similar display in China. This matter she consulted with her Ministers, but they gave the usual evasive answer, viz.: "There is plenty of time for that." From this you will see that Her Majesty was not able to introduce reforms entirely alone, even though she might desire to do so, but had to consult the Ministers, who would always agree with Her Majesty, but would suggest that the matter be put off for a time.

My experience while at the Palace was that everybody seemed to be afraid to suggest anything new for fear they might get themselves into trouble.

When Her Majesty came out from the Audience Hall, Miss Carl went up to her and kissed Her Majesty's hand, which caused her great surprise, although she did not show it at the time. Afterwards, however, when we were alone, she asked me why Miss Carl had done this, as it was not a Chinese custom. She naturally thought that it must be a foreign custom, and therefore said nothing about it.

Her Majesty then proceeded on foot to her own Palace, to change her dress for the portrait. It was a beautiful morning, and when she had posed for about ten minutes, she told me that she felt too tired to proceed, and asked if it would be all right to ask Miss Carl to postpone it. I explained that as Miss Carl was going to be at the Palace for some time, the postponement of one day's sitting would not make much difference at that time, although I knew that Miss Carl would naturally be disappointed. Still, I had to humor Her Majesty as much as possible, otherwise she might have thrown up the whole thing. Miss Carl said that if Her Majesty wished to go to rest, she could be working painting the screen and the throne, and Her Majesty could pose again later on if she felt like it. This pleased Her Majesty, and she said that she would try to sit again after taking her afternoon's rest. Her Majesty ordered me to give Miss Carl her lunch in my own room at twelve o'clock each day, my mother, my sister and myself keeping her company. Dinner at the Palace was usually taken about six o'clock, and it was arranged that Miss Carl should take dinner with the Young Empress and the Court ladies at that hour, after Her Majesty had finished dining. Her Majesty also ordered that champagne or any other wine which Miss Carl preferred, should be served, as she said she knew it was the custom for all foreign ladies to take wine with their meals. Where she got hold of this idea, nobody knew. I was sure that Her Majesty had been misinformed by somebody, but it would have been bad policy to have tried to tell her different at the moment. She disliked very much to be told that she was wrong in any of these things, and it could only be done by waiting and casually introducing the subject at some other time.

After Miss Carl had gone to rest during the afternoon, Her Majesty sent for me and asked the usual question, viz.: What had Miss Carl been saying? etc., etc. She seemed particularly anxious to know what Miss Carl thought of her, and when I told her that Miss Carl had said that she was very beautiful and quite young looking, she said: "Oh! well, of course Miss Carl would say that to you." However, on my assuring her that Miss Carl had given this opinion without being asked for it, she showed very plainly that she was not at all displeased with the compliment.

Suddenly Her Majesty said: "I have been thinking that if Miss Carl can paint the screen and the throne, surely she ought to be able to paint my clothes and jewels, without it being necessary for me to pose all the time." I told her that would be quite impossible, as nobody could hold the things for Miss Carl to get the proper effect. To my surprise she answered: "Well, that is easily gotten over. You wear them in my place." I hardly knew what to say, but thought I would get out of the difficulty by telling her that perhaps Miss Carl would not like such an arrangement. Her Majesty, however, could see no possible objection on Miss Carl's part, as she herself could pose when the time came for painting her face. So I put the matter as nicely as possible to Miss Carl, and it was finally arranged that I should dress in Her Majesty's robes and jewels whenever Her Majesty felt too tired to do the posing herself. In this manner the portrait of the Empress Dowager was painted, and with the exception of just a few hours to enable Miss Carl to get Her Majesty's facial expression, I had to sit for two hours each morning, and for another two hours each afternoon until the portrait was finished.

# CHAPTER FOURTEEN

## The Emperor's Birthday

MY father's four months' leave having expired, he was received in audience by their Majesties on the first day of the sixth moon. He was much improved in health, but his rheumatism was still very troublesome. This was particularly noticeable when climbing the steps to the Audience Hall, and Her Majesty ordered two of the eunuchs to assist him.

First he thanked Her Majesty for her kindness towards my sister and myself, and, as was the custom, took off his hat and knelt down, bowing his head until it struck the ground. This ceremony was always gone through by any official who had received special favors from Their Majesties.

He then replaced his hat on his head and remained kneeling before the throne. Her Majesty then questioned him about his life in Paris, from time to time complimenting him on his work. Seeing that remaining in this kneeling position appeared to be making him tired, Her Majesty ordered one of the eunuchs to bring a cushion for him to use, which was another great honor, as this cushion was only used by the President of the Grand Council.

Her Majesty told him that as he was now getting to be a very old man, she did not intend sending him away from China again, as she wanted to keep my sister and myself at the Court, which she could not do if she sent him to some foreign country, as he would want to take his daughters with him. She said she was pleased, that although we had been away from China for such a long time, we were well acquainted with the Manchu customs. My father replied that it had been his care that we should be brought up according to the customs of our own country.

Her Majesty when asked the Emperor if he had anything to say, and he replied by asking my father if he spoke French, and thought it very strange on learning that he did not. My father explained that he had never had the time to study it, besides which he considered himself too old to learn a foreign language.

The Emperor next asked what was the feeling in France towards China.

My father replied that they were very friendly at that time, but that immediately after the Boxer trouble the post of Minister had been a very embarrassing one. Her Majesty said that it had been an unfortunate affair, but she was glad that everything was now settled satisfactorily. She told my father that he was to get well again as quickly as possible, and the audience came to an end.

Afterwards Her Majesty said that my father was looking very old since his return from France and that he would have to be careful and take things easy until he got stronger again. She was pleased that he had shown appreciation of her interest in my sister and myself.

Preparations were now commenced for celebrating the birthday of His Majesty, the Emperor Kwang Hsu, which was to take place on the 28th of that month. The actual date of the Emperor's birthday was the 26th of the sixth moon, but this day, being the anniversary of the death of a previous Emperor of China, we were unable to hold any festivities, and so it was always celebrated on the 28th day instead. The official celebration lasted for seven days, three days before and four days after the actual date. During that time the whole of the Court dressed in official robes, and no business of any kind whatever was attended to. This being the Emperor's 32nd birthday, and as the full celebrations only took place every tenth year, i. e. On his 20th birthday, his 30th birthday, and so on, the festivities were not carried out on a very grand scale. However, it was quite sufficient to interfere with all business, and the usual morning audiences did not take place during these seven days. The Empress Dowager herself was the only person who did not dress especially during these celebrations, and who did not take any active part in the festivities. Another reason why the celebrations were not carried out on a very large scale was the fact that the Empress Dowager, being alive, she took precedence, according to the Manchu custom, over the Emperor himself, in fact she was the actual ruler of the country, the Emperor being second. The Emperor was quite aware of this fact, and when the Empress commanded that preparations be commenced for the celebrations, the Emperor would always suggest that it was not at all necessary to celebrate the occasion unless it happened to be a tenth year, and would very reluctantly agree to the festivities taking place. Of course this was more out of politeness on the part of the Emperor and to conform to the recognized etiquette, but the nation recognized this birthday and naturally celebrated according to the usual custom. During this period, therefore, the painting of the portrait was postponed.

When the morning of the 25th arrived, the Emperor dressed himself in his official robe-yellow gown, embroidered with gold dragons and coat of a reddish black color. Of course, being the Emperor, in place of the usual button on the hat he wore a large pearl. I might mention that the Emperor was the only person who could wear this particular pearl in place of a button. He came as usual to wish Her Majesty Chi Hsiang and then proceeded to the temple to worship before the ancestral tablets. After this ceremony was over he returned to the Empress Dowager and kowtowed to her. All the Chinese adopt this rule of kowtowing to their parents on their own birthdays, as a sign of reverence and respect. The Emperor next proceeded to the Audience Hall, where all the Ministers were assembled, and received their salutations and congratulations. This ceremony very often caused amusement, for to see several hundred people all bobbing their heads up and down, especially when they did not all manage to do it together, was a very funny sight. Even the Emperor himself had to laugh, it was such an extraordinary spectacle.

The musical instruments which were used during the ceremony deserve a little description. The principal instrument is made of hard wood, and has a flat bottom about three feet in diameter, with a dome-shaped top raised about three feet from the ground. The inside is quite hollow. A long pole made of the same material is used as a drumstick, and an official, specially appointed, beats with all his might on the drum. The noise can be better imagined than described. This is used as a signal to announce when the Emperor takes his seat upon the throne. In addition to the above, a full sized model of a tiger, also made of similar hard wood, and having twenty-four scales on its back, is brought into the courtyard. In this case they did not beat the instrument, but scraped along its back over the scales, which emitted a noise similar to the letting off simultaneously of innumerable crackers. This noise was kept up during the whole of the ceremony, and what with the drum and this tiger instrument it was sufficient to deafen one. During the ceremony, an official crier used to call out the different orders, such as when to kneel, bow, stand up, kowtow, etc., etc., but with the noise it was quite impossible to hear a single word of what he uttered. Another instrument was composed of a frame made of wood, about eight feet high by three feet broad. Across this frame were three wooden bars, from which was suspended twelve bells, made out of pure gold. When these were struck with a wooden stick the sound was not at all unlike the dulcimer, only, of course, very much louder. This was placed on the right side of the Audience Hall. On the left side a similar instrument was placed, with the exception that the bells were carved out of white jade. The music which could be brought out of the instrument was very sweet.

When this ceremony of receiving the Ministers was concluded, the Emperor proceeded to his private Palace, where the Young Empress (his wife), the Secondary wife and all the Court ladies were gathered, and, after kowtowing, all of the Court ladies present, led by the Young Empress, knelt before him and presented him with a Ru Yee. This is a kind of sceptre. Some are made out of pure jade, while others are made out of wood inlaid with jade. This Ru Yee is a symbol of good luck and was supposed to bring happiness and prosperity to the person to whom it was presented. The ceremony was gone through to the accompaniment of music played on string instruments, which was very sweet.

Next the eunuchs were received by the Emperor, and they similarly congratulated him, but without the accompaniment of music. After the eunuchs came the servant girls, and the whole of the ceremony was over. The Emperor next proceeded to Her Majesty's Palace, where he knelt before Her Majesty and thanked her for the celebration which had been given in his honor, after which Her Majesty, accompanied by the whole Court, went to the theatre to see the play. On arrival at the theatre we were all presented by Her Majesty with sweetmeats, this being the custom on these occasions, and after a little while Her Majesty retired for her afternoon rest. Thus the celebration ended.

Two days after the celebration the seventh moon commenced. The seventh day of the seventh moon was the occasion of another important anniversary.

The two stars, Niu Lang (Capricorn) and Chih Nu (Lyra) are supposed to be the patrons of agriculture and weaving and, according to tradition, were at one time man and wife. As the result of a quarrel, however, they were doomed to live apart, being separated from each other by the "Milky Way." But on the seventh day of the seventh moon of each year they are allowed to see each other and the magpies are supposed to build a bridge to enable them to meet.

The ceremony is rather peculiar. Several basins full of water were placed so that the sun's rays would fall upon them. Her Majesty then took several tiny needles and dropped one into each basin. These floated on the water, casting a shadow across the bottom of the basins. These shadows took different forms, according to the position of the needle, and if the shadow took certain prescribed forms, the person throwing in the needle was supposed to be very lucky and clever, while if they represented certain other forms, they were despised by the gods as being ignorant. In addition, Her Majesty burned incense and offered up prayers to the two gods referred to.

This was always a sad moon for Her Majesty, it being the anniversary of the death of her husband, the Emperor Hsien Feng, who died on the 17th of that month. The fifteenth of the seventh moon each year is the day of the festival for the dead, and early in the morning the Court moved to the Sea Palace in order to sacrifice. The Chinese hold that when a person dies, his soul still remains on the earth, and on these anniversaries they burn imitation money, the belief being that the soul of the departed one will benefit to the extent of the amount of money so represented. On the anniversary above referred to Her Majesty sent for hundreds of Buddhist priests to pray for those unfortunate people who had died without leaving anyone who could sacrifice for them. On the evening of this day, Her Majesty and all her Court ladies set out in open boats on the lake, where imitation lotus flowers were arranged as lanterns, with a candle placed in the centre, which formed a sort of floating light, the idea being to give light to the spirits of those who had departed during the year, so as to enable them to come and receive the blessings which had been prepared for them. Her Majesty ordered us to light the candles and place the flowers on the water ourselves, as she said it would be appreciated by the spirits of the dead. Some of the eunuchs had told Her Majesty that they had actually seen some of these spirits, which assertion was thoroughly believed. Although she had never seen them herself, she accounted for this by the fact that she was of too high a rank and the spirits were afraid of her, but she ordered all the rest of us to keep a sharp lookout and tell her if we saw anything. Of course we didn't see anything, but many of the Court ladies were so frightened that they closed their eyes for fear they might see something supernatural.

Her Majesty was devoted to the late Emperor Hsien Feng, and she was very sad and morose during this period. We all had to be very careful indeed not to upset her in any way, as she would find fault on the slightest provocation. She hardly had a word to say to any of us, and cried almost incessantly. I could hardly understand the reason for such grief, seeing that the Emperor had died so many years previously. None of the Court ladies were allowed to dress in light-coloured gowns during the whole of the seventh moon. We all dressed either in dark blue or pale blue, while Her Majesty herself dressed in black every day without exception. Even her handkerchiefs were black. The theatres which were usually opened on the first and fifteenth of each month, were closed during the seventh moon. There was no music, and everything was conducted in the most solemn manner; in fact, the whole Court was in deep mourning.

On the morning of the seventeenth day of the seventh moon, Her Majesty visited the late Emperor's tablet, and knelt there crying for quite a while. In order to show respect for the late Emperor, none of us were allowed to eat meat for three days. This being my first year at the Palace, it appeared to me very strange, after the customary gaiety and noise. Of course I felt very sorry for Her Majesty, as I could see that it was a genuine display of grief and was not in any way put on. As I was her favorite at that time, she kept me close to her side during this sad period. The Young Empress said to me one day: "Her Majesty is very much attached to you, and I think you had better stay with her for the time being." This I did, and I was so miserable myself that when Her Majesty commenced crying I would cry also. When she saw that I was crying, Her Majesty would immediately stop and ask me not to cry. She would tell me that I was too young to cry, and that in any case I did not know what real sorrow was as yet. During the conversations we had at that time she would tell me quite a lot about herself. On one occasion she said: "You know I have had a very hard life ever since I was a young girl. I was not a bit happy when with my parents, as I was not the favorite. My sisters had everything they wanted, while I was, to a great extent, ignored altogether. When I first came to the Court, a lot of the people were jealous of me because I was considered to be a beautiful woman at that time. I must say myself that I was a clever one, for I fought my own battles, and won them, too. When I arrived at Court the late Emperor became very much attached to me and would hardly glance at any of the other ladies. Fortunately, I was lucky in giving birth to a son, as it made me the Emperor's undisputed favorite; but after that I had very bad luck. During the last year of his reign the Emperor was seized with a sudden illness. In addition to this the foreign soldiers burnt down the Palace at Yuen Ming Yuen, so we fled to Jehol. Of course everybody knows what took place at that time. I was still a young woman, with a dying husband and a young son. The East Empress Dowager's nephew was a bad man, who coveted the throne, which he had no right to in any event, as he was not of royal blood. I would not wish anyone to experience what I myself passed through at that time. When the Emperor was in a dying condition, being practically unconscious of what was taking place around him, I took my son to his bedside and asked him what was going to be done about his successor to the throne. He made no reply to this, but, as has always been the case in emergencies, I was equal to the occasion, and I said to him: 'Here is your son,' on hearing which he immediately opened his eyes and said: 'Of course he will succeed to the throne.' I naturally felt relieved when this was settled once and for all. These words were practically the last he spoke, for he died immediately afterwards. Although it is now so many years ago, I can see him now in that dying condition, just as though it all happened only yesterday.

"I thought that I could be happy with my son as the Emperor Tung Chi, but unfortunately he died before he was twenty years of age. Since that time I have been a changed woman, as all happiness was over as far as I was concerned when he died. I had also quite a lot of trouble with the East Empress Dowager and found it very difficult to keep on good terms with her. However, she died five years after the death of my son. In addition to all this, when the Emperor Kwang Hsu was brought to me as a baby three years old, he was a very sickly child, and could hardly walk, he was so thin and weak. His parents seemed to be afraid of giving him anything to eat. You know his father was Prince Chung, and his mother was my sister, so of course he was almost the same as my own son, in fact I adopted him as such. Even now, after all my trouble on his account, he is not in perfect health. As you know, I have had plenty of other troubles beside these, but it is useless to mention them now. I am disappointed with everything, as nothing has turned out as I had expected." With this remark Her Majesty commenced crying afresh. Continuing, she said: "People seem to think that just because I am the Empress Dowager that I am bound to be happy, but what I have just told you is not all. I have gone through much more than that. If ever anything went wrong, I was always the one who was blamed. The censors even dare to impeach me once in a while. However, I am philosopher enough to take things for what they are worth, otherwise I would have been in my own grave long, long ago. Just imagine how small minded these people are. Amongst other things they objected to my transferring my Court to the Summer Palace during the hot weather, although I could do no harm by being there. Even in the short time you have spent at Court, you can see that I am unable to decide anything alone, while whenever they want anything they consult with each other and then present their petition to me, which, unless it is something of a very serious nature, I never think of refusing."

After the time set apart for mourning had expired, we all went back to the Summer Palace, where Miss Carl re-commenced her work on Her Majesty's portrait. Her Majesty apparently soon got tired of this portrait painting, for one day she asked me when I thought it would be finished. She was afraid that it would not be finished by the time the cold weather came on, when we always removed the Court to the Forbidden City, and she said it would be a lot of trouble and inconvenience to have to continue the portrait there. I told Her Majesty that it could easily be arranged and that she need not worry herself.

After I had been posing in Her Majesty's place for several days Her Majesty asked me whether Miss Carl had said anything about it, and if she did, I was to inform her that it was a command from Her Majesty, and that I dare not make any further suggestions in that respect. So we had no further trouble with Miss Carl after that. I had, however, quite a lot of trouble with the eunuchs, who, in spite of Her Majesty's instructions, were anything but polite to Miss Carl. Of course Miss Carl herself did not know this. I tried to make them behave better by threatening to tell Her Majesty about them, which had a good effect for a while, but they were soon as bad as ever.

At the commencement of the eighth moon, Her Majesty always attended to the transplanting of her chrysanthemums, which was one of her favorite flowers, so each day she would take us with her to the west side of the lake and, assisted by us, would cut the tops of the young plants and set them in flower pots. I was very much surprised at this, as there were no roots, only the stems of the flowers, but Her Majesty assured me that they would soon grow into very pretty plants. Every day we went over to water these flowers until they began to bud. In case it rained heavily, Her Majesty would order some of the eunuchs to go over and cover up these chrysanthemum plants with mats, so that they would not be broken. It was characteristic of Her Majesty that, no matter what other business she had to attend to, her flowers had her first consideration and she would, if necessary, even go without her usual rest in order to superintend them personally. She also spent quite a time in looking after her orchard, where she had planted apple trees, pear trees, etc. Another thing which I began to notice was that when the spring and summer days had passed, she got quite irritable and sad, while in the winter she was simply unbearable. She loathed cold weather.

One day, during the eighth moon, Her Majesty was taken slightly ill, and complained of suffering from severe headaches. This was the only time I ever saw Her Majesty actually sick. She, however, got up as usual in the morning, and held audience, but was unable to take her luncheon, and very soon had to retire to her bed. Several doctors were summoned, each of whom took her pulse. This was quite a ceremony in itself. The doctors knelt at the bedside, and Her Majesty stretched forth her arm, resting her hand upon a small pillow which was provided for that purpose. After this each doctor wrote out his prescription, all of which were different from each other. We handed them to Her Majesty, who chose the one which she thought was the nicest to take, and two attendants and the doctor himself had to take a dose in her presence before she would touch it. Then she would take it all right.

During this time it rained a great deal and was very hot. The climate at this time of the year is very damp, which causes the flies to make their appearance in millions. If there was one thing more than another that Her Majesty detested it was these flies. During the actual summer they were not so troublesome as at this particular time. Of course every precaution was taken to keep them away, a eunuch being posted at each door, provided with sort of a switch made of horse hair fastened at the end of a bamboo pole. We were never troubled by mosquitoes, however; in fact I never saw a mosquito curtain in the Palace during the whole of my stay there. These flies were an abomination, and in spite of all that could be done a few would find their way into the rooms. Whenever they alighted on Her Majesty she would scream, while if by any chance one were to alight on her food she would order the whole lot to be thrown away. This would spoil her appetite for the whole day and put her into a terrible temper as well. Whenever she saw one anywhere near her, she would order whoever happened to be present to go and catch it. I myself often received this order, but I detested them almost as much as Her Majesty did, they were so dirty, and stuck to one's hands whenever they touched them.

After her illness Her Majesty was indisposed more or less for quite a long time, and doctors were constantly in attendance. She took so many different kinds of medicine that instead of getting better she got worse and eventually contracted a fever. Her Majesty was very much afraid of fevers of any kind and we had to stay with her all night and all day and had to take our meals whenever we could get away from her bedside for a few minutes. Another peculiarity was Her Majesty's aversion for any kind of perfume near her when she was sick, while when she was feeling well she was simply smothered in it. The same applied to fresh flowers; in spite of her love for them under ordinary conditions, when she was sick she could not bear them anywhere near. Her nerves became absolutely unstrung, as she was unable to sleep during the day, and consequently the time passed very slowly to her. In order to make the time pass a little less tediously, she gave instructions for one of the better educated eunuchs to read to her during the daytime. This reading generally consisted of ancient Chinese history, poetry and all kinds of Chinese lore, and while the eunuch was reading to her we had to stand by her bedside, one of us being told off to massage her legs, which seemed to soothe her somewhat. This same program was gone through every day until she was completely herself again – some ten days later.

One day Her Majesty asked me: "What kind of medicine does a foreign doctor usually give in case of a fever? I have heard that they make you take all kinds of pills. This must be very dangerous, as you never know what they are made of. Here in China all medicines are made from roots, and I can always find out whether I am receiving the right medicine, as I have a book which explains what each different medicine is for. Another thing I have heard is that foreign doctors generally operate on you with a knife, while we cure the same sickness by means of our medicine. Li Lien Ying told me that one of our little eunuchs had a boil on his wrist and someone advised him to go to the hospital. Of course they didn't know what they would do, and the foreign doctor there opened the boil with a knife, which frightened the child very much. I was very much surprised when I heard he was all right again in a couple of days." Continuing, Her Majesty said: "A year ago one of the foreign ladies came to the Palace, and hearing me cough a lot, gave me some black pills and told me to swallow them. I did not like to offend her, so I took the pills and told her I would take them by and bye. However, I was afraid to take them and threw them away." Of course I answered that I didn't know much about medicines, to which she replied that she had seen me take foreign medicines whenever I was not feeling well. She then said: "Of course I know there are people in Peking who do take the medicines given them by foreign doctors and even some of my own relatives patronize these foreigners also. They try not to let me know, but I do know for all that. In any case, if they choose to kill themselves by taking these things, it is none of my business; that is the reason why, when they are sick, I never send my own doctors to attend them."

When Her Majesty had completely recovered from her illness she used to go out on the lake a great deal, sometimes in an open boat and at other times in a steam launch. She always appeared to enjoy this kind of thing. For some reason or other she always insisted on taking the west side of the lake, which was very shallow, and invariably the launch would get stuck fast in the mud, which seemed to afford Her Majesty great enjoyment; she simply loved to feel the launch strike the bottom. The open boats would then come alongside and we would have to get out of the launch and enter the boats and proceed to the top of the nearest hill to watch the efforts of the eunuchs trying to refloat the launch. It was a characteristic of Her Majesty to experience a keen sense of enjoyment at the troubles of other people. The eunuchs knew this quite well, and whenever opportunity offered, they would do something which they thought would amuse Her Majesty. So long as it was nothing of a serious nature Her Majesty would always overlook it, but in case it proved serious or was carelessness, she would always order them to be severely punished. Thus it was very hard to tell just what to do in order to please her.

Another of Her Majesty's peculiarities was inquisitiveness. For example: As I have stated before, it was the custom for Her Majesty to have sweetmeats brought to her before every meal, and after she had finished with them, the remainder were distributed among the Court ladies. Whenever it happened that we were very busy, we did not bother with the sweetmeats at all, which Her Majesty very soon found out. One day, after she had finished dining, she came and looked through the window to see what we were doing, and saw some of the eunuchs eating the sweetmeats which she had given to us. She did not say anything, but simply ordered that the sweetmeats should be brought back again, making us believe that she wanted some more herself. I knew that there was something wrong, as she never ordered them back before. When she saw what was left of them, she asked who had been eating so many, as they were nearly all finished, but she got no reply – we were all too scared. However, after thinking it over, I came to the conclusion that it would be best to tell her the truth, for I was quite certain that she knew anyhow. So I told her that we had all been very busy and had forgotten all about the sweetmeats, and that the eunuchs had come and taken them themselves, and I added that this was not the first time they had done so. I was rather glad that she had given me this opportunity to report the eunuchs, for Her Majesty replied that if she intended the eunuchs to have sweetmeats, she herself could give them some, but thought it a lack of appreciation on our part not eating them ourselves after she had been so kind as to provide them for us. She turned to me, and said: "I am glad that you have told the truth, as I saw myself what was happening." She gave orders that the offending eunuchs should each have three months' wages deducted as a punishment, but of course I knew very well they didn't mind that, as they were making many times the amount of their salary in other ways. On my return to the sitting room, one of the Court ladies said: "You should not have told Her Majesty about the eunuchs, they are sure to revenge themselves in some way." I asked how they could possibly injure me in any way, as they were only servants, but she told me that they would find some underhand way in which to get even with me, this being their general custom. Of course I knew the eunuchs were a bad lot, but could not see what cause they had to be against me in any way. I knew they dare not say anything against me to Her Majesty, so I forgot all about the matter. I found out afterwards that one of the tricks they used to play on any of the Court ladies who offended them was to try and prejudice Her Majesty against us. For instance, if Her Majesty told one of the eunuchs that a certain thing should be done, instead of telling me what Her Majesty wanted, the eunuch would go off to one of the other ladies and tell her. In this way Her Majesty would get the impression that I was too lazy to wait upon her myself, and of course the other lady would get all the credit. Although Her Majesty was very kind to me, also the Young Empress, it was very hard to get along with eunuchs, and it was not good policy to offend them in any way. They regarded themselves as being exclusively the servants of Her Majesty, the Empress Dowager, and refused to take instructions from anybody else, consequently they were often very rude to the other ladies of the Court, not even excepting the Young Empress.

Everything proceeded as usual until the eighth moon, when the Emperor was to sacrifice at the "Temple of the Sun." On this occasion the Emperor wore a red robe.

About this time Mrs. Conger asked for a private audience, as she wanted to see Her Majesty and at the same time see how the portrait was progressing. Her Majesty replied that she would receive her and gave orders accordingly. At this private audience Mrs. Conger brought into the Court two of her relatives to be presented to Her Majesty, besides Miss Campbell and a missionary lady. As it was a private audience, the guests were conducted to Her Majesty's private Palace. They were received in the hall which was being used as studio for this lady artist, although Her Majesty was out of patience with the portrait painting, and talked to us a great deal about it, yet when she saw Mrs. Conger and the others she was extremely polite and told them that the portrait was going to be a masterpiece. She was in an unusually good humor that day and told me to give orders to the eunuchs to open all the buildings and show them to her guests. Her Majesty led the way from one room to another and showed them her curios in the different rooms, until she came to rest in one of the bedrooms, when she ordered chairs to be brought in for the guests. There were many chairs in this room, but they were really small thrones of Her Majesty's, although they looked like any ordinary chairs. The custom is that no matter what kind of a chair it may be, as soon as she uses it, it is at once called her throne and no one is allowed to sit on it thereafter unless the order is given by her.

During the time the eunuchs were bringing in the chairs kept purposely for foreigners to use, one of the ladies of the party made a mistake and sat upon one of Her Majesty's thrones. I noticed her at once, and before I had a chance to warn her, Her Majesty made a sign of annoyance to me. I went to this lady at once and told her I wanted to show her something and naturally she was obliged to get up. The trouble was this, although Her Majesty felt that no one had the right to sit upon her throne, she expected me to get this lady off the chair and at the same time not to tell her the reason why. While I was busy interpreting for her, she said in an undertone: "There she is again, sitting on my bed. We had better leave this room." After this the ladies were conducted to the refreshment room, and when they had partaken of lunch, bade Her Majesty good-bye, leaving Miss Carl with us. As usual we reported to her that we had seen the guests safely off. She said to me: "That was a funny lady: first she sat upon my throne, and then upon my bed. Perhaps she does not know what a throne is when she sees one, and yet foreigners laugh at us. I am sure that our manners are far superior to theirs. Another thing – did you notice that Mrs. Conger handed a parcel to Miss Carl out in the courtyard when she came in?" I replied that I had noticed her passing something like a parcel, but could not tell what the parcel contained. She thereupon told me to go and ask Miss Carl what it was. At that time I had received so many peculiar orders from Her Majesty that I was beginning to get accustomed to them and used my own discretion in carrying out her instructions. Therefore I did not ask Miss Carl, but set about finding out for myself. However, when I began to look around for the parcel, it had mysteriously disappeared and I could not find the thing anywhere. This naturally worried me, knowing as I did that Her Majesty liked her instructions carried out quickly. While I was searching, one of the eunuchs came in and told me that Her Majesty wanted to see me, and of course I had to go to her. Before she could say anything to me, I informed Her Majesty that I had not been able to ask Miss Carl about the parcel as she was asleep, but would do so immediately she got up. Her Majesty said: "I don't want Miss Carl to think I have told you to ask what the parcel contains, otherwise she might think I am suspicious of what is going on, so you must manage to get the information somehow without mentioning the matter; you are clever enough to do that much." Shortly afterwards, while I was walking along with Miss Carl to Her Majesty's Palace, to proceed with the portrait, I noticed that she was carrying the parcel in question, which was a great relief to me, I can assure you. On arrival at the Palace, Miss Carl said to me: "You need not trouble to pose at present, as it is rather dark, and I can be painting the throne; you can look through this magazine, if you like, to pass the time away." So I opened up the parcel, which proved to contain nothing more than an ordinary American monthly magazine. After glancing through the book, I made an excuse to hurry away and inform Her Majesty. However, she had already gone out for her usual trip on the lake, so I took my chair and followed. When I reached the lake, Her Majesty, who had seen me, sent a small boat and I was rowed out to the launch. Before I could get a chance to speak, Her Majesty said with a smile: "I know all about it, it was a book and Miss Carl handed it to you to read." I was very much disappointed that I had had my journey for nothing. I knew that the eunuchs would report it to Her Majesty at the first opportunity, but I hardly expected they would have done so already. Her Majesty was now quite satisfied, and simply asked whether Miss Carl suspected that she had enquired about the matter.

As I was about to return to Miss Carl, Her Majesty called me and said: "There is one thing I want to tell you and that is whenever any foreign ladies are visiting the Palace, always keep close to the Emperor so that in the event of their speaking to him you can interpret." I answered that so far whenever any foreigners were present I was present also and did not think that anybody had held any conversation with the Emperor whatsoever. She explained that her reason for mentioning this was that she wanted me to be just as courteous to the Emperor as I was to herself, and I was to place myself entirely at his disposal whenever visitors were present. Of course I knew very well that this was not the true reason at all but that she wanted to take every precaution to preclude the possibility of foreigners influencing the Emperor in matters of reform, etc.

# CHAPTER FIFTEEN

## The Mid-Autumn Festival

ON the fifteenth day of the eighth moon came the celebration of the Mid-Autumn Festival, sometimes called the Moon Festival.

This name is derived from the belief which the Chinese hold that the moon is not permanently round when full, but that on this particular day it is a perfect circle. The ceremony which is gone through is conducted entirely by the Court ladies and consists of worshiping the moon as soon as it appears in the sky. In other respects the celebrations are exactly the same as in the Dragon Boat Festival, presents were exchanged between Her Majesty and the Court officials. The festival concluded with a theatrical performance which describes a scene in the moon. The belief is that a beautiful maiden lives in the moon, her only companion being a white rabbit, called a Jade Rabbit. According to the play this rabbit escapes from the moon to the Earth and becomes a young and beautiful girl. A golden rooster which lives in the sun, becoming aware of the rabbit's descent to the earth, himself descends from the sun and changes into a handsome prince. Of course they very naturally meet and immediately fall in love. Now, on the earth lived another rabbit – a red one, who, on finding out what was going on, changed himself into a prince also and set about making love to the beautiful maiden with the object of cutting out the rooster. However, he was seriously handicapped inasmuch as he was unable to change the color of his face, which remained red, therefore his love making met with no success and the rooster prince had it all his own way. At this point, the beautiful maiden in the moon, on discovering her loss, sent the soldiers of Heaven to re-capture her rabbit, with the result that she was taken back to the moon and the rooster being left alone, had no alternative but to reluctantly return to his home in the sun.

During this performance the head eunuch brought a young man into the courtyard, who kowtowed to Her Majesty. This was such an unusual occurrence that everybody noticed it. I could see that he was a stranger and did not belong to the Court and I wondered who he could be. At the other end of the veranda I saw two or three of the Court ladies whispering together and smiling. They finally came over to me and asked if I knew who he was. I told them that he was a stranger to me and they ought to know better than I did as they had been at the Court much longer. Anyhow I gave it as my opinion that he was decidedly ugly. That same evening Her Majesty asked me whether I had noticed this young man, and told me that he was the son of a very high Manchu official; that his father was dead and that he had succeeded to the title and to a large amount of money. I was surprised that Her Majesty should give such a lengthy explanation about this young man, but I told her that I did not think him very handsome. Her Majesty was talking in a very serious manner but I did not think anything of the occurrence at the time but a few days later while I was posing for the portrait I heard Her Majesty whispering to my mother at the other end of the room. I saw that Her Majesty was holding a photograph in her hands which she showed to my mother, at the same time asking whether my mother considered him good looking. My mother answered "not very." On Her Majesty replying that beauty was not everything I began to suspect that there was something going on which directly concerned me. I began to think of some excuse in order to get out of what I could plainly see was a proposed marriage between myself and this gentleman. I knew that if Her Majesty had made up her mind that I was to marry him I could not help myself, but, at the same time, I made up my own mind that rather than marry anyone whom I did not like, especially one I had never seen before, I would leave the Court altogether. When Her Majesty retired for her usual afternoon rest she told me she wanted to see me for a moment. After beating about the bush for some time, she asked me whether I would like to stay with her always or whether I would like to go away again to some foreign country. I at once answered that I was quite satisfied to stay with her as long as she cared to have me but that when she was tired of me she could then send me away. Her Majesty informed me that it had been her intention to marry me to this young gentleman and asked my opinion. I told her that I did not want to get married at all, especially seeing that my father was sick at this time, and leaving home to go to live apart from my family would break his heart and perhaps be the cause of his premature death. Her Majesty said that was no excuse as I should not have to go out of China but would be able to see my father and family any time I wished. I told Her Majesty that I would much rather stay with her altogether and that I did not want to marry anybody. Her Majesty then said: "I won't listen to any excuse. I have already explained everything to your mother, but much to my surprise she said it would be better to mention it to you first, on account of your having been brought up differently from the rest of the Court ladies. Had it not been for this fact I would simply have arranged everything with your mother and the matter would have been settled so far as you were concerned." I could not say anything in answer to this, so commenced to cry. I told Her Majesty that I was not like the rest of the Court ladies who pretended they did not want to marry, when all the time they were simply looking forward to getting married, if only for the change from the monotony of Court life. I promised that I would stay with her forever, and that I had no desire to go away from China again. I explained that I should not have gone away at all had it not been that my father was transferred to Paris. Her Majesty said: "Oh, well, I am very glad that you did go away as you are more useful to me than you would have been had you stayed in China all your life." After a lot more discussion Her Majesty said: "Well, I will leave you to think the matter over. If you don't like the young man I have chosen there are plenty of others," which remark did not help me very much as I could see that she meant to marry me off anyway. However, I had managed to get out of it this time, and thought I would be able to arrange matters satisfactorily should the question come up again. Nothing further was said about the matter until nearly a month later when I heard that a marriage had been arranged between this gentleman and the daughter of one of the princes. So everything ended very satisfactorily from my point of view.

The twenty-sixth day of the eighth moon was the occasion of another celebration. At the time the Manchu Dynasty began, Emperor Shung Chih, who had fought very hard to gain the throne, found himself on the twenty-sixth day of the eighth moon, absolutely out of provisions of every kind and it was necessary for him and his army to live on the leaves of trees, which was the only form of food obtainable at the time. Thus the anniversary of this day, even up to the present time, is always celebrated by the Manchu people, who deny themselves all luxuries, especially at the Court. We did not eat any meat on that day, but only rice wrapped in lettuce leaves. Chopsticks were also discarded and the food was conveyed to the mouth by the hands alone. Even the Empress Dowager was no exception to this rule. This is done in order to remind the present generation of the privation suffered by their ancestors who established the Manchu Dynasty.

Towards the close of the eighth moon Her Majesty's gourd plants, which had been planted early in the spring, were ripening, and each day she would take us all to see what progress they were making. She would pick out those which she considered to be the most perfect in form, i. e., those with the smallest waist and tie ribbons around them so as not to lose sight of them. She pointed to one of these plants one day, and said to me: "This reminds me of yourself when dressed in foreign clothes. Surely you feel more comfortable in the clothes you are now wearing." When these gourds were quite ripe they were cut down and Her Majesty would scrape the outer skin with a bamboo knife, afterwards wiping the fruit with a wet cloth. They were then allowed to dry and after a few days they would assume a brownish color, when they were ready for hanging as ornaments in the Summer Palace. In one room alone there were over 10,000 of these gourds, of different shapes. It was the duty of the Court ladies to periodically wipe these gourds with a cloth, in order to give them a shiny appearance, and also to scrape any new ones which were pulled and prepare them for the Palace. None of us cared very much about this work excepting Her Majesty. One day whilst attending to these gourds I happened to knock the top off one of the old ones which was Her Majesty's particular favorite. I dared not go and tell Her Majesty what had happened and one of the Court ladies suggested throwing the thing away altogether and saying nothing about it as Her Majesty would not be likely to find it out, having so many of them. However, I finally decided to go and tell Her Majesty about it, and take punishment if necessary. For a wonder Her Majesty did not make much bother about it. She said: "Well it was quite an old one in any case and the top was ready to drop off at any time; it so happens that you were the one to wipe it, and of course it came off. It can't be helped." I told Her Majesty that I was very much ashamed at being so careless, especially as I knew it was one of her favorites, and there the matter ended. All the rest of the Court ladies were in the waiting room and were anxious to know how I would get out of it, and when I told them they said that had it been any of them there would have been a fine row. They laughed, and said it must be nice to be a favorite which made me feel very uncomfortable. I told the Young Empress exactly what had happened, and she said I was quite right to tell Her Majesty the truth and told me to be very careful as there was much jealousy going on.

At the beginning of the ninth moon the chrysanthemums commence to bud and it was the duty of the ladies of the Court to go and trim them each day by cutting away all the buds except one on each stalk. This trimming gives the flower a better chance of developing, a much larger blossom being the result. Even Her Majesty would help with this work. She was very particular about these plants, and would not allow any of us to meddle with them if our hands were not perfectly cool, as to touch them with hot hands would cause the leaves to shrivel up. These flowers are generally in full bloom about the end of the ninth moon or beginning of the tenth moon. Her Majesty had a wonderful gift of being able to tell what kind of flower would bloom from each separate plant, even before the buds appeared. She would say: "This is going to be a red flower," and we would place a bamboo stick in the flower pot, with the name written on it. Then another, Her Majesty would declare to be a white one and we would place a similar bamboo stick in the flower pot, with the description, and so on. Her Majesty said: "This is your first year at the Palace and no doubt you are surprised at what you have just seen and heard me say, but I have never yet made a mistake. For you will see when the flowers commence to bloom." It was a fact as everything turned out exactly as she had predicted. None of us ever knew how she was able to distinguish one from the other, but she was always right. I did once ask her to explain how she was able to tell but she answered that it was a secret.

All this time the portrait was proceeding very slowly and one day Her Majesty asked me how long I thought it would be before it was finished and what the custom in Europe was as regards remuneration for such a portrait. I replied that it was customary to pay very handsomely, but she would not hear of such a suggestion, saying that in China it was not the custom and that it would be regarded as an insult to offer money for such a service. She suggested decorating Miss Carl as a reward for her services, which she considered would be appreciated far more than a money present. There was nothing for me to say at this time but I determined to mention the matter again when a favorable opportunity occurred.

During the ninth moon a Russian circus visited Peking and of course everybody talked of little else. Her Majesty, hearing so much talk about this circus asked what it was like, and after we had explained to her, she became very interested and said that she would like to see it. My mother thought it would be a good idea to have the circus brought up to the Summer Palace, where they could perform, so she asked Her Majesty whether this might be done. Her Majesty was delighted with the idea, and arrangements were accordingly made for the performance. While everything was being fixed, the people belonging to the circus, and the animals, were quartered near our own house and we had to feed them at our own expense. However, we wanted to show Her Majesty what a circus was like so the expense did not matter. It took them two days to erect the tent and make all necessary preparations, and during this time Her Majesty received reports as to what was being done, and the progress they were making.

The day before the performance, we noticed that Her Majesty, on coming from her audience, looked very angry, and on our enquiring what was the matter she informed my mother and myself that some censors had raised objections against having this circus in the Palace grounds, as there had never been anything of this kind allowed before and they had begged Her Majesty to give up the idea. Her Majesty was very angry, and said: "You see how much power I have here; I cannot even have a circus without somebody raising objections. I think we had better pay them something and let them go away." Of course we agreed to anything she thought best. After considering for a time Her Majesty jumped up and said: "They have the tent up already; they will talk just the same whether we have the circus or not; I will have it anyway." So the performance duly took place and Her Majesty and all the Court were delighted. One item consisted of a young girl walking and dancing on a large globe. This especially pleased Her Majesty and she insisted on the performance being repeated several times. Another item of interest was the trapeze act. Of course nobody present with the exception of my mother, sister and myself had ever seen a circus performance before, and Her Majesty was very much afraid that the man would fall from the trapeze and kill himself. Another thing which interested Her Majesty was the bare-back riding, which she thought simply wonderful. The only objection to the whole show which she raised was when it was suggested to bring in the lions and tigers, etc. She said it was not safe to bring wild beasts into the Palace and that she would rather not see this part of the performance. The proprietor of the circus, however, brought in a small baby elephant which performed several clever tricks. This delighted Her Majesty more than anything else and when the proprietor saw how pleased she was he offered the elephant as a present, which she accepted. However, after the performance was over we tried to make him go through his tricks again but he would not budge an inch, so we had to give it up as a bad job and send him away to be placed along with the other elephants belonging to the Palace.

Altogether there were three performances given by the circus, and before the final performance, the circus Manager told me that he would very much like to show the lions and tigers: there was no chance of any accident and it really would be worth seeing. So after a lot of discussion Her Majesty finally consented to allow them to be brought in but on the distinct understanding that they should not be let out of their cages.

When they were brought in the ring all the eunuchs gathered around Her Majesty, and after remaining in the ring for a few minutes Her Majesty ordered them to be taken away again. She said: "I am not afraid for myself, but they might get loose and hurt some of the people." This item finished the whole of the performance and the circus departed richer by some Taels 10,000 which Her Majesty had ordered to be given to them.

For the next couple of days we discussed the merits of the circus but afterwards, Her Majesty, when referring to the subject, expressed great disappointment with the whole thing. She said she had expected something entirely different and far more wonderful. This was another characteristic of Her Majesty; nothing pleased her for more than five minutes at a time. She said to me: "I don't see anything at all wonderful in foreign accomplishments. Take for instance this portrait which this lady is painting. I don't think it is going to be at all a good picture, it seems so rough. (Her Majesty did not understand oil painting). Then again why should she always want to have the things before her while painting them. An ordinary Chinese artist could paint my dress, shoes, etc., after seeing the things once. She cannot be very much of an artist in my opinion, though you need not tell her that I said so." Continuing, Her Majesty said: "By the way, what do you talk about when you are posing for this portrait of mine; although I don't understand what she is saying, still I can see she has a lot to say. Be sure not to tell her anything connected with the Court life and do not teach her any Chinese. I hear that she often asks what different things are called in Chinese, but don't tell her. The less she knows the better for us. I can see that she has seen nothing of our ordinary Court life, as yet. I wonder what she would say if she were to see one of the eunuchs being punished, or anything like that. She would think that we were savages, I suppose. I noticed the other day, when I was angry, that you took this lady artist away. This was very wise of you; it is better that she should not see me in a temper, she might talk about it afterwards. I wish this portrait was finished. The cool weather is coming on and we have to open up the boxes and get our winter clothes ready. You girls need winter clothes I know as you have none but foreign dresses. Then, again, my birthday is next month and there will be the usual celebrations. After that we return to the Sea Palace, and what can we do with this artist? I suppose she will have to go back and stay at the American Legation and come to the Sea Palace each day until the work is finished. This will be a lot of trouble as it is not ten minutes' drive as at present, but nearer an hour's drive. And even if this can be satisfactorily arranged, what about the Winter Palace in the Forbidden City? Try and get to know how long she expects to be before it is finished." This gave me an opportunity to tell Her Majesty that Miss Carl was just as anxious to get the work finished as she was to have it finished, but explained that Miss Carl had very little time to paint as Her Majesty could spare very little time to give personal sittings, and again, when Her Majesty went to lie down each afternoon, Miss Carl had to stop painting as she was working in the next room to Her Majesty's bedroom. Her Majesty replied: "Well, if she expects me to sit for her all day long I will give up the whole thing at once," and then added: "I think you yourself are getting tired of sitting, and want me to take it up again, but I have already had quite enough of it." Of course, I told her that instead of being tired of it, I enjoyed sitting on Her Throne, which I regarded as a great honor. I explained to Her Majesty that Miss Carl did not like me to pose in her place, as she could not get along so quickly as if she were to sit herself; but she simply said that I was acting under her commands, and that should be sufficient for me.

For the next ten days we were kept very busy selecting materials for winter clothing and also official robes for my sister and myself to be worn during the forthcoming birthday celebrations. These dresses were full winter Court dresses, of red satin embroidered with golden dragons and blue clouds, and were trimmed with gold braid and lined with grey squirrel. The cuffs and collars (which were turned down) were of sable. While Her Majesty was giving one of the eunuchs instructions as to how these were to be made, the Young Empress beckoned to me, and I went out. She said: "You go and kowtow to Her Majesty as it is a great favor for her to give you a dress trimmed with sable. This is usually only worn by a Princess." So when I returned to the room I availed myself of the first opportunity to kowtow and thank Her Majesty for the great favor she had granted me. She answered: "You deserve it, and I see no reason why you should not be treated as a Princess anyway; many of the Princesses are not of the Imperial family. Any title may be bestowed for special services rendered to the country and you have been of more help to me than any other Court lady I have ever had, and I can see that you are faithful in the discharge of your duties. You may think I do not notice these things, but I do. You are certainly entitled to be ranked as a Princess, and in fact I never treat you different from the Princesses, but rather better in many ways." Turning to a eunuch she said: "Bring my fur cap here." This cap was made of sable, trimmed with pearls and jade and Her Majesty explained that our caps would be something after the same style except that the crown, instead of being yellow as in the case of Her Majesty's cap, would be red. I was naturally delighted. In addition to the cap and full Court dress Her Majesty had two ordinary dresses made for everyday wear, one lined with sheepskin and the other lined with grey squirrel. Then she gave us four other dresses of finer material, lined with black and white fox skin, and all trimmed with gold braid and embroidered ribbons. In addition there were two other dresses, one of a pale pink color, embroidered with one hundred butterflies and the other of a reddish color embroidered with green bamboo leaves. Several short jackets, also lined with fur, were also included in Her Majesty's present, and several sleeveless jackets went to complete the lot.

On coming out of the room, one of the Court ladies remarked that I was very lucky to receive so many clothes from Her Majesty and said that she had never received so many during the whole time she had been at the Palace – nearly ten years. I could see she was jealous. The young Empress, overhearing this conversation, joined us and told her that when I arrived at the Palace I had nothing but foreign clothes and how was I to manage if Her Majesty did not get me the proper dresses. This incident was the beginning of another unpleasant time for me with the ladies of the Court. At first I took no notice until one day one of the girls attached to the Palace joined in the unkind remarks. She said that before my arrival she had been Her Majesty's particular favorite, but I gave her to understand that she had no right to discuss me in any way whatsoever. The Young Empress, who was present, spoke to them about their treatment of me and said that some fine day I would be telling Her Majesty about it. This seemed to have a good effect for they never troubled me much afterwards with their talk.

# CHAPTER SIXTEEN

## The Summer Palace

JUST about the end of the ninth moon Her Majesty began to tire of doing nothing day after day, and said: "What is the use of waiting until the first of the month to have the theatrical performance? Let us have a performance to-morrow." So she gave instructions for the eunuchs to prepare for the play, which should be staged without the assistance of any outside actors. I might here mention that certain of the eunuchs were specially trained as actors and used to study their parts every day. Indeed, they were far cleverer than the professionals from outside.

Her Majesty gave the head eunuch the list of the plays she wished to be performed, which were for the most part dramatised fairy tales, and we had a performance the next day.

After Her Majesty had gone to rest in the afternoon, during the theatrical performance I met the Emperor returning to his own Palace. I was surprised to see only one eunuch in attendance. This was the Emperor's own private eunuch and he trusted him implicitly. He asked me where I was going and I told him I was going to my room to rest a while. He remarked that he had not seen me for quite a long time, which made me laugh as I saw him every morning at the audience. He said: "I don't get as much chance of chatting with you as formerly since this portrait painting began. I am afraid I am not making much progress with my English as I have nobody to help me now that your time is occupied with this lady artist. You appear to enjoy her company very much. All the same I suppose it is very monotonous. Has she found out yet that you are there simply to keep an eye upon her?" I told him that I was very careful not to betray myself in any way and that I did not think she suspected she was being watched.

The Emperor then said: "I understand there is a rumor to the effect that when this lady has finished Her Majesty's portrait she is going to paint mine. I should very much like to know who says so." I told him this was the first I had heard about it so could not say. I asked him whether he would like to have his portrait painted but he only answered: "That is rather a difficult question for me to answer. You know best whether I ought to have it painted or not.

"I see Her Majesty having so many photographs taken and even the eunuchs are in the picture." I understood at once what he meant, so I asked him if he wished me to take him with my little kodak. He looked surprised and asked: "Can you take pictures, too? If it is not too risky for us, we might try it some day when we have an opportunity. Don't forget, but I think we must be very careful."

He then changed the conversation by saying: "Well, now that we have time to talk I want to ask you a question and I expect you to answer me truly. What is the general opinion amongst the foreigners regarding myself? Do they consider me a man of character and do they think me clever? I am very anxious to know." Before I could say anything in answer to this question he continued: "I know very well that they regard me as nothing more than a boy, and as being of no consequence at all. Tell me, is not this so?" I replied that many foreigners had asked me about him – as to what kind of man he was, but that they had never expressed any opinion of their own regarding him excepting that they understood he was in the best of health. "If any wrong impression does exist regarding myself and my position at the Court," continued the Emperor, "it is owing to the very conservative customs of the Chinese Court. I am not expected to either say or do anything on my own initiative, consequently outsiders never hear much about me and I am regarded as being nothing more than a figure-head. I know this is so. Whenever they ask you about me in the future just explain to them exactly what my position here is. I have plenty of ideas regarding the development of this country but you know I am not able to carry them out as I am not my own master. I don't think the Empress Dowager herself has sufficient power to alter the state of things existing in China at present, and even if she has, she is not willing to. I am afraid it will be a long time before anything can be done towards reform."

The Emperor went on to say how nice it would be if he were allowed to travel about from place to place the same as the European monarchs, but of course such a thing was out of the question for him. I told him that several Princesses had expressed a wish to visit the St. Louis Exposition and said I thought it would be a good thing if that could be arranged as they would see for themselves the difference between their own country and customs and foreign countries and customs. The Emperor expressed doubts as to this permission being granted as such a thing had never been heard of before.

We talked for quite a long time, mostly about foreign customs, and the Emperor remarked that he would very much like to visit Europe and see for himself how things were carried on there.

Just then one of my eunuchs came and said that Her Majesty was awake, so I had to hurry off to her room.

We now arrive at the tenth moon.

The first day it snowed, and the head eunuch enquired of Her Majesty whether it was her intention to celebrate her birthday at the Summer Palace as usual. As previously explained the Summer Palace was Her Majesty's favorite place of abode; so she replied in the affirmative and arrangements were accordingly made for the celebration to be held there as usual. The head eunuch then brought Her Majesty a list giving the names and ranks of all the Princesses and the names of the wives and daughters of the Manchu officials, and she selected those whom she wished to be present at the celebrations. On this occasion she selected forty-five ladies, who were duly informed that she desired their presence at the Palace. I was standing behind Her Majesty's chair all this time, and she turned and said: "Usually I do not ask many people to my birthday celebrations, but on this occasion I have made an exception as I want you to see the way they dress and how ignorant they are of Court etiquette."

The celebrations commenced on the sixth day of the tenth moon. Miss Carl, having returned to the American Legation in Peking for the time being, my mother, my sister and myself went back to the Palace again. Early on the morning of the sixth, the eunuchs decorated the verandas with different colored silks and hung lanterns all over the place and amongst the trees. At about seven o'clock in the morning the visitors began to arrive and I quite agreed with what Her Majesty had told me about them. The eunuchs introduced them to all the Court ladies, but they seemed to have very little to say, appearing very shy. They were then conducted to the waiting room, but there were so many of them that we Court ladies had to stand outside on the veranda. Some of them were very expensively dressed, but their colors were, for the most part, very old fashioned, and their manners very awkward. We watched them for quite a while and then went off to report to Her Majesty.

On such occasions as this Her Majesty was generally in pretty good spirits. She commenced asking us a lot of questions. Amongst other things she asked whether we had noticed an elderly lady among the visitors, dressed as a bride. She explained that this lady was the only Manchu lady present who was married to a Chinese official, and had been invited because of her previous connection with the Court. Her Majesty said she had never seen her herself, but understood that she was a very clever woman. We had not noticed such a person, and suggested that perhaps she had not yet arrived.

Her Majesty dressed very quickly, and as soon as she was ready she came into the hall, where the head eunuch brought in the visitors and presented them to Her Majesty. We Court ladies were all standing in a row behind the Throne. As they came in, some kowtowed; others courtesied, while others did not do anything at all, in fact nobody appeared to know what to do with herself. Her Majesty spoke a few words of welcome and thanked them for the presents they had sent her.

I would like to say here that, contrary to the general idea which exists, Her Majesty always expressed her thanks for any present or service rendered, no matter how insignificant.

Her Majesty could see plainly that everybody was embarrassed and ordered the head eunuch to show them to their respective rooms, and told them to make themselves at home and to go and take a rest. They hesitated a moment, not knowing whether to go or not, until Her Majesty said to us: "Take them and present them to the Young Empress."

When we arrived at the Palace of the Young Empress they were duly presented and were not nearly so shy as before. The Young Empress informed them that in case they desired to know anything or to be put right on any point of Court etiquette, the Court ladies would be pleased to give them all necessary information and she decided that the best way would be for each Court lady to have charge of so many of the visitors, as it would not be nice to have any mistakes occur during the ceremony, on the tenth. So we each were allotted so many guests and had to look after them and instruct them how to act on the different occasions.

During Her Majesty's afternoon rest I paid a visit to the guests I was to take charge of. Among them was the bride referred to by Her Majesty. So I went and made myself agreeable to her and found her very interesting. She had evidently received a good education, unlike the majority of Manchu ladies, as I found she could read and write Chinese exceptionally well. I then explained to all of them what they would have to do, and how to address Her Majesty, should it be necessary to do so. I don't know whether I have mentioned it previously, but whenever anybody spoke to Her Majesty, they always addressed her as "Great Ancestor," and when referring to themselves, instead of the pronoun

"I," they would say "Your slave." In all Manchu families a similar rule is observed, the pronouns "You" and "I" being dispensed with and the titles "Mother" and "Father" and the son's or daughter's first name being substituted.

Her Majesty was very particular about this rule being strictly observed.

For the next four days, until the day of the ceremony, these visitors passed their time in learning the Court etiquette and going to the theatre.

Every morning, as usual, we waited on Her Majesty and reported anything of interest which had occurred during the previous day. Then we all preceded Her Majesty to the theatre, where we awaited her arrival standing in the courtyard. On Her Majesty appearing, we would all kneel down until she had passed into the building opposite the stage, kneeling in rows – first the Emperor, behind him the Young Princess, next the Secondary wife, then the Princesses and Court ladies, and last of all the visitors. The first two days everything went of all right, but on the third morning the Emperor, from whom we received the signal, suddenly turned and said: "Her Majesty is coming." Down we all went on our knees, the Emperor alone remaining standing and laughing at us. Of course there was no sign of Her Majesty and everybody joined in the laugh. He was never so happy as when he could work off a joke like this.

On the evening of the ninth, none of the Court ladies went to bed, as we all had to be up betimes on the morning of the tenth. The visitors were told to proceed by chair to Her Majesty's special Audience Hall on the top of the hill, where they were to await our arrival. They arrived at the Audience Hall at three o'clock in the morning, and we followed soon afterwards, arriving there about daybreak. By and bye Her Majesty arrived and the ceremony commenced. This ceremony in no way differed from the one previously described in connection with the Emperor's birthday, so there is no need to give particulars, except one thing. Very early on the morning of the tenth, we had to bring another present to her and each of us brought a hundred birds of various kinds. Each year, on her birthday, Her Majesty did a very peculiar thing. She would buy 10,000 birds with her own money, from her private purse and set them free. It was a very pretty sight to see those huge cages hung in the courtyard of the Audience Hall. Her Majesty would select the most lucky hour and order the eunuchs to carry the cages and to follow her. The hour selected was four o'clock in the afternoon. Her

Majesty took the whole Court with her to the top of the hill, where there was a Temple. First she burnt sandal wood and offered up prayers to the Gods, then the eunuchs, each with a cage of birds, knelt in front of Her Majesty and she opened each cage one after another and watched the birds fly away, and prayed to the Gods that these birds should not be caught again. Her Majesty did this very seriously and we asked each other in whispers which bird we thought was the prettiest and would like to keep it for ourselves. Among this lot there were a few parrots. Some were pink; others were red and green; all were chained on stands, and when the eunuchs broke the chains, the parrots would not move. Her Majesty said: "How funny; each year a few parrots will not go away at all and I have kept them until they died. Look at them now. They won't go away." By this time the head eunuch arrived. Her Majesty told him what had happened and he immediately knelt down and said: "Your Majesty's great luck. These parrots understand Your Majesty's kindness and would rather stay here and serve Your Majesty." This ceremony is called "Fang Sheng." It is considered a very meritorious action and will not fail of reward in Heaven.

One of the Court ladies asked me what I thought of the parrots that would not fly away, and I told her that it was really very strange. She said: "It is very simple and not strange at all. These eunuchs, ordered by the head one, have bought these parrots long ago and trained them. During Her Majesty's afternoon rest, these parrots were brought to the top of the very same hill every day to accustom them to the place. The object of this is just to please and otherwise fool Her Majesty, to make her feel happy and believe that she is so merciful that even such dumb things would rather stay with her." Continuing, she said: "The huge joke is this: while Her Majesty is letting the birds free, there are a few eunuchs waiting at the rear of the hill to capture them and sell them again, and so, no matter how Her Majesty prays for their freedom, they will be caught at once."

The celebrations were continued until the thirteenth day. Nobody did any work and all was gaiety and enjoyment, the theatre being open every day. Towards the close of the thirteenth day the visitors were informed that the celebrations were at an end and they made arrangements to leave early the next morning. They all bade Her Majesty good-bye that evening and departed early the following day.

For the next few days we were all busy preparing for removing to the Sea Palace. Her Majesty consulted her book and finally selected the 22d as being the most favorable day for this removal. So at six o'clock on the morning of the 22d the whole Court left the Summer Palace. It was snowing very heavily and the journey was only accomplished with great difficulty. Of course we were all in chairs, as usual, and the eunuchs who were not employed as chair-bearers rode horseback. Many of the horses fell on the slippery stones and one of Her Majesty's chair-bearers also slipped and brought Her Majesty to the ground. All of a sudden I thought something dreadful had happened, horses galloping and eunuchs howling: "Stop! Stop!!" I heard someone saying: "See if she is still alive." The whole procession stopped and blocked the way. This happened on the stone road just before entering the Western Gate. Finally we saw that Her Majesty's chair was resting on the ground, so we all alighted and went forward to see what had happened. A great many people were talking excitedly all at the same time, and for a moment I was rather frightened (for just about that time we heard a rumor that some of the revolutionists were going to take the life of the whole Court, and, although we heard that, we did not dare tell Her Majesty), so I immediately went to her chair and found her sitting there composedly giving orders to the chief eunuch not to punish this chair-bearer, for he was not to blame, the stones being wet and very slippery. Li Lien Ying said that would never do, for this chair-bearer must have been careless, and how dare he carry the Old Buddha in this careless way. After saying this, he turned his head to the beaters (these beaters, carrying bamboo sticks, went everywhere with the Court, for such occasions as this) and said: "Give him eighty blows on his back." This poor victim, who was kneeling on the muddy ground, heard the order. The beaters took him about a hundred yards away from us, pushed him down and started to do their duty. It did not take very long to give the eighty blows and, much to my surprise, this man got up, after receiving the punishment, as if nothing had happened to him. He looked just as calm as could be. While we were waiting a eunuch handed me a cup of tea, which I presented to Her Majesty, and asked her if she was hurt. She smiled and said it was nothing, ordering us to proceed on our journey. I must explain about this tea; the eunuchs had it prepared all the time and always carried a little stove along with hot water. Although this went every time when the Court moved, it was seldom used.

As usual, all the Court ladies take a short cut to the Palace, so as to be ready to receive Her Majesty, when she arrived. After waiting in the courtyard for quite a long time, during which we were nearly frozen, Her Majesty arrived, and we all knelt until she had passed, and then followed her into the Palace. Her Majesty also complained of the cold and ordered that fires should be brought into the hall. These fires were built in brass portable stoves lined with clay, and were lighted outside and brought into the hall after the smoke had passed off somewhat. There were four stoves in all. All the windows and doors were closed, there being no ventilation of any description, and very soon I began to feel sick. However, I went on with my work getting Her Majesty's things in order until I must have fainted, for the next thing I remembered was waking up in a strange bed and inquiring where I was, but on hearing Her Majesty giving orders in the next room, I knew it was all right. One of the Court ladies brought me a cup of turnip juice which Her Majesty said I was to drink. I drank it and felt much better. I was informed that Her Majesty had gone to rest, and so I went off to sleep again myself. When I awoke, Her Majesty was standing by my bedside. I tried to get up, but found that I was too weak, so Her Majesty told me to lie still and keep quiet and I would soon be all right again. She said that I had better have a room close to her bedroom, and gave instructions for the eunuchs to remove me there as soon as it was prepared. Every few minutes Her Majesty would send to inquire how I was progressing and whether I wanted anything to eat. It was the custom to stand up whenever receiving a message from Her Majesty, but it was out of the question for me to do so, although I tried, with the result that I made myself worse than ever.

Towards evening the head eunuch came to see me and brought several plates of sweetmeats. He was very nice, and told me that I was very fortunate, as Her Majesty very rarely bothered herself about any of the Court ladies and that evidently she had taken a fancy to me. He sat talking for some little time, and told me to eat some of the sweetmeats. Of course I was not able to eat anything at all, let alone sweetmeats, so I told him to leave them and I would eat them later. Before leaving he said that in case I wanted anything I was to let him know. This visit was a great surprise to me, as usually he took very little notice of any of us, but I was told afterwards that the reason he was so nice was because Her Majesty showed such an interest in me.

The next morning I was able to get up and resume my duties. I went in to see Her Majesty and kowtowed to her, thanking her for her kindness during my indisposition. Her Majesty said that the head eunuch had told her the previous evening that I was much better and that she was glad I was up and about again. She said it was nothing serious, simply that I was unaccustomed to the fumes from the fires, which had gone to my head.

As the snow had stopped falling, Her Majesty decided that the next day we would go and choose a place for Miss Carl to continue the painting. I suggested that perhaps it would be better if we waited until Miss Carl arrived herself, so that she could choose a suitable place for her work, but Her Majesty said that would not do at all, because if it were left to Miss Carl, doubtless she would choose some impossible place. Of course there were many parts of the Palace which were kept quite private and Miss Carl would not be allowed to go there. So the next day Her Majesty and myself set out to find a place. After visiting many different rooms, all of which were too dark, we finally fixed on a room on the lake side of the Palace. Her Majesty said: "This is very convenient, as you can go to and fro either by chair or by water. I found that it took about three-quarters of an hour by chair to get to the Palace Gate, and rather less than that by boat. I was expecting to return to stay at the Palace with Her Majesty, but it was finally decided that this would not do, as it would not be policy to allow Miss Carl, who was staying at the American Legation, to go in and out of the Palace Gate alone, so Her Majesty said it would be better for me to stay at my father's place in the city and bring Miss Carl to the Palace each morning, returning with her in the evening. This was anything but pleasant, but I had no other alternative than to obey Her Majesty's instructions.

When Miss Carl arrived at the Palace the next day and saw the room which had been selected for her to work in, she was not at all pleased. In the first place she said it was too dark, so Her Majesty ordered the paper windows to be replaced by glass. This made the room too bright, and Miss Carl asked for some curtains so as to focus the light on the picture. When I informed Her Majesty of this request, she said: "Well, this is the first time I have ever changed anything in the Palace except to suit myself. First I alter the windows, and she is not satisfied, but must have curtains. I think we had better take the roof off, then perhaps she may be suited." However, we fixed up the curtains to Miss Carl's satisfaction.

When Her Majesty examined the portrait to see how it was progressing, she said to me: "After all the trouble we have had over this picture, I am afraid it is not going to be anything very wonderful. I notice that the pearls in my cape are painted in different colors; some look white, some pink, while others are green. You tell her about it." I tried to explain to Her Majesty that Miss Carl had simply painted the pearls as she saw them, according to the different shades of light, but Her Majesty could not understand that at all and asked if I could see anything green about them, or pink either. I again explained that this was simply the tints caused by the light falling on the pearls, but she replied that she could not see any shade except white. However, after a while she did not seem to trouble any further about the matter.

Situated in a room near Her Majesty's bedroom in the Sea Palace was a Pagoda, about ten feet in height, made of carved sandalwood. This contained various images of Buddha, which Her Majesty used to worship every morning. The ceremony consisted of Her Majesty burning incense before the Pagoda, while a Court lady was told off each day to kowtow before the images. Her Majesty told me that this Pagoda had been in the Palace for more than a hundred years. Among the different images was one representing the Goddess of Mercy. This image was only about five inches in height and was made of pure gold. The inside was hollow and contained all the principal anatomical parts of the human body, made out of jade and pearls. This Goddess of Mercy was supposed to possess wonderful powers and Her Majesty often worshiped before it when in any trouble, and maintained that on many occasions her prayers had been answered. She said: "Of course, when I pray to the image, I pray earnestly, not the same as you girls, who simply kowtow because it is your duty and then get away as quickly as possible." Her Majesty went on to say that she was quite aware that many of the people in China were discarding the religion of their ancestors in favor of Christianity, and that she was very much grieved that this was so.

Her Majesty was a firm believer in the old Chinese superstitions connected with the Sea Palace, and during one of our conversations she told me I was not to be surprised at anything I saw. She said it was quite a common occurrence for a person walking beside you to suddenly disappear altogether, and explained that they were simply foxes who took human shape to suit their purpose. They had probably lived in the Sea Palace for thousands of years and possessed this power of changing their form at will. She said that no doubt the eunuchs would tell me they were spirits or ghosts, but that was not true: they were sacred foxes and would harm nobody. As if to confirm this superstition, one evening, a few days later, my fire having gone out, I sent my eunuch to see if any of the other Court ladies were awake, and if so, to try to get me some hot water. He went out taking his lantern along with him, but he returned almost immediately with a face as white as chalk. On inquiring what was the matter, he replied: "I have seen a ghost: a woman, who came up to me, blew the light out and disappeared." I told him that perhaps it was one of the servant girls, but he said "No"; he knew all the women attached to the Palace and he had never seen this one before. He stuck to it that it was a ghost. I told him that Her Majesty had said there were no ghosts, but that it might be a fox which had taken human shape. He replied: "It was not a fox. Her Majesty calls them foxes, because she is afraid to call them ghosts." He went on to tell me that many years previously the head eunuch, Li Lien Ying, while walking in the courtyard back of Her Majesty's Palace, saw a young servant girl sitting on the edge of the well. He went over to ask her what she was doing there, but on getting closer he found that there were several other girls there also, and on seeing him approach, they all deliberately jumped down the well. He immediately raised the alarm, and on one of the attendants coming forward with a lantern, he explained what had occurred. The attendant showed him that it was impossible for anybody to jump into the well, as it was covered with a large stone. My eunuch said that a long time before this several girls did actually commit suicide by jumping down this well, and that what Li Lien Ying had seen were the ghosts of these girls, and nothing more. It is believed by the Chinese that when a person commits suicide their spirit remains in the neighborhood until such time as they can entice somebody else to commit suicide, when they are free to go to another world, and not before. I told him that I did not believe such things and that I would very much like to see for myself. He replied: "You will only want to see it once; that will be sufficient."

Things went along in the usual way until the first day of the eleventh moon, when Her Majesty issued orders to the Court that as the eleventh moon contained so many anniversaries of the deaths of previous rulers of China, the usual theatrical performance would be eliminated and the Court dress would in addition be modified to suit the occasion. On the ninth day the Emperor was to go and worship at the Temple of Heaven. So, as was customary on all these occasions, he confined himself to his own private apartments for three days before the ninth, during which time he held no communication whatsoever with anybody excepting his private eunuchs. Not even the Young Empress, his wife, was allowed to see him during these three days.

This ceremony did not differ very materially from the other sacrifices, except that pigs were killed and placed on the numerous altars of the Temple, where they remained for a time, after which they were distributed among the different officials. The eating of the flesh of these pigs, which had been blessed, was believed to bring good luck and prosperity, and the officials who were presented with them considered themselves greatly favored by Her Majesty. Another difference was that the Emperor could not appoint a substitute to officiate for him; but must attend in person, no matter what the circumstances might be. The reason for this was, that according to the ancient law, the Emperor signs the death warrant of every person sentenced to death, record of which is kept in the Board of Punishments. At the end of the year the name of each person executed is written on a piece of yellow paper and sent to the Emperor. When the time for worshiping at the Temple arrives, he takes this yellow paper and burns it in order that the ashes may go up to Heaven and his ancestors know that he has been fearless and faithful, and has done his duty according to the law.

As this ceremony of worshiping at the Temple of Heaven was to take place in the Forbidden City, in spite of Her Majesty's dislike to the place, she commanded that the whole of the Court be transferred there, her reason for this being that she did not wish to be away from the Emperor's side even for an hour. So we all moved to the Palace in the Forbidden City. After the ceremony was over, the Court was to return to the Sea Palace, but as the thirteenth day was the anniversary of the death of the Emperor Kang Hsi, it was decided that we should remain in the Forbidden City, where the ceremony was to be held. The Emperor Kang Hsi ruled over the Chinese Empire for sixty-one years, the longest reign of any Chinese Ruler up to the present time, and Her Majesty told us that he was the most wonderful Emperor China had ever had and that we must respect his memory accordingly.

# CHAPTER SEVENTEEN

## The Audience Hall

ON the fourteenth day of the eleventh moon, after the morning audience, Her Majesty informed us that there was a likelihood of war breaking out between Russia and Japan and that she was very much troubled, as although it actually had nothing whatever to do with China, she was afraid they would fight on Chinese territory and that in the long run China would suffer in some way or other. Of course we did not bother ourselves about it much at the moment, but the next morning the head eunuch reported to Her Majesty that fifty eunuchs were missing. As there was no apparent reason for this, everybody was much excited. There was no rule against any of the eunuchs going into the city after their duties were ended, providing they returned before the Palace Gate was closed, but when on the following morning it was reported that another hundred eunuchs had also disappeared, Her Majesty at once said: "I know now what the trouble is; they must have heard what I said about this war coming on and are afraid there may be a repetition of the Boxer trouble, and so they have cleared out." It was the custom whenever a eunuch was missing to send out search parties and have him brought back and punished, but in the present instance Her Majesty gave instructions that nothing was to be done about recapturing them. One morning, however, one of Her Majesty's personal attendants was missing, which made her furious. She said that she had been very kind to this particular eunuch in many ways, and this was all the thanks she got; he ran away at the first sign of trouble. I myself had noticed how good she had been to this eunuch, but I was not really sorry that he had left, as he used to take advantage of every opportunity of getting some of the Court ladies into trouble.

These disappearances continued from day to day until Her Majesty decided that it would be safer for us to remain in the Forbidden City until the following spring at any rate.

On inquiring from my eunuch the cause of these disappearances, he said that it was just as Her Majesty suspected; they were afraid of getting mixed up in another such affair as the Boxer trouble, and added that he was not a bit surprised at Her Majesty's favorite eunuch going along with the rest. He further told me that even Li Lien Ying himself was not to be absolutely relied upon, as at the time of Her Majesty's leaving Peking for Shi An during the Boxer movement, he had feigned sickness, and followed a little later, so that in the event of anything happening, he would be able to return and make his escape. While talking about Li Lien Ying, my eunuch told me in confidence that he was responsible for the death of many innocent people, mostly eunuchs. He had unlimited power at the Court, and it was very easy for him to get anybody put away who offended him or to whom, for some reason or another, he took a dislike. Furthermore, the eunuch informed me that, although not generally known, Li Lien Ying was addicted to opium-smoking, which habit he indulged in very freely. Even Her Majesty was unaware of this, as opium-smoking was strictly forbidden in the Palace.

Each morning there was fresh news regarding the trouble between Russia and Japan, and of course everybody gradually became very much excited at the Palace. One day Her Majesty summoned the whole of the Court to a special audience and there informed us that there was no need for us to get excited at all; that if any trouble did occur, it was none of our business and we should not be interfered with, as the spirits of our ancestors were watching over us, and she did not want to hear any more talk and gossip on the subject. However, she summoned all of the Court ladies to her apartment and there commanded us to pray to the spirits of our ancestors to protect us, which plainly showed that she was just as much worried as we were ourselves. In spite of what she had said with reference to gossiping about this trouble, Her Majesty often spoke about it herself, and during one of our conversations she said she wished she could get information each day as to what was actually occurring, so I suggested that it would be very easy to get all the latest news by taking the foreign papers and also Reuter's specials. Her Majesty jumped at the suggestion and told me to have these sent each day to my father's house in his name, and have them brought to the Palace, where I could translate them for her. I told her that my father received all these papers as they were published, so I arranged that they should be brought along as directed by Her Majesty. Each morning during the audience I translated into Chinese all the war news, but the telegrams began to arrive so rapidly that it soon became quite impossible for me to write them all out in Chinese, so I told Her Majesty that I would read and translate them into Chinese as they arrived. This was much quicker and interested Her Majesty so much that she insisted on my not only translating the war news, but everything else of interest in the papers. Especially was she interested in all news appertaining to the movements, etc., of the crowned heads of Europe, and was very plainly astonished when she learned that their every movement was known. She said: "Here, at any rate, it is more private, for nobody outside the Palace ever knows what is going on inside, not even my own people. It would be a good thing if they did know a little more, then perhaps all these rumors about the Palace would stop."

Of course, during our stay in the Forbidden City, Miss Carl attended each morning to work on the portrait. We had given her a nice room, which seemed to suit her very well, and Her Majesty had instructed me to let her have every convenience possible to assist her, as she was getting tired of the business and would like to see it finished quickly. Her Majesty hardly ever went near the place herself, but when she did go, she would be most affable and, really, one would think that it was the greatest pleasure of her life to go and inspect the portrait.

Things went very slowly during this eleventh moon on account of the Court being in mourning, so one day Her Majesty suggested that she should show us round the Forbidden City. First we proceeded to the Audience Hall. This differs somewhat from the Audience Hall of the Summer Palace. To enter, one must mount some twenty odd steps of white marble, with rails on either side of the steps made of the same material. At the top of the steps a large veranda, supported by huge pillars of wood, painted red, surrounded the building. The windows along this verandah were of marvellously carved trellis-work, designed to represent the character "Shou" arranged in different positions. Then we entered the hall itself. The floor is of brick, and Her Majesty told us that all these bricks were of solid gold and had been there for centuries. They were of a peculiar black color, doubtless painted over, and were so slippery that it was most difficult to keep on one's feet. The furnishing was similar to that in the Audience Halls in the Summer Palace and in the Sea Palace, with the exception that the throne was made of dark brown wood inlaid with jade of different colors.

The Hall was only used for audience on very rare occasions, such as the birthday of the Empress Dowager and New Year's Day, and no foreigner has ever entered this building. All the usual audiences were held in a smaller building in the Forbidden City.

After spending some little time in the Audience Hall, we next visited the Emperor's quarters. These were much smaller than those occupied by Her Majesty, but were very elaborately furnished. There were thirty-two rooms, many of which were never used, but all were furnished in the same expensive style. In the rear of this building was the Palace of the Young Empress, which was smaller still, having about twenty-four rooms in all, and in the same building three rooms were set apart for the use of the Secondary wife of the Emperor. Although close together, the Palaces of the Emperor and his wife were not connected by any entrance, but both buildings were surrounded by verandas connecting with Her Majesty's apartments, which were quite a distance away. There were several other buildings, which were used as waiting rooms for visitors. In addition to the above, there were several buildings which were not used at all; these were sealed and nobody seemed to know what they contained, or whether they contained anything at all. Even Her Majesty said she had never been inside these buildings, as they had been sealed for many years. Even the entrance to the enclosure containing these buildings was always closed, and this was the only occasion that any of us ever even passed through. They were quite different in appearance from any other buildings in the Palace, being very dirty and evidently of great age. We were commanded not to talk about the place at all.

The apartments of the Court ladies were connected with those of Her Majesty, but the rooms were so small one could hardly turn round in them; also they were very cold in winter. The servants' quarters were at the end of our apartments, but there was no entrance and they could only be reached by passing along our veranda, while the only entrance we ourselves had to our rooms was by passing along Her Majesty's veranda. This was Her Majesty's own idea, in order that she could keep an eye on all of us and could see when we either went out or came in.

Her Majesty now conducted us to her own Palace, and pausing a little said: "I will now show you something which will be quite new to you." We entered a room adjoining her bedroom, which was connected by a narrow passage some fifteen feet in length. On either side the walls were painted and decorated very beautifully. Her Majesty spoke to one of the eunuch attendants, who stooped down and removed from the ground at each end of this passage two wooden plugs which were fitted into holes in the basement. I then began to realize that what I had hitherto regarded as solid walls were in reality sliding panels of wood. These panels when opened revealed a kind of grotto. There were no windows, but in the roof was a skylight. At one end of this room or grotto was a large rock, on the top of which was a seat with a yellow cushion, and beside the cushion an incense burner. Everything had the appearance of being very old. The room contained no furniture of any description. One end of this room led into another passage similar to the one already described, having sliding panels, which led into another grotto, and so on; in fact the whole of the palace walls were intersected by these secret passages, each concealing an inner room. Her Majesty told us that during the Ming dynasty these rooms had been used for various purposes, principally by the Emperor when he wished to be alone. One of these secret rooms was used by Her Majesty as a treasure room where she kept her valuables. During the time of the Boxer trouble, she hid all her valuables here before she fled. When she returned and opened this secret room she found everything intact, not one of the vandals who ransacked the Palace even suspecting there was such a place.

We returned to our veranda, and on looking around for the rooms we had just vacated, could see nothing excepting black stone walls, so well were they hidden. One of the principal reasons for Her Majesty's dislike to the Forbidden City was the mysteries which it contained, many of which she did not know of herself. She said: "I don't even talk about these places at all, as people might think that they were used for all kinds of purposes."

While at the Palace in the Forbidden City I met the three Secondary wives of the previous Emperor Tung Chi, son of the Empress Dowager, who, since the death of the Emperor, had resided in the Forbidden City and spent their time in doing needlework, etc., for Her Majesty. When I got to know them I found that they were highly educated, one of them, Yu Fai, being exceptionally clever. She could write poetry and play many musical instruments, and was considered to be the best educated lady in the Empire of China. Her knowledge of western countries and their customs surprised me very much; she seemed to know a little bit of everything. I asked how it was that I had never seen them before, and was informed that they never visited Her Majesty unless commanded by her to do so, but that when Her Majesty stayed in the Forbidden City, of course they had to call and pay their respects each day. One day I received an invitation to visit them in their Palace. This was separated from all the other buildings in the city. It was rather a small building, and very simply furnished, with just a few eunuchs and servant girls to wait upon them. They said they preferred this simple life, as they never received any visitors and had nobody to please but themselves. Yu Fai's room was literally packed with literature of all descriptions. She showed me several poems which she had written, but they were of a melancholy character, plainly showing the trend of her thoughts. She was in favor of establishing schools for the education of young girls, as only very few could even read or write their own language, and she suggested that I should speak to Her Majesty about it at the first opportunity. In spite of her desire to see western reforms introduced into China, however, she was not in favor of employing missionary teachers, as these people always taught their religion at the expense of other subjects, which she feared would set the Chinese against the movement.

Toward the end of the eleventh moon Her Majesty granted an audience to the Viceroy of Chihli, Yuan Shih Kai, and as this particular day was a holiday and Miss Carl was absent, I was able to attend. Her Majesty asked him for his opinion of the trouble between Russia and Japan. He said that although these two countries might make war against each other, China would not be implicated in any way, but that after the war was over, there was sure to be trouble over Manchuria. Her Majesty said she was quite aware of that, as they were fighting on Chinese territory, and that the best thing for China to do would be to keep absolutely neutral in the matter, as she had quite enough of war during the China-Japan war. She said it would be best to issue orders to all the officials to see that the Chinese did not interfere in any way, so as not to give any excuse for being brought into the trouble.

She then asked his opinion as to what would be the result in the event of war – who would win. He said that it was very hard to say, but that he thought Japan would win. Her Majesty thought that if Japan were victorious, she would not have so much trouble over the matter, although she expressed doubts as to the outcome, saying that Russia was a large country and had many soldiers, and that the result was far from certain.

Her Majesty then spoke about the condition of things in China. She said that in case China were forced into war with another nation, we should be nowhere. We had nothing ready, no navy and no trained army, in fact nothing to enable us to protect ourselves. Yuan Shih Kai, however, assured her there was no need to anticipate any trouble at present so far as China was concerned. Her Majesty replied that in any event it was time China began to wake up and endeavor to straighten things out in some way or other, but she did not know where to begin; that it was her ambition to see China holding a prominent position among the nations of the world and that she was constantly receiving memorials suggesting this reform and that reform, but that we never seemed to get any further.

After this audience was over, Her Majesty held an audience with the Grand Council. She told them what had been said during her interview with Yuan Shih Kai, and of course they all agreed that something should be done. Several suggestions were discussed with regard to national defense, etc., but a certain Prince said that although he was in perfect sympathy with reform generally, he was very much against the adoption of foreign clothing, foreign modes of living, and the doing away with the queue. Her Majesty quite agreed with these remarks and said that it would not be wise to change any Chinese custom for one which was less civilized. As usual, nothing definite was decided upon when the audience was over.

For the next few days nothing was talked of but the war, and many Chinese generals were received in audience by Her Majesty. These audiences were sometimes very amusing, as these soldiers were quite unaccustomed to the rules of the Court and did not know the mode of procedure when in the presence of Her Majesty. Many foolish suggestions were made by these generals. During one of the conversations Her Majesty remarked on the inefficiency of the navy and referred to the fact that we had no trained naval officers. One of the generals replied that we had more men in China than in any other country, and as for ships, why we had dozens of river boats and China merchant boats, which could be used in case of war. Her Majesty ordered him to retire, saying that it was perfectly true that we had plenty of men in China, but that the majority of them were like himself, of very little use to the country. After he had retired, everybody commenced to laugh, but Her Majesty stopped us, saying that she did not feel at all like laughing, she was too angry to think that such men held positions as officers in the army and navy. One of the Court ladies asked me why Her Majesty was so angry with the man for mentioning the river boats, and was very much surprised when I informed her that the whole of them would be worse than useless against a single war vessel.

Just about the end of the eleventh moon Chang Chih Tung, Viceroy of Wuchang, arrived, and was received in audience. Her Majesty said to him: "Now, you are one of the oldest officials in the country, and I want you to give me your unbiased opinion as to what effect this war is going to have on China. Do not be afraid to give your firm opinion, as I want to be prepared for anything which is likely to happen." He answered that no matter what the result of the war might be, China would in all probability have to make certain concessions to the Powers with regard to Manchuria for trade purposes, but that we should not otherwise be interfered with. Her Majesty repeated what had been discussed at the previous audiences on this subject and also regarding reform in China. Chang Chih Tung replied that we had plenty of time for reform, and that if we were in too great a hurry, we should not accomplish anything at all. He suggested that the matter be discussed at length before deciding upon anything definite. In his opinion it would be foolish to go to extremes in the matter of reform. He said that ten or fifteen years ago he would have been very much against any reform whatsoever, but that he now saw the need for it to a certain extent, as circumstances had changed very much. He said that we should adhere strictly to our own mode of living and not abandon the traditions of our ancestors. In other words, he simply advised the adoption of western civilization where it was an improvement on our own, and nothing more. Her Majesty was delighted with the interview, for Chang Chih Tung's opinions coincided exactly with her own.

During the whole of these audiences the Emperor, although present each time, never opened his lips to say a word, but sat listening all the time. As a rule, Her Majesty would ask his opinion, just as a matter of form, but he invariably replied that he was quite in accord with what Her Majesty had said or decided upon.

Of the many religious ceremonies in connection with the Buddhist religion the "La-pachow" was the most important. This was held on the 8th day of the twelfth moon each year. According to the common belief, on this eighth day of the twelfth moon, many centuries ago, a certain Buddhist priest Ju Lai set out to beg for food, and after receiving a good supply of rice and beans from the people, he returned and divided it with his brother priests, giving each an equal share, and he became celebrated for his great charity. This day was therefore set apart as an anniversary to commemorate the event. The idea was that by practising self-denial on this day, one would gain favor in the sight of this Buddha Ju Lai, therefore the only food eaten was rice, grain and beans, all mixed together in a sort of porridge, but without any salt or other flavoring. It was not at all pleasant to eat, being absolutely tasteless.

# CHAPTER EIGHTEEN

## The New Year Festivals

WE now reached the time set apart for cleaning the Palace in preparation for the New Year festivals. Everything had to be taken down and thoroughly overhauled, and all the images, pictures, furniture and everything else were subjected to a thorough scrubbing. Her Majesty again consulted her book in order to choose a lucky day on which to commence these operations, finally choosing the twelfth day as being most favorable. As we had all received our orders previously, we commenced early on the morning of the twelfth. Several of the Court ladies were told off to take down and clean the images of Buddha and prepare new curtains for them. The rest of the cleaning was done by the eunuchs. I asked Her Majesty whether I was to clean her jewelry, but she answered that as nobody but herself ever wore it, it didn't need cleaning.

After everything had been cleaned to Her Majesty's satisfaction, she prepared a list of names of the people she desired to attend the ceremony of Tzu Sui. This ceremony was held on the last day of each year and was something like the midnight services usually held in Europe on the last night of each old year – just a farewell ceremony to bid the old year adieu. The guests were invited about a fortnight ahead, so as to give them plenty of time to get ready. Her Majesty also ordered new winter clothing for the Court ladies. The only difference between these new garments and those we were then. wearing was that they were trimmed with the fur of the silver fox instead of the gray squirrel.

The next thing was to prepare cakes, which were to be placed before the Buddhas and ancestors, during the New Year. It was necessary that Her Majesty should make the first one herself. So when Her Majesty decided that it was time to prepare these cakes the whole Court went into a room specially prepared for the purpose and the eunuchs brought in the ingredients-ground rice, sugar and yeast. These were mixed together into a sort of dough and then steamed instead of baked, which caused it to rise just like ordinary bread, it being believed that the higher the cake rises, the better pleased are the gods and the more fortunate the maker. The first cake turned out fine and we all congratulated Her Majesty, who was evidently much pleased herself at the result. Then she ordered each of the Court ladies to make one, which we did, with disastrous results, not one turning out as it should.

This being my first year, there was some excuse for my failure, but I was surprised that none of the older Court ladies fared any better, and on inquiring from one of them the reason, she replied: "Why, I did it purposely, of course, so as to flatter Her Majesty's vanity. Certainly I could make them just as well as she, if not better, but it would not be good policy." After we had all finished making our cakes, the eunuchs were ordered to make the rest, and needless to say they were perfect in every way.

The next thing was to prepare small plates of dates and fresh fruits of every kind. These were decorated with evergreens, etc., and placed before the images of Buddha. Then we prepared glass dishes of candy, which were to be offered to the God of the Kitchen. On the twenty-third day of the last moon the God of the Kitchen left this earth to go on a visit to the King of Heaven, to whom he reported all that we had been doing during the past year, returning to earth again on the last day of the year. The idea of offering him these sweets was in order that they should stick to his mouth and prevent him from telling too much. When these candies were prepared, we all adjourned to the kitchen and placed the offering on a table specially placed for the purpose. Turning to the head cook, she said: "You had better look out now; the God of the Kitchen will tell how much you have stolen during the past year, and you will be punished."

The following day another ceremony had to be gone through, that of writing out the New Year Greetings for the guests and Court, so in the morning we all went with Her Majesty to the Audience Hall, where the eunuchs had prepared large sheets of yellow, red and pale green paper. Her Majesty took up a large brush and commenced to write. On some of these sheets she wrote the character "Shou" (Long Life) and on others "Fu" (Prosperity). By and bye, when she began to feel tired, she would get either one of the Court ladies or one of the official writers to finish them for her. When finished, they were distributed to the guests and different officials, the ones Her Majesty had written herself being reserved for her special favorites. These were given out a few days before the New Year.

Her Majesty received New Year presents from all the Viceroys and principal officials. She would examine each present as it was received, and if it found favor in her eyes, she would use it, but if not, she would have it locked away in one of the storerooms and probably never see it again. These presents consisted of small pieces of furniture, curios, jewelry, silks, in fact everything – even clothing. The present sent by

Viceroy Yuan Shih Kai was a yellow satin robe, embroidered with different colored precious stones and pearls designed to represent the peony flower; the leaves were of green jade. It was really a magnificent thing, and must have cost a fortune. The only drawback was its weight; it was too heavy to wear comfortably. Her Majesty appeared delighted with this gown, and wore it the first day, after which it was discarded altogether, although I often suggested that she should wear it, as it was the most magnificent gown I ever saw. Once when Her Majesty was granting an audience to the Diplomatic Corps, I suggested that she should wear this dress, but she refused, giving no reason, so nobody outside the Court has ever seen this wonderful garment.

Another costly present was received from the Viceroy of Canton, and consisted of four bags of pearls, each bag containing several thousands. They were all perfect in shape and color, and would have brought fabulous prices in Europe or America. However, Her Majesty had so many jewels, especially pearls, that she hardly paid any attention to them beyond remarking that they were very nice.

The Young Empress and the Court ladies were also expected to give presents to Her Majesty each New Year. These were for the most part articles that we had made ourselves, such as shoes, handkerchiefs, collars, bags, etc. My mother, my sister and myself made presents of mirrors, perfumes, soaps and similar toilet accessories which we had brought with us from Paris. These Her Majesty appreciated very much; she was very vain. The eunuchs and servant girls gave fancy cakes and other food stuffs.

The presents were so numerous that they filled several rooms, but we were not allowed to remove them until Her Majesty gave orders to do so.

The Court ladies also exchanged presents among themselves, which often led to confusion and amusement. On this occasion I had received some ten or a dozen different presents, and when it came my turn to give something, I decided to use up some of the presents I had received from my companions. To my surprise, the next day I received from one of the Court ladies an embroidered handkerchief which I immediately recognized as the identical handkerchief I had myself sent her as my New Year's present. On mentioning the fact, this lady turned and said: "Well, that is rather funny; I was just wondering what had made you return the shoes I sent you." Of course everybody laughed very heartily, and still further merriment was caused when, on comparing all the presents, it was found that quite half of us had received back our own presents. In order to settle the matter, we threw them all into a heap and divided them as evenly as possible, everybody being satisfied with the result.

About a week before New Year's day all audiences ceased and the seals were put away until after the holidays. During this time no business was transacted by Her Majesty. Everything was much more comfortable and we could see that Her Majesty also appreciated the change from bustle to quietness. We had nothing whatever to do but to take things easy until the last day of the year.

Early on the morning of the thirtieth Her Majesty went to worship before the Buddhas and Ancestral Tablets. After this ceremony was finished, the guests began to arrive, until by midday, all the guests, numbering about fifty, were present. The principal guests were: The Imperial Princess (Empress Dowager's adopted daughter), Princess Chung (wife of Emperor Kwang Hsu's brother), Princesses Shun and Tao (wives of the Emperor's younger brothers), Princess hung (wife of the nephew of the Imperial Princess), and Prince Ching's family. All these ladies were frequent visitors to the Court. Next day many other Princesses, not of the Imperial family, but whose titles were honorary titles bestowed by previous rulers, came. Next, the daughters of the high Manchu officials and many other people whom I had never seen before. By midday all the guests had arrived, and, after being presented to Her Majesty, were taken to their different apartments and told to rest a while. At two o'clock in the afternoon everybody assembled in the Audience Hall, lined up according to their different ranks and, led by the Young Empress, kowtowed to Her Majesty. This was the ceremony Tzu Sui already referred to, and was simply a last goodbye to Her Majesty before the New Year set in. When it was all over, Her Majesty gave each of us a small purse made of red satin embroidered with gold, containing a sum of money. This is to enable each one to commence the New Year with a kind of reserve fund for a rainy day, when they would have this money to fall back upon. It is an old Manchu custom and is still kept up.

The evening was spent in music and enjoyment, and was carried on right through the night, none of us going to bed. At Her Majesty's suggestion we commenced gambling with dice, Her Majesty providing each of us with money, sometimes as much as $200. She told us to be serious about it, and to try and win, but of course we took good care not to win from Her Majesty. When Her Majesty began to tire, she stopped the game and said: "Now, all this money I have won I am going to throw on the floor, and you girls can scramble for it." We knew that she wanted to see some fun, so we fought for it as hard as we could.

At midnight the eunuchs brought into the room a large brass brazier containing live charcoal. Her Majesty pulled a leaf from a large evergreen tree, which had been placed there for the purpose, and threw it into the fire. We each followed her example, adding large pieces of resin, which perfumed the whole atmosphere. This ceremony was supposed to bring good luck during the coming year.

The next item was making cakes or pies for New Year's day. On the first of the New Year, nobody is allowed to eat rice, these cakes taking its place. They were made of flour paste, with minced meat inside. While some of us were preparing these cakes, others were peeling lotus seeds for Her Majesty's breakfast.

It was now well on into the morning hours and Her Majesty said that she was tired and would go and rest a while. She was not going to sleep, however, so we could carry on our noise as much as we liked. This we did for some time, and on visiting Her Majesty's bedroom, we found that she was fast asleep. We then all repaired to our various rooms and commenced to make ourselves tidy for the day. As soon as Her Majesty was awake, we all proceeded to her bedroom, taking with us plates of apples (representing "Peace"), olives ("Long Life"), lotus seeds (Blessing). She suitably acknowledged these gifts and wished us all good luck in return. She inquired whether we had been to bed and, on learning that we had been up all night, she said that was right. She herself had not meant to sleep, only to rest a little, but somehow she had not been able to keep awake, and gave as a reason that she was an old woman. We waited on her until she had finished her toilet and then wished her a Happy New Year. We then proceeded to pay our respects to the Emperor and to the Young Empress. There was nothing further to be done in the way of ceremonies, and we therefore all accompanied Her Majesty to the theatre. The performance took place on a stage erected in the courtyard, and Her Majesty closed in one part of her veranda for the use of the guests and Court ladies. During the performance I began to feel very drowsy, and eventually fell fast asleep leaning against one of the pillars. I awoke rather suddenly to find that something had been dropped into my mouth, but on investigation I found it was nothing worse than a piece of candy, which I immediately proceeded to eat. On approaching Her Majesty, she asked me how I had enjoyed the candy, and told me not to sleep, but to have a good time like the rest. I never saw Her Majesty in better humor. She played with us just like a young girl, and one could hardly recognize in her the severe Empress Dowager we knew her to be.

The guests also all seemed to be enjoying themselves very much. In the evening, after the theatrical performance was over, Her Majesty ordered the eunuchs to bring in their instruments and give us some music. She herself sang several songs, and we all sang at intervals. Then Her Majesty ordered the eunuchs to sing. Some were trained singers, and sang very nicely, but others could not sing at all and caused quite a lot of amusement by their efforts to please Her Majesty. The Emperor appeared to be the only one present who was not having a good time; he never smiled once. On meeting him outside, I asked him why he looked so sad, but he only answered: "A Happy New Year" in English, smiled once, and walked away.

Her Majesty rose very early next morning and proceeded to the Audience Hall to worship the God of Wealth. We all accompanied her and took part in the ceremony. During the next few days we did nothing but gamble and scramble for Her Majesty's winnings. This was all very nice in its way, until one day one of the Court ladies began to cry, and accused me of stepping on her toes in the scramble. This made Her Majesty angry and she ordered the offender to go to her room and stay there for three days, saying that she did not deserve to be enjoying herself if she could not stand a little thing like that.

The tenth of the first moon was the birthday of the Young Empress, and we asked Her Majesty whether we would be allowed to give presents. She gave us permission to give whatever presents we might wish to. However, we submitted all our presents to Her Majesty for her approval, before giving them to the Young Empress, and we had to be very discreet and not choose anything which Her Majesty might think was too good. It was very difficult to tell what to send, as Her Majesty might take a fancy to any of the presents herself, even though they might not be of much value intrinsically. In such a case Her Majesty would tell us that she would keep it, and to give the Young Empress something else.

The celebration was very similar to that of the Emperor's birthday, but not on such an elaborate scale. We presented the Ru Yee to the Young Empress and kowtowed to her. She was supposed to receive these tokens of respect sitting on her throne, but out of deference to Her Majesty (we were Her Majesty's Court ladies) she stood up. She always was very polite to us under all circumstances.

On this day, as on the Emperor's birthday, the Emperor, Young Empress and Secondary wife dined together. These were the only two occasions when they did so, always dining separately at other times. Her Majesty sent two of her Court ladies to wait upon the Empress, I myself being one of them. I was very pleased, as I wanted to see for myself how they conducted themselves when together. I went into the Young Empress' room and informed her that Her Majesty had ordered us to wait upon them, to which she simply answered: "Very well." So we went to the dining room and set the table, placing the chairs into position. The meal was much different from what I expected. Instead of being stiff and serious like Her Majesty when dining they were quite free and easy, and we were allowed to join in the conversation and partake of some of the food and wine. A very pretty ceremony was gone through at the commencement of the meal. The Emperor and Young Empress seated themselves, and the Secondary wife filled their cups with wine and presented it to them in turn as a sign of respect, the Emperor first. When the meal was over we returned to Her Majesty's apartment and told her that everything had passed off nicely. We knew very well that we had been sent simply to act as spies, but we had nothing interesting to tell Her Majesty. She asked if the Emperor had been very serious and we answered "Yes."

The New Year celebrations terminated with the Festival of Lanterns on the fifteenth day of the first moon. These lanterns were of different shapes, representing animals, flowers, fruits, etc., etc. They were made of white gauze, painted in different colors. One lantern representing a dragon about fifteen feet long was fastened to ten poles, and ten eunuchs were required to hold it in position. In front of this dragon a eunuch was holding a lantern representing a large pearl, which the dragon was supposed to devour. This ceremony was gone through to the accompaniment of music.

After the lanterns came a firework display. These fireworks represented different scenes in the history of China, grape vines, wisteria blossoms, and many other flowers. It was a very imposing sight. Portable wooden houses had been placed near the fireworks from which Her Majesty and the rest of the Court could see them without being out in the cold air. This display lasted for several hours without a stop, and thousands of firecrackers were set off during the time. Her Majesty seemed to enjoy the noise very much. Altogether it was a good finish to the celebrations and we all enjoyed it very much.

The next morning all the guests departed from the Palace and we recommenced our everyday life.

As usual after the guests had departed Her Majesty began to criticise their mode of dressing, their ignorance of Court etiquette, etc., but added that she was rather glad, as she didn't want them to know anything about Court life.

As Spring soon arrived it was time for the farmers to commence sowing seed for the rice crop, and of course there was another ceremony. The Emperor visited the Temple of Agriculture where he prayed for a good harvest. Then he proceeded to a small plot of ground situated in the temple and after turning the earth over with a hand plow he sowed the first seeds of the season. This was to show the farmers that their labors were not despised and that even the Emperor was not ashamed to engage in this work. Anybody could attend this ceremony, it being quite a public affair, and many farmers were present.

About this same time the Young Empress went to see the silkworms and watch for the eggs to be hatched. As soon as they were out, the Young Empress gathered mulberry leaves for the worms to feed upon and watched until they were big enough to commence spinning. Each day a fresh supply of leaves were gathered and they were fed four or five times daily. Several of the Court ladies were told off to feed the worms during the night and see that they did not escape. These silkworms grow very rapidly and we could see the difference each day. Of course when they became full grown they required more food and we were kept busy constantly feeding them. The Young Empress was able to tell by holding them up to the light when they were ready to spin. If they were transparent then they were ready, and were placed on paper and left there. When spinning the silkworm does not eat, therefore all we had to do was to watch that they did not get away. After spinning for four or five days their supply of silk becomes exhausted and they shrivel up and apparently die. These apparently dead worms were collected by the Young Empress and placed in a box where they were kept until they developed into moths. They were then placed on thick paper and left there to lay their eggs.

If left to themselves, the silkworms when ready for spinning will spin the silk around their bodies until they are completely covered up, gradually forming a cocoon. In order to determine when they have finished spinning it was customary to take the cocoon and rattle it near the ear. If the worm was exhausted you could plainly hear the body rattle inside the cocoon. The cocoon is then placed in boiling water until it becomes soft. This, of course, kills the worm. In order to separate the silk a needle is used to pick up the end of the thread which is then wound on to a spool and is ready for weaving. A few of the cocoons were kept until the worms had turned into moths, which soon ate their way out of the cocoons when they were placed on sheets of paper and left to lay their eggs, which are taken away and kept in a cool place until the following Spring, when the eggs are hatched and become worms.

When the silk had all been separated we took it to Her Majesty for inspection and approval. On this particular occasion Her Majesty ordered one of the eunuchs to bring in some silk which she herself had woven when a young girl in the Palace, and on comparing it with the new silk it was found to be just as good in every way although many years had passed since it was made.

All this was done with the same object as the Emperor sowing the seeds, viz.: – to set the people a good example and to encourage them in their work.

# CHAPTER NINETEEN

## The Sea Palace

THIS year we had a very hot spring and Her Majesty was desirous of getting back again to the Sea Palace. However, as war had already been declared between Russia and Japan it was thought best to remain in the Forbidden City until things were more settled. Her Majesty was very much worried over this war and spent most of her time in offering prayers to the different divinities for the welfare of China and we, of course, were expected to join her. Things were very monotonous about this time and nothing particular occurred until the beginning of the second moon. By this time Her Majesty was quite sick of staying in the Forbidden City and said that no matter what happened she would remove the Court to the Sea Palace, where Miss Carl could get along and finish the portrait which had been hanging on for nearly a year. So on the sixth day of the second moon we moved back to the Sea Palace. Everything looked fresh and green and many of the trees had commenced to blossom. Her Majesty took us around the lake and we were in such good spirits that Her Majesty remarked that we acted more like a lot of wild animals escaped from a menagerie than human beings. She was much brighter now, but said that she would be happier still to get to the Summer Palace.

Miss Carl was summoned to the Palace, and Her Majesty visited her and asked to see the portrait. She again asked me how long it would be before it was finished, and I told her that unless she gave a little more of her time to posing it might not be finished for quite a long time. After a lot of consideration Her Majesty finally agreed to give Miss Carl five minutes each day after the morning audience, but that she desired it to be distinctly understood that she did not intend to pose for anything but the face. She accordingly sat for two mornings, but on the third morning she made an excuse saying that she was not feeling well. I told her that Miss Carl could not proceed further unless she sat for the face, so, although she was very angry, she gave Miss Carl a few more sittings until the face was finished. She absolutely refused to sit again whether it was finished or not, saying that she would have nothing more to do with the portrait. I myself sat for the remainder of the portrait, viz.: — for Her Majesty's dress, jewels, etc., and so by degrees the portrait was completed.

When Her Majesty learned that the portrait was nearing completion she was very much pleased, and I thought it a good opportunity to again broach the subject of payment. Her Majesty asked me whether I really thought it necessary to pay cash for the portrait and how much. I told her that as painting was Miss Carl's profession, if she had not been engaged on painting Her Majesty's portrait she would most probably have been engaged on other similar work for which she would have received compensation, and that therefore she would naturally expect to be paid even more handsomely in this instance. It was difficult to make Her Majesty understand this and she asked if I was quite certain that Miss Carl would not be offended by an offer of money, also Mrs. Conger who had presented her. I explained that in America and Europe it was quite customary for ladies to earn their own living either by painting, teaching or in some other similar manner, and that it was no disgrace but rather the opposite. Her Majesty seemed very much surprised to learn this, and asked why Miss Carl's brother did not support her himself. I told Her Majesty that Miss Carl did not desire him to provide for her, besides which he was married and had a family to support. Her Majesty gave it as her opinion that this was a funny kind of civilization. In China when the parents were dead it was the duty of the sons to provide for their unmarried sisters until such time as they married. She also said that if Chinese ladies were to work for their living it would only set people talking about them. However, she promised to speak with Her Ministers about paying Miss Carl, and I felt somewhat relieved as there seemed to be a probability of something satisfactory being arranged after all.

The twelfth day of the second moon was the anniversary of another interesting ceremony, viz.: – the birthday of the flowers and trees. After the morning audience we all went into the Palace grounds, where the eunuchs were waiting with huge rolls of red silk. These we all commenced to cut into narrow strips about two inches wide and three feet long. When we had cut sufficient Her Majesty took a strip of red silk and another of yellow silk which she tied round the stem of one of the peony trees (in China the peony is considered to be the queen of flowers). Then all the Court ladies, eunuchs and servant girls set to work to decorate every single tree and plant in the grounds with red silk ribbons, in the same manner as Her Majesty had done. This took up nearly the entire morning and it made a very pretty picture, with the bright costumes of the Court ladies, green trees and beautiful flowers.

We then went to a theatrical performance. This represented all the tree fairies and flower fairies celebrating their birthday. The Chinese believe that all the trees and flowers have their own particular fairies, the tree fairies being men and the flower fairies being women. The costumes were very pretty and were chosen to blend with the green trees and flowers which were on the stage. One of the costumes worn by a lotus fairy was made of pink silk, worked so as to represent the petals of the flower, the skirt being of green silk to represent the lotus leaves. Whenever this fairy moved about the petals would move just as though wafted by the breeze, like a natural flower. Several other costumes representing different flowers were made in the same manner. The scene was a woodland dell, surrounded with huge rocks perforated with caves, out of which came innumerable small fairies bearing decanters of wine. These small fairies represented the smaller flowers, daisies, pomegranate blossoms, etc. The result can be better imagined than described. All the fairies gathered together and drank the wine, after which they commenced to sing, accompanied by stringed instruments, played very softly. The final scene was a very fitting ending to the performance. It represented a small rainbow which gradually descended until it rested on the rocks; then each fairy in turn would sit upon the rainbow which rose again and conveyed them through the clouds into Heaven. This completed the celebration and we all retired to our rooms.

On the fourteenth day of the second moon (March 2, 1904), I completed my first year at Court. I had quite forgotten this fact until Her Majesty reminded me of it. She asked whether I was comfortable and happy where I was or did I long to return to Paris. I answered truly that although I had enjoyed myself while in France still I preferred the life of the Court, it was so interesting, besides which I was in my own native land and among all my friends and relations, and naturally I preferred that to living in a strange land. Her Majesty smiled and said she was afraid that sooner or later I would tire of the life in the Palace and fly away again across the ocean. She said that the only way to make sure of me was to marry me off. She again asked me what was my objection to getting married; was I afraid of having a mother-in-law, or what was it? If that was all, I need not worry, for so long as she was alive there was nothing to be afraid of. Her Majesty said that even if I were married it would not be necessary for me to stay at home all the time, but that I would be able to spend my time in the Palace as usual. Continuing, she said: "Last year when this marriage question came up I was willing to make allowances as you had been brought up somewhat differently from the rest of my Court ladies, but do not run away with the idea that I have forgotten all about it. I am still on the lookout for a suitable husband for you." I simply answered as before – that I had absolutely no desire to marry, but that I wanted to stay where I was and live at the Court so long as Her Majesty was willing to have me there. She made some remark about my being stubborn and said that I should probably change my mind before long.

During the latter part of the second moon Miss Carl worked very hard to get the portrait finished and Her Majesty again consulted her book in order to select a lucky day on which to put the final touches to the picture. The 19th of April, 1904, was chosen by Her Majesty as the best time, and Miss Carl was duly notified. Miss Carl most emphatically stated that it was quite impossible to finish the portrait properly by the time named, and I told Her Majesty what Miss Carl said, explaining that there were many small finishing touches to be added and I suggested it would be better to give Miss Carl a few days longer if possible. However, Her Majesty said that it must be finished by four o'clock on the 19th day of April, and therefore there was nothing further to be said.

About a week before the time fixed for completion Her Majesty paid a visit to the studio to finally inspect the picture. She seemed very much pleased with it, but still objected to her face being painted dark on one side and light on the other. As I have said before, I had explained that this was the shading, but Her Majesty insisted on my telling Miss Carl to make both sides of her face alike. This led to a pretty hot discussion between Miss Carl and myself but she finally saw that it was no use going against Her Majesty's wishes in the matter, so consented to make some slight alteration. Happening to catch sight of some foreign characters at the foot of the painting Her Majesty inquired what they were and on being informed that they were simply the artist's name, said: "Well, I know foreigners do some funny things, but I think this about the funniest I ever heard of. Fancy putting her own name on my picture. This will naturally convey the impression that it is a portrait of Miss Carl, and not a portrait of myself at all." I again had to explain the reason for this, saying that it was always customary for foreign artists to write their names at the foot of any picture they painted, whether portrait or otherwise. So Her Majesty said she supposed it was all right, and would have to remain, but she looked anything but satisfied with it.

By working practically all night and all day, Miss Carl managed to get the portrait finished by the time stipulated, and Her Majesty arranged that Mrs. Conger and the other ladies of the Diplomatic Corps should come to the Palace and see the portrait. This was quite a private audience and Her Majesty received them in one of the small Audience Halls. After the usual greetings Her Majesty ordered us to conduct the ladies to the studio, which we did, Her Majesty bidding them good-bye and remaining in her own apartments. The Young Empress in accordance with instructions from Her Majesty, accompanied us to the studio, and acted as hostess. Everybody expressed great admiration for the portrait and it was voted a marvellous likeness. After inspecting the picture we all adjourned for refreshments. The Young Empress sat at the head of the table and asked me to sit next to her. Shortly after everybody was seated a eunuch came and asked the Young Empress to inform these ladies that the Emperor was slightly indisposed and was unable to be present. I interpreted this, and everybody appeared satisfied. As a matter of fact the Emperor was quite well, but we had forgotten all about him. And so the guests departed without seeing him on this occasion.

On reporting everything to Her Majesty as usual, she asked what they thought of the portrait, and we told her that they had admired it very much. Her Majesty said: "Of course they did, it was painted by a foreign artist." She didn't appear to be very much interested and was quite cross about something, which caused me great disappointment after all the trouble Miss Carl had taken to finish the portrait. Her Majesty then remarked that Miss Carl had taken a long time to get the portrait finished, and asked why nobody had reminded her to inform the Emperor about the audience, being particularly angry with the head eunuch on this occasion. Her Majesty said that as soon as she remembered, she immediately sent a eunuch to make excuses, as the ladies might very well think that something had happened to the Emperor and it might cause talk. I told her that I explained to them that the Emperor was not well and they evidently thought nothing further of his absence.

By the next day the carpenters in the Palace had finished the frame for the portrait and when it had been properly fitted Her Majesty ordered my brother to take a photograph of it. This photograph turned out so well that Her Majesty said it was better than the portrait itself.

The picture being now quite finished, Miss Carl prepared to take her leave, which she did a few days later, having received a handsome present in cash from Her Majesty in addition to a decoration and many other presents as remuneration for her services. For quite a long time after Miss Carl had left the Palace I felt very lonely, as during her stay I had found her a genial companion and we had many things in common to talk about. Her Majesty noticed that I was rather quiet, and asked me the cause. She said: "I suppose you are beginning to miss your friend, the lady artist." I did not care to admit that this was so, for fear she might think me ungrateful to herself, besides which I knew she did not like the idea of my being too friendly with foreigners. So I explained to Her Majesty that I always did regret losing old friends but that I would get used to the change very soon. Her Majesty was very nice about it and said she wished that she was a little more sentimental over such small things, but that when I got to her age I should be able to take things more philosophically.

After Miss Carl had left the Court, Her Majesty asked me one day: "Did she ever ask you much about the Boxer movement of 1900?" I told her that I knew very little of the Boxer movement myself, as I was in Paris at the time and I could not say very much. I assured her that the lady artist never mentioned the subject to me. Her Majesty said: "I hate to mention about that affair and I would not like to have foreigners ask my people questions on that subject. Do you know, I have often thought that I am the most clever woman that ever lived and others cannot compare with me. Although I have heard much about Queen Victoria and read a part of her life which someone has translated into Chinese, still I don't think her life was half so interesting and eventful as mine. My life is not finished yet and no one knows what is going to happen in the future. I may surprise the foreigners some day with something extraordinary and do something quite contrary to anything I have yet done. England is one of great powers of the world, but this has not been brought about by Queen Victoria's absolute rule. She had the able men of parliament back of her at all times and of course they discussed everything until the best result was obtained, then she would sign the necessary documents and really had nothing to say about the policy of the country. Now look at me. I have 400,000,000 people, all dependent on my judgment. Although I have the Grand Council to consult with, they only look after the different appointments, but anything of an important nature I must decide myself. What does the Emperor know? I have been very successful so far, but I never dreamt that the Boxer movement would end with such serious results for China. That is the only mistake I have made in my life. I should have issued an Edict at once to stop the Boxers practising their belief, but both Prince Tuan and Duke Lan told me that they firmly believed the Boxers were sent by Heaven to enable China to get rid of all the undesirable and hated foreigners. Of course they meant mostly missionaries, and you know how I hate them and how very religious I always am, so I thought I would not say anything then but would wait and see what would happen. I felt sure they were going too far as one day Prince Tuan brought the Boxer leader to the Summer Palace and summoned all the eunuchs into the courtyard of the Audience Hall and examined each eunuch on the head to see if there was a cross. He said, 'This cross is not visible to you, but I can identify a Christian by finding a cross on the head.' Prince Tuan then came to my private Palace and told me that the Boxer leader was at the Palace Gate and had found two eunuchs who were Christians and asked me what was to be done. I immediately became very angry and told him that he had no right to bring any Boxers to the Palace without my permission; but he said this leader was so powerful that he was able to kill all the foreigners and was not afraid of the foreign guns, as all the gods were protecting him. Prince Tuan told me that he had witnessed this himself. A Boxer shot another with a revolver and the bullet hit him, but did not harm him in the least. Then Prince Tuan suggested that I hand these two eunuchs supposed to be Christians to the Boxer leader, which I did. I heard afterwards that these two eunuchs were beheaded right in the country somewhere near here. This chief Boxer came to the Palace the next day, accompanied by Prince Tuan and Duke Lan, to make all the eunuchs burn incense sticks to prove that they were not Christians. After that Prince Tuan also suggested that we had better let the chief Boxer come every day and teach the eunuchs their belief; that nearly all of Peking was studying with the Boxers. The next day I was very much surprised to see all my eunuchs dressed as Boxers. They wore red jackets, red turbans and yellow trousers. I was sorry to see all my attendants discard their official robes and wear a funny costume like that. Duke Lan presented me with a suit of Boxer clothes. At that time Yung Lu, who was the head of the Grand Council, was ill and asked leave of absence for a month. While he was sick, I used to send one of the eunuchs to see him every day, and that day the eunuch returned and informed me that Yung Lu was quite well and would come to the Palace the next day, although he still had fifteen days more leave. I was puzzled to know why he should give up the balance of his leave. However, I was very anxious to see him, as I wished to consult him about this chief Boxer. Yung Lu looked grieved when he learned what had taken place at the Palace, and said that these Boxers were nothing but revolutionaries and agitators. They were trying to get the people to help them to kill the foreigners, but he was very much afraid the result would be against the Government. I told him that probably he was right, and asked him what should be done. He told me that he would talk to Prince Tuan, but the next day Prince Tuan told me that he had had a fight with Yung Lu about the Boxer question, and said that all of Peking had become Boxers, and if we tried to turn them, they would do all they could to kill everyone in Peking, including the Court; that they (the Boxer party) had the day selected to kill all the foreign representatives; that Tung Fou Hsiang, a very conservative General and one of the Boxers, had promised to bring his troops out to help the Boxers to fire on the Legations. When I heard this I was very much worried and anticipated serious trouble, so I sent for Yung Lu at once and kept Prince Tuan with me. Yung Lu came, looking very much worried, and he was more so after I had told him what the Boxers were going to do. He immediately suggested that I should issue an Edict, saying that these Boxers were a secret society and that no one should believe their teaching, and to instruct the Generals of the nine gates to drive all the Boxers out of the city at once. When Prince Tuan heard this he was very angry and told Yung Lu that if such an Edict was issued, the Boxers would come to the Court and kill everybody. When Prince Tuan told me this, I thought I had better leave everything to him. After he left the Palace, Yung Lu said that Prince Tuan was absolutely crazy and that he was sure these Boxers would be the cause of a great deal of trouble. Yung Lu also said that Prince Tuan must be insane to be helping the Boxers to destroy the Legations; that these Boxers were a very common lot, without education, and they imagined the few foreigners in China were the only ones on the earth and if they were killed it would be the end of them. They forgot how very strong these foreign countries are, and that if the foreigners in China were all killed, thousands would come to avenge their death. Yung Lu assured me that one foreign soldier could kill one hundred Boxers without the slightest trouble, and begged me to give him instructions to order General Nieh, who was afterwards killed by the Boxers, to bring his troops to protect the Legations. Of course I gave him this instruction at once, and also told him that he must see Prince Tuan at once and Duke Lan to tell them that this was a very serious affair and that they had better not interfere with Yung Lu's plans. Matters became worse day by day and Yung Lu was the only one against the Boxers, but what could one man accomplish against so many? One day Prince Tuan and Duke Lan came and asked me to issue an Edict ordering the Boxers to kill all the Legation people first and then all remaining foreigners. I was very angry and refused to issue this Edict. After we had talked a very long time, Prince Tuan said that this must be done without delay, for the Boxers were getting ready to fire on the Legations and would do so the very next day. I was furious and ordered several of the eunuchs to drive him out, and he said as he was going out: 'If you refuse to issue that Edict, I will do it for you whether you are willing or not,' and he did. After that you know what happened. He issued these Edicts unknown to me and was responsible for a great many deaths. He found that he could not carry his plans through and heard that the foreign troops were not very far from Peking. He was so frightened that he made us all leave Peking." As she finished saying this, she started to cry, and I told her that I felt very sorry for her. She said: "You need not feel sorry for me for what I have gone through; but you must feel sorry that my fair name is ruined. That is the only mistake I have made in my whole life and it was done in a moment of weakness. Before I was just like a piece of pure jade; everyone admired me for what I have done for my country, but the jade has a flaw in it since this Boxer movement and it will remain there to the end of my life. I have regretted many, many times that I had such confidence in, and believed that wicked Prince Tuan; he was responsible for everything."

By the end of the third moon Her Majesty had had enough of the Sea Palace and the Court moved into the Summer Palace. This time we travelled by boat as it was very beautiful weather. On reaching the water-gates of the Palace we found everything just lovely and the peach blossoms were in full bloom. Her Majesty plainly showed how glad she was to be back once more and for the time being seemed to have forgotten everything else, even the war.

# CHAPTER TWENTY

## Conclusion

MY second year at the Palace was very much the same as the first. We celebrated each anniversary and festival in the same way as before: the usual audience was held each morning by Her Majesty, after which the day was given up to enjoyment. Amongst other things Her Majesty took great interest in her vegetable gardens, and superintended the planting of the different seeds. When vegetables were ready for pulling, from time to time, all the Court ladies were supplied with a kind of small pruning fork and gathered in the crop. Her Majesty seemed to enjoy seeing us work in the fields, and when the fit seized her she would come along and help. In order to encourage us in this work, Her Majesty would give a small present to the one who showed the best results so we naturally did our best in order to please her, as much as for the reward. Another hobby of Her Majesty's was the rearing of chickens, and a certain number of birds were allotted to each of the Court ladies. We were supposed to look after these ourselves and the eggs had to be taken to Her Majesty every morning. I could not understand why it was that my chickens gave less eggs than any of the others until one day my eunuch informed me that he had seen one of the other eunuchs stealing the eggs from my hen house and transferring them to another, in order to help his mistress to head the list.

Her Majesty was very particular not to encourage untidyness or extravagance among the Court ladies. On one occasion she told me to open a parcel which was lying in her room. I was about to cut the string when Her Majesty stopped me and told me to untie it. This I managed to do after a lot of trouble, and opened the parcel. Her Majesty next made me fold the paper neatly and place it in a drawer along with the string so that I would know where to find it should it be wanted again. From time to time Her Majesty would give each of us money for our own private use and whenever we wanted to buy anything, say flowers, handkerchiefs, shoes, ribbons, etc., these could be bought from the servant girls who used to make them in the Palace and we would enter each item in a small note book supplied by Her Majesty for the purpose. At the end of each month Her Majesty examined our accounts and in case she considered that we had been extravagant she would give us a good scolding, while on the other hand, if we managed to show a good balance she would compliment us on our good management. Thus under Her Majesty's tuition we learned to be careful and tidy against such time as we might be called upon to look after homes of our own.

About this time my father began to show signs of breaking down and asked for permission to withdraw from public life. However, Her Majesty would not hear of this and decided to give him another six months vacation instead. It was his intention to go to Shanghai and see the family physician, but Her Majesty did not approve of this, maintaining that her own doctors were quite as good as any foreign doctor. These doctors therefore attended him for some time, prescribing all kinds of different concoctions daily. After a while he seemed to pick up a little but was still unable to get about on account of having chronic rheumatism. We therefore again suggested that it would be better for him to see his own doctor in Shanghai, who understood my father thoroughly, but Her Majesty could not be made to see it in that light. She said that what we wanted was a little patience, that the Chinese doctors might be slow, but they were sure, and she was convinced they would completely cure my father very soon. The fact of the matter was she was afraid that if my father went to stay in Shanghai the rest of the family would want to be there with him, which was not in her programme at all. So we decided to remain in Peking unless my father showed signs of getting worse.

In due course the time arrived on which it had been arranged to hold the Spring Garden Party for the Diplomatic Corps, and as usual one day was set apart for the Ministers, Secretaries and members of the various Legations, and the following day for their wives, etc. This year very few guests attended the Garden Party but among those who did come were several strangers. About half a dozen ladies from the Japanese Legation came with Madame Uchida, wife of the Japanese Minister. Her Majesty was always very pleased to see this lady whom she very much admired on account of her extreme politeness. After the usual presentation we conducted the ladies to luncheon, showed them over the Palace grounds, after which we wished them good-bye and they took their leave. We reported everything to Her Majesty, and as usual were asked many questions. Among the guests there was one lady (English so far as I could make out) dressed in a heavy tweed travelling costume, having enormous pockets, into which she thrust her hands as though it were extremely cold. She wore a cap of the same material. Her Majesty asked if I had noticed this lady with the clothes made out of "rice bags," and wasn't it rather unusual to be presented at Court in such a dress. Her Majesty wanted to know who she was and where she came from. I replied that she certainly did not belong to any of the Legations as I was acquainted with everybody there. Her Majesty said that whoever she was she certainly was not accustomed to moving in decent society as she (Her Majesty) was quite certain that it was not the thing to appear at a European Court in such a costume. "I can tell in a moment," Her Majesty added, "whether any of these people are desirous of showing proper respect to me, or whether they consider that I am not entitled to it. These foreigners seem to have the idea that the Chinese are ignorant and that therefore they need not be so particular as in European Society. I think it would be best to let it be understood for the future what dress should be worn at the different Court Functions, and at the same time use a certain amount of discretion in issuing invitations. In that way I can also keep the missionary element out, as well as other undesirables. I like to meet any distinguished foreigners who may be visiting in China, but I do not want any common people at my Court." I suggested that the Japanese custom could be followed, viz.: to issue proper invitation cards, stipulating at the foot the dress to be worn on each particular occasion. Her Majesty thought this would meet the case and it was decided to introduce a similar rule in China.

Whenever the weather permitted, Her Majesty would pass quite a lot of her time in the open air watching the eunuchs at work in the gardens. During the early Spring the lotus plants were transplanted and she would take keen interest in this work. All the old roots had to be cut away and the new bulbs planted in fresh soil. Although the lotus grew in the shallowest part of the lake (the West side) it was necessary for the eunuchs to wade into the water sometimes up to their waists in order to weed out the old plants and set the young ones. Her Majesty would sit for hours on her favorite bridge (The Jade Girdle Bridge) and superintend the eunuchs at their work, suggesting from time to time as to how the bulbs were to be planted. This work generally took three or four days, and the Court ladies in attendance would stand beside Her Majesty and pass the time making fancy tassels for Her Majesty's cushions, in fact doing anything so long as we did not idle.

It was during the Spring that Yuan Shih Kai paid another visit to the Palace, and among other subjects discussed was the Russo-Japan war. He told Her Majesty that it was developing into a very serious affair and that he feared China would be the principal sufferer in the long run. Her Majesty was very much upset by this news, and mentioned that she had been advised by one of the censors to make a present to the Japanese of a large quantity of rice, but had decided to take no action whatever in the matter, which resolve Yuan Shih Kai strongly supported.

I was still working each day translating the various newspaper reports and telegrams relating to the war and one morning, seeing a paragraph to the effect that Kang Yu Wei (Leader of the Reform Movement in China in 1898) had arrived at Singapore from Batavia, I thought it might interest Her Majesty and so translated it along with the rest. Her Majesty immediately became very much excited which made me feel frightened as I did not know what could be the matter. However, she explained to me that this man had caused all kinds of trouble in China, that before meeting Kang Yu Wei the Emperor had been a zealous adherent to the traditions of his ancestors but since then had plainly shown his desire to introduce reforms and even Christianity into the country. "On one occasion," continued Her Majesty, "he caused the Emperor to issue instructions for the Summer Palace to be surrounded by soldiers so as to keep me prisoner until these reforms could be put into effect, but through the faithfulness of Yung Lu, a member of the Grand Council, and Yuan Shill Kai, Viceroy of Chihli, I was able to frustrate the plot. I immediately proceeded to the Forbidden City, where the Emperor was then staying and after discussing the question with him he replied that he realized his mistake and asked me to take over the reins of government and act in his stead."

(The result of this was, of course, the Edict of 1898 appointing the Empress Dowager as Regent of China.)

Her Majesty had immediately ordered the capture of Kang Yu Wei and his followers, but he had managed to effect his escape and she had heard nothing further about him until I translated this report in the newspaper. She seemed relieved, however, to know where he was, and seemed anxious to hear what he was doing. She suddenly became very angry again and asked why it was that the foreign governments offered protection to Chinese political agitators and criminals. Why couldn't they leave China to deal with her own subjects and mind their own business a little more? She gave me instructions to keep a lookout for any further news of this gentleman and report to her immediately, but I made up my mind that in any case, I would not mention anything about him again and so the matter gradually died away.

During one of our visits to the Sea Palace Her Majesty drew attention to a large piece of vacant ground and said that it had formerly been the site of the Audience Hall which had been destroyed by fire during the Boxer trouble. Her Majesty explained that this had been purely an accident and was not deliberately destroyed by the foreign troops. She said that it had long been an eyesore to her as it was so ugly, and that she had now determined to build another Audience Hall on the same site, as the present Audience Hall was too small to accommodate the foreign guests when they paid their respects at New Year. She therefore commanded the Board of Works to prepare a model of the new building in accordance with her own ideas, and submit it for her approval. Up to that time all the buildings in the Palace Grounds were typically Chinese but this new Audience Hall was to be more or less on the foreign plan and up to date in every respect. This model was accordingly prepared and submitted to Her Majesty. It was only a small wooden model but was complete in every detail, even to the pattern of the windows and the carving on the ceilings and panels. However, I never knew anything to quite come up to Her Majesty's ideas, and this was no exception. She criticised the model from every standpoint, ordering this room to be enlarged and that room to be made smaller: this window to be moved to another place, etc., etc. So the model went back for reconstruction. When it was again brought for Her Majesty's inspection everybody agreed that it was an improvement on the first one, and even Her Majesty expressed great satisfaction. The next thing was to find a name for the new building and after serious and mature consideration it was decided to name it Hai Yen Tang (Sea Coast Audience Hall). Building operations were commenced immediately and Her Majesty took great interest in the progress of the work. It had already been decided that this Audience Hall was to be furnished throughout in foreign style, with the exception of the throne, which, of course, retained its Manchu appearance. Her Majesty compared the different styles of furniture with the catalogues we had brought with us from France and finally decided on the Louis Fifteenth style, but everything was to be covered with Imperial Yellow, with curtains and carpets to match. When everything had been selected to Her Majesty's satisfaction, my mother asked permission to defray the expense herself and make a present of this furniture. This Her Majesty agreed to and the order was accordingly placed with a well-known Paris firm from whom we had purchased furniture when in France. By the time the building was completed the furniture had arrived, and it was quickly installed. Her Majesty went to inspect it and, of course, had to find fault as usual. She didn't seem at all pleased with the result of the experiment and said that after all a Chinese building would have been the best as it would have had a more dignified appearance. However, the thing was finished and it was no use finding fault now, as it could not be changed.

During the Summer months I had plenty of leisure time and devoted about an hour each day to helping the Emperor with his English. He was a most intelligent man with a wonderful memory and learned very quickly. His pronunciation, however, was not good. In a very short time he was able to read short stories out of an ordinary school reader and could write from dictation fairly well. His handwriting was exceptionally fine, while in copying old English and ornamental characters, he was an expert. Her Majesty seemed pleased that the Emperor had taken up this study, and said she thought of taking it up herself as she was quite sure she would learn it very quickly if she tried. After two lessons she lost patience, and did not mention the matter again.

Of course these lessons gave me plenty of opportunity to talk with His Majesty, and on one occasion he ventured the remark that I didn't seem to have made much progress with Her Majesty in the matter of reform. I told him that many things had been accomplished since my arrival at Court, and mentioned the new Audience Hall as an instance. He didn't appear to think that anything worth talking about, and advised me to give up the matter altogether. He said when the proper time arrived – if it ever did arrive – then I might be of use, but expressed grave doubts on the subject. He also enquired about my father and I told him that unless his health improved very soon it would be necessary for us to leave the Court for a while at any rate. He replied that although he should very much regret such a necessity, he really believed that it would be for the best. He said he felt certain that I should never be able to settle down permanently to Court life after spending so many years abroad, and for his part would put no obstacles in the way of my leaving the Court if I desired to do so.

Her Majesty had given me permission to visit my father twice every month, and everything appeared to be going along nicely until one day one of Her Majesty's servant girls told me that Her Majesty was trying to arrange another marriage for me. At first I did not take any notice of this, but shortly afterwards Her Majesty informed me that everything was arranged and that I was to be married to a certain Prince whom she had chosen. I could see that Her Majesty was waiting for me to say something, so I told her that I was very much worried at that time about my father and begged her to allow the matter to stand over for the time being at any rate. This made Her Majesty very angry, and she told me that she considered me very ungrateful after all she had done for me. I didn't reply, and as her Majesty did not say anything more at the time, I tried to forget about it. However, on my next visit home, I told my father all about it, and as before he was strongly opposed to such a marriage. He suggested that on my return to the Palace I should lay the whole matter before Li Lien Ying, the head eunuch, and explain my position, for if anybody could influence Her Majesty, he was the one. I, therefore, took the first opportunity of speaking to him. At first he appeared very reluctant to interfere in the matter, and said he thought I ought to do as Her Majesty wished, but on my stating that I had no desire to marry at all, but was quite willing to remain at Court in my present position, he promised to do his best for me. I never heard anything further about my marriage, either from Her Majesty or Li Lien Ying, and therefore concluded that he had been able to arrange the matter satisfactorily.

The Summer passed without anything further important occurring. During the eighth moon the bamboos were cut down and here again the Court ladies were called upon to assist, our work being to carve designs and characters on the cut trees, Her Majesty assisting. These were afterwards made into chairs, tables and other useful articles for Her Majesty's teahouse. During the long Autumn evenings Her Majesty would teach us Chinese history and poetry and every tenth day would put us through an examination in order to find out how much we had learned, prizes being awarded for proficiency. The younger eunuchs also took part in these lessons and some of their answers to Her Majesty's questions were very amusing. If Her Majesty were in a good humor she would laugh with the rest of us, but sometimes she would order them to be punished for their ignorance and stupidity. However, as they were quite accustomed to being punished they did not seem to mind very much and forgot all about it the next minute.

As Her Majesty's seventieth birthday was approaching the Emperor proposed to celebrate this event on an unusually grand scale, but Her Majesty would not give her consent to this proposal on account of the war trouble, for fear people might comment on it. The only difference, therefore, between this birthday and former ones was that Her Majesty gave presents to the Court, in addition to receiving them. These included the bestowal of titles, promotions and increases in salary. Among the titles conferred by Her Majesty, my sister and myself received the title of Chun Chu Hsien (Princess). These titles, however, were confined to members of the Court, and were granted specially by the Empress Dowager. Similar promotions to outside officials were always conferred by the Emperor. It was proposed to hold the celebrations in the Forbidden City as it was more suited for such an important event. However, Her Majesty did not like this idea at all, and gave instructions that the Court should not be moved until three days before the 10th of the tenth moon, the date of her birthday. This entailed a lot of unnecessary work as it necessitated decorating both the

Summer Palace and the Forbidden City. Everything was hurry and bustle. To add to this, it snowed very heavily during the few days previous to the tenth. Her Majesty was in a very good mood. She was very fond of being out in the snow and expressed a wish to have some photographs taken of herself on the hillside. So my brother was commanded to bring his camera, and took several very good pictures of Her Majesty.

On the seventh day the Court moved into the Forbidden City and the celebrations commenced. The decorations were beautiful; the Courtyards being covered with glass roofs to keep out the snow. The theatres were in full swing each day. The actual ceremony, which took place on the tenth, did not differ in any respect from previous ones. Everything passed off smoothly, and the Court removed again into the Sea Palace.

While at the Sea Palace we received news that my father's condition was becoming serious, and he again tendered his resignation to Her Majesty. She sent her eunuchs to find out exactly what the matter was, and on learning that he was really very ill, accepted his resignation. Her Majesty agreed that it might be better for him to go to Shanghai and see if the foreign physicians could do him any good. She said she supposed it would be necessary for my mother to accompany him to Shanghai, but did not consider it serious enough to send my sister and myself along also. I tried to explain that it was my duty to go along with him as he might be taken worse and die before I could get down to see him again, and I begged Her Majesty to allow me to go. She offered all kinds of objections but eventually, seeing that I was bent on going, she said: "Well, he is your father, and I suppose you want to be with him, so you may go on the understanding that you return to Court as soon as ever possible." We did not get away until the middle of the eleventh moon, as Her Majesty insisted on making clothes for us and other preparations for our journey. Of course we could do nothing but await Her Majesty's pleasure.

When everything was ready Her Majesty referred to her book to choose a suitable day for our departure, and fixed on the thirteenth as being the best. We therefore left the Palace for our own house on the twelfth. We kowtowed and said good-bye to Her Majesty, thanking her for her many kindnesses during our stay with her. Everybody cried, even Her Majesty. We then went to say good-bye to the Emperor and Young Empress. The Emperor simply shook hands and wished us "Good Luck" in English. Everybody appeared sorry to see us leave. After standing about for a long time Her Majesty said it was no use wasting any more time and that we had better start. At the gate the head eunuch bade us good-bye and we entered our carriage and drove to my father's house, our own eunuchs accompanying us to the door. We found everything prepared for our journey, and early the next morning we took train to Tientsin where we just managed to catch the last steamer of the season leaving for Shanghai. As it was, the water was so shallow that we ran aground on the Taku bar.

On arrival in Shanghai my father immediately consulted his physician who examined him and prescribed medicine. The trip itself seemed to have done him a lot of good. I very soon began to miss my life at Court, and, although I had many friends in Shanghai and was invited to dinner parties and dances; still I did not seem to be able to enjoy myself. Everything seemed different to what I had been accustomed to in Peking and I simply longed for the time when I should be able to return to Her Majesty. About two weeks after our arrival, Her Majesty sent a special messenger down to Shanghai to see how we were getting along. He brought us many beautiful presents and also a lot of medicine for my father. We were very glad to see him. He informed us that we were missed very much at Court and advised us to return as soon as it was possible for us to do so. As my father began to show signs of improvement he suggested that there was no further need for me to stay in Shanghai, and thought it better that I should return to Peking and resume my duties at Court. I therefore returned early in the New Year. The river was frozen and I had to travel by boat to Chinwantao, from thence by rail to Peking. It was a most miserable journey and I was very glad when it was over. Her Majesty had sent my eunuchs to the station to meet me and I at once proceeded to the Palace. On meeting Her Majesty we both cried again by way of expressing our happiness. I informed her that my father was progressing favorably and that I hoped to be able to remain with her permanently.

I resumed my previous duties, but this time I had neither my sister for a companion nor my mother to chat with and everything appeared changed. Her Majesty was just the same, however, and treated me most kindly. Still, I was not comfortable, and heartily wished myself back again in Shanghai. I stayed at the Court, going through pretty much the same daily routine as before until the second moon (March 1905), when I received a telegram summoning me to Shanghai as my father had become worse, and was in a critical condition and wished to see me. I showed Her Majesty the telegram and waited for her decision. She commenced by telling me that my father was a very old man, and therefore his chances of recovery were not so great as if he were younger, finally winding up by telling me that I could go to him at once. I again wished everybody good-bye, fully expecting to return very soon; but this was not to be. I found my father in a very dangerous condition, and after a lingering illness, he died on the 18th of December, 1905. Of course we went into mourning for one hundred days which in itself prevented my returning to the Court.

While in Shanghai I made many new friends and acquaintances and gradually began to realize that after all, the attractions of Court life had not been able to eradicate the influences which had been brought to bear upon me while in Europe. At heart I was a foreigner, educated in a foreign country, and, having already met my husband the matter was soon settled and I became an American citizen. However, I often look back to the two years I spent at the Court of Her Majesty, the Empress Dowager of China, the most eventful and happiest days of my girlhood.

Although I was not able to do much towards influencing Her Majesty in the matter of reform, I still hope to live to see the day when China shall wake up and take her proper place among the nations of the world.

THE END.

Lightning Source UK Ltd.
Milton Keynes UK
26 August 2009

143088UK00003B/10/P